GREAT MEN BOW DOWN

To Blake —

Be inspired !

GREAT MEN BOW DOWN

150 Legendary Men of History
Reveal Their Source
Of True Greatness

Gordon Lawrence

Sword Point Publishing
Lawrenceville, Georgia

Sword Point Publishing, Lawrenceville, Georgia
Order online from: gordon @ greatmenbowdown.com
Order by phone: 770-682-8855

Scripture quotations taken from the New American Standard Bible.
© Copyright 1960, 1962, 1963, 1968, 1971, 1972, 1973, 1975, 1977, 1995
by the Lockman Foundation. Used by permission. (www.lockman.org)

Some Scripture quotations are paraphrased by the author for emphasis.

Cover Design: 1976 © Arnold Friberg,
For more information on "The Prayer at Valley Forge" contact Friberg Fine Art, Inc.,
5206 Pinemont Drive, Salt Lake City, UT 84123 www.fribergfineart.com.
Local (801) 261.5111
Toll-free Fax (800) 783.1256

All photographs and likenesses of great men have been selected from public domain.

Library of Congress Catalog Pending

Lawrence, J. Gordon (1950 -)
        Great Men Bow Down
        Legendary Men of History Reveal Their Source of True Greatness.
        390 pages

Printed in the United States of America

ISBN - 978-0-9830823-0-9

Great Men in My Life

Through the years there have been individuals who have shaped my thinking,
my behavior and my concept of how to function as a minister of the gospel.
They have been role models, disciplers, mentors and an inspiration to me
at various stages of my pilgrimage. They have given me opportunities,
and encouraged me along the way. To these men I pay tribute, and I hope,
that in small, but significant ways, I can model the same for the next generation.

Michael D. Smith
Asheville, North Carolina

Dr. John F. MacArthur
Sun Valley, California

Dr. Billy H. Cline
Asheville, North Carolina

C. Thomas Wright, Ph.D
Mobile, Alabama

Loy Witherspoon, Ph.D
Charlotte, North Carolina

Charles L. Chaney, Ph.D
Fort Worth, Texas

Dr. Raymond Sanderson
Charlotte, North Carolina

Glyn W. McWhorter, R.A.
Alpharetta, Georgia

Rev. Dave R. Pierceall
Charlotte, North Carolina

Alan L Montgomery
Snellville, Georgia

R. Allen Brown, P.E.
Clemmons, North Carolina

Rev. R. Doyle McDaniel
Snellville, Georgia

Donald R. Poteat
Charlotte, North Carolina

Carl V. Thomas
Lawrenceville, Georgia

Dr. Waylon B. Moore
Tampa, Florida

Marvin J. Rosenthal
Orlando, Florida

Dedication

To my son Tyler.

To my sons-in-law,
Scott and Jason.

To my sons in the faith,
Brett and Aaron.

Hoping that this book
will inspire each of these young men
to constantly bow down
before the Sovereign God
of all Great Men.

And to the memory of my dad, Robert D. Lawrence.

In Appreciation

To my mom Lucy and my wife Sandra,
my two ladies of grace, for their constant support,

To my siblings, Becky, Cathy and Charlie, who have shared my journey.

To my architectural staff
Lori, Tracy, Dena, Jayne, Maty, John, Kevin, Ryan and Jared - for proofreading;
and to Johnathan for technical expertise.

To my songwriter / author friend, Carol J. Smith
for her abilities to craft words with inspiration and impact.

To my publisher, Mel Guinn
and my editors: Anne Alexander, John Crayton,
Beth Wilson (author of "Under His Rainbow")
and Bill Thurber (author of "A Moment of Truth"),
who have fine-tuned the text
and given me accountability and encouragement.

Table of Contents

Great Men by Vocation

Great Men of Government Bow Down.

Jefferson, Washington, Franklin, Patrick Henry, Abraham Lincoln. These men stood on principle to provide basic human rights as a nation forged the documents that would guarantee the rights of citizenship. They bowed down to the Creator God who gave us the rights of life, liberty and the pursuit of happiness.

Great Men of Military Bow Down.

Douglas MacArthur, Eisenhower, Ulysses S. Grant, Robert E. Lee, Stonewall Jackson. These men waged wars on home and foreign soil to insure that freedom would not be forfeited to tyrants and evil empires. They bowed down to the sovereign God of all authority and all power.

Great Men of Literature Bow Down.

Charles Dickens, Longfellow, Hawthorne, Emerson, Mark Twain, Tolstoy, G.K. Chesterton. These men have crafted words over the centuries which have shaped our imaginations and inspired our hunger for learning. They bowed down to the God of history, and they understood the power of words.

Great Men of Science Bow Down.

Francis Bacon, Da Vinci, Isaac Newton, George Washington Carver, Einstein and Wernher von Braun. These men made discoveries regarding natural laws of the universe that have allowed science and technology to advance each generation toward a better understanding of how God created the planet and the order of living creatures. They bowed down to the infinite God who holds time and space in His hands.

Great Men of Sports Bow Down.

George Foreman, Tom Landry, Vince Lombardi. These men fought battles in a controlled environment with rules of engagement that taught young men how to win and how to live. Daily discipline and fierce competition were the fuel that motivated them. They bowed down to the God of victory, who wants us to win in the arenas of life, and they understood that God gives victory to the faithful.

Great Men of World Missions Bow Down.

William Carey, David Brainerd, Jim Elliot, Eric Liddell. These men left the comfort zone of their own culture to cross boundaries of race and nationality. Perhaps sacrificing more than any other group, these men were drawn to the conviction that the gospel must be preached in all the world. They bowed down to God because they understood the words: "For God so loved the World."

Great Men of Business Bow Down.

Andrew Carnegie, John Wanamaker. These men were entrepreneurs who learned how to accumulate and distribute wealth in the arena of capitalism. They used their wealth to encourage personal success in others. They bowed down to the God "who owns the cattle on a thousand hills" - a God who blesses those who honor Him.

Great Men of Philosophy Bow Down.

Kierkegaard, Immanuel Kant, William James, Francis Schaeffer. These men have asked the hard questions. They have challenged traditional values and ideologies in an attempt to establish a rock solid conviction based on truth. They bowed down to the God of all wisdom, who has hidden His treasures from the proud and revealed them to the innocent.

Great Men of Adventure Bow Down.

Christopher Columbus, David Livingstone, Charles Lindbergh. These men caught a vision of doing something that had never been done before. They were pioneer spirits who left us a legacy of courage and discovery. They bowed down to the God who promises that "our hearts cannot begin to imagine what God has prepared for those that love Him."

Great Men of Art Bow Down

William Blake, Leonardo Da Vinci, Arnold Friberg. These men understood that God is an artist, who created a world of wonder with only a few broad strokes of His celestial paintbrush, and who desires that we enjoy the beauty of His creation. They bowed down to the designer God who gives us light and color and texture and breathtaking beauty.

Great Men of Music Bow Down.

Bach, Beethoven, Handel and Haydn. These masters of the piano and the stringed instruments captivated the world with their sometimes soft, sometimes powerful display of timeless melody and medley. They bowed down to the God of praise, who opened the portals of heaven to give them a glimpse of heaven's worship and majestic glory.

Great Men of Medicine Bow Down.

Albert Schweitzer, Sir William Osler. Louis Pasteur. These men gave their lives to the quest of studying and treating the human body to cure the diseases that plague mankind. They bowed down to the God who has "fearfully and wonderfully" created the body of man. They understood the awesome responsibility of being an agent of healing.

Great Men of Theology Bow Down.

Calvin, Luther, Bunyan and Jonathan Edwards. These men left secular fields of endeavor to follow a calling which sought to define and reveal the God of Creation. They bowed down to the living God who became personal to them, and they bowed down because they understood the need for humility before an awesome God.

Find Us Faithful

We're pilgrims on the journey of the narrow road
And those who've gone before us line the way
Cheering on the faithful, encouraging the weary
Their lives a stirring testament to God's sustaining grace.
Surrounded by so great a cloud of witnesses
Let us run the race not only for the prize
But as those who've gone before us
Let us leave to those behind us
The heritage of faithfulness passed on through godly lives

Oh may all who come behind us find us faithful
May the fire of our devotion light their way
May the footprints that we leave
Lead them to believe
And the lives we live inspire them to obey
Oh may all who come behind us find us faithful

After all our hopes and dreams have come and gone
And our children sift through all we've left behind
May the clues that they discover
and the memories they uncover
Become the light that leads them
to the road we each must find
Oh may all who come behind us find us faithful

———

Words and Music by Jon Mohr
Sung by Steve Green
Copyright 1988 Birdwing Music/Jonathan Mark Music
(administrated By The Sparrow Corp.)
All Rights Reserved. International Copyright secured.

Reflections from the Author

A book about great men will probably stir up many "great" men to wonder why they are not included. One of the criteria for selection in this book is that you are not alive to read it. There are some exceptions, however, whom I have chosen because their lives are so influential that their absence from these pages would be a shortcoming. This book is written from a Judeo-Christian, or western cultural perspective, which mostly ignores the global cultures of the Far East and the Middle East. The first criteria for inclusion in this book is an outstanding quotation about Jehovah God, Christ or the Bible, which is missing from their indigenous religious traditions.

While this book has been written from the perspective of an evangelical Christian, my target audience is not necessarily the church crowd. It is my hope to attract a readership of open minded liberals who might be overwhelmed by the reality that there are hundreds of historical figures whose worldview had a godly foundation. The selections have come from the ranks of those men whom I considered to be heroic figures and worthy of mention. Though you may not agree with all selections, it is my hope you can find inspiration from all of them.

Allow me to clarify that those I refer to as great men are on the left-hand side of the page. Though I have quoted from another three hundred men (and women), I have used their quotes to enhance the character qualities of the great men themselves. It should also be noted that I have not included women in this particular work - not because there are not great women to be featured - but because I have chosen to make a strong appeal to the men of this world who need to see their male counterparts as bold and courageous and full of faith. I have promised my niece Rachel that she can write the sequel called "Great Women Stand Up."

I have always loved great quotes from great men. This book came into being when I woke up one day to realize that I knew nothing about many of the men whose quotes I cherished so much. I began to cross reference the many quotes from great men about God, or Christ, or the Bible, and was surprised to find that I could fill up a book with great quotes and simple vignettes from their lives. The one page format is my contribution to a busy culture which is gradually eroding the attention span of its future leaders.

I have not written this book to give the illusion that my name should be placed in the context of these great and noble men of history, nor to leverage my name by association with the ranks of these great men. I am a sinner saved by God's grace, and my personal resume falls far short of these heroes of history. It is a legacy we all share since we have in common a congenital flaw that we call "the fall of man." Perhaps it is finally this acknowledgement in my life that has given me the clear vision to write this book. Proverbs 25:6 says: "Do not claim honor in the presence of the king, and do not stand in the place of great men."

Great Men Bow Down is a book for students and teachers and families and churches. It is a book for coaches and athletes and businessman. It is a book that can quickly introduce the reader to 150 heroes throughout history that have acknowledged the God of the Bible as their source of strength. It is a book for college kids who need to know the truth about how faith has played a vital role in the development of our great men of history. It is my vision that young readers can personalize their own heroes of history by reading these pages.

But I also have a vision for **giving** this book to every U.S. soldier who wants to read short profiles about great men of achievement and great men of history. These men deserve to be inspired daily by stories which will motivate them to achieve their own goals. I also have a vision for **giving** this book to every U.S. prisoner who wants to rise above the consequences of his life and to anchor himself in the occupation of new aspirations - to submit himself to the God of the Bible, the God who can exchange guilt with forgiveness and despair with hope. This is my vision.

Life is brief and history is but a parenthesis as eternity unfolds. These men of renown help us to understand that greatness is best understood only in the context of humbling one's self before a sovereign God.

Introduction

Every parent that reads these words knows that the world is changing. We watch with bated breath as the arenas of education, technology and culture continue to rumble with a seismic force that threatens the very fabric of predictability. With one hand we hold onto tradition - where we live, who we know, and how we function; with the other hand we stretch toward a future of progress, basking in the inventions of convenience and efficiency, thankful that our kids have new opportunities and new horizons of experience awaiting them. Or are we really thankful for what is to come?

There is a new reality emerging in the world today. It is no longer called a "paradigm shift." I would suggest to you that the new term is "paradigm inversion." Yes, the world is not only turning and stretching and shifting. It is now morphing into a new reality, slowly changing generations of history and tradition and predictability. As an example, I write this book like writers for 500 years have written: anticipating that a volume will be produced and then reproduced and then distributed across the free world. But you KNOW that it is possible that technology in this generation may truly make the paginated book as obsolete as the scroll was 300 years ago. Not only do we fear that the beloved books that we have known could become obsolete by technology, we also understand that the ideologies of other despotic cultures could seek to undermine, and condemn and eradicate the very book that you are reading today.

Enter the great men of history. Upon what common thread was woven the fabric which provided our tapestry of life, liberty and the pursuit of happiness? Emerson said: **"There is properly no history - only biography. All history is but the lengthened shadow of a great man."** If that is true, then we are indebted to the valiant men of the past, who have fought our battles, defined our government and molded our character. But again, I suggest to you that the paradigm is not only shifting, but being inverted. The following diagram represents the world we have known and the world as it is becoming.

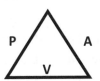 

The trinity of man, his body, mind and spirit are symbolized in each triangle. We could also call these three the physical, mental and spiritual components of man. In each triangle you see P, which stands for Possessions; A, which stands for Abilities; and V, which stands for Values. On the left you observe that Values are the foundational component of the trinity of man. On the right you observe that Possessions and Abilities form a point, providing a very small and precarious foundation. To parallel these two systems, the physical part of man is Possessions; the mental part of man is Abilities; and the spiritual part of man is Values. Another way to say this is that man is composed of three essential parts: what we HAVE, what we DO and what we BELIEVE.

For thousands of years, man has possessed relatively little. Food, clothing and shelter were the mantra for a contented life. I would suggest to you that the generation after World War II began to experience the paradigm shift that would eventually become inverted. The baby boomer generation of the '60s began to experience Possessions in a whole new dimension: cars, houses, televisions, computers, mobile phones, etc. For the first time in history a generation of kids were born who had more than the average king in the not-too-ancient past. Possessions took on a new significance in our lives and we coined a word that symbolized the emptiness of being possessed by your possessions: MATERIALISM.

Then comes "the next generation." After the baby boomers were the "x" generation. Possessions were already a commodity in their culture, so experience became the new high for them. Not only did they have more, but they now would push the envelope to experience more. Their Abilities were tested and challenged, and what they DO would reach a new level of sophistication, called HEDONISM. The Greeks coined this term to describe a life of raucous pleasure. Nothing wrong with fun. Nothing wrong with recreation. But this generation would push adventure to its limits - drugs and parties and sex and the entitlement of global vacations seem to be the siren call that lured this generation to a life of meaningless activity.

Now comes the "millennial generation." The last leg of the trinity paradigm is about to change. For a generation that has it all and done it all, there is not much left except to explore the outer limits of the Value system itself. This generation does not have a historic value system, nor a traditional value system. Their value system is rooted, or should I say "not rooted" in a society that believes anything and tolerates anything. In the words of Malcolm Muggeridge: **"It has been said that when human beings stop believing in God they believe in nothing. The truth is much worse; they believe in anything."** Relativism used to be a word in a philosophy class; today it is a reality which threatens to force us to shelter or even quarantine our kids, for fear that the poisonous air of HUMANISM will suck the very life out of them. No longer is what you believe the stable foundation of the trinity. The inversion is now complete.

Perhaps now you can appreciate the traditions that have been handed down from generation to generation. We now have a culture, an ideology, that no longer believes that "the glass is half full" - that we are royally blessed by God with health and food and employment and hope for the future; our culture now trains us to believe "the glass is half empty" - that somehow, in this cosmic accident that we call humanity, we are indoctrinated by the educators to believe that we evolved from a random pattern of stars that exploded millions of years ago, creating a complex life form that could sustain itself and morph into a creature that, even by evolutionary standards, would be a miracle every time a new life is born.

It is because of this inversion that we now begin to cling tenaciously to the great men who have come before us. They were great thinkers and achievers, yes. But most of all they understood that if the trinity of man was to have order and predictability and stability and wisdom and hope - the VALUE component of man would have to be the foundational component. What we believe has to be the driving force. It has to be stabilized, unlike the tottering legs of Materialism and Hedonism, and there must be a value system that becomes the lens through which all of life is seen. For you see, humanism is having **FAITH** in the wrong things. Hedonism is having **HOPE** in the wrong things; and materialism is having **LOVE** for the wrong things. Sound familiar? So what was it that the great men of the past had or saw or experienced that we need so desperately today? The Bible implies that faith, hope and love are the lifeblood of mankind. Faith in the Messiah of the Bible, hope in the destiny of the Bible and love for the truth of the Bible.

The great men who have been exposed to the Judeo-Christian message for two thousand years have been building on a solid foundation. What I believe IS who I am. What I believe must be more than what I possess or what I have experienced. What I believe must be rooted and grounded in the reality of Jehovah God, the God of the Bible, who is the Creator, Sustainer and Redeemer of life. Any other religion or ideology or philosophy will ultimately crumble under the weight of man's relentless march toward destruction.

The Post Modern Culture of Globalism is slowly eradicating the history we have known and the heroes we have admired. As western culture concedes its place of prominence in world politics, and levels the playing field to allow other cultures, religions and ideologies to rewrite our history books, we will find that "they" are not as sympathetic to our Founding Fathers as we are. In fact, we will find that there is an insidious jealousy which seeks to undermine our heritage and strip away our national (or cultural) dignity and pride. Nationalism and pride of country and culture are seen as a primitive tool to those whose own global agenda is a far worse form of civil management - stripping away individualism, private ownership, free enterprise and the general dignity that our Judeo-Christian culture values so much.

Since the dawn of human history, men have bowed down to authority - first by brute force, then to difficult taskmasters, and finally by emperors whose kingdoms demanded their allegiance. There will always be those in authority, and those who are subservient to authority. The premise of this book is that truly great men bow down to a power greater than kings and emperors. Truly great men recognize the ultimate authority of sovereign God, who rules over creation and conscience and circumstance.

In his book *On Heroes, Hero-Worship and the Heroic in History*, Thomas Carlyle paints a clear picture of one who is a hero. He says a hero is a man who willingly devotes his life to the divine and inner truth, and shares his vision with the rest of the world. Carlyle would further define a great man as one who is a deep and spiritual being, living his life by divine truths. It is based on the CONFIDENCE of those divine truths that Carlyle observed overwhelming CONVICTION in the life of the hero. He also said: **"the Great Man was always as lightning out of Heaven; the rest of men waited for him like fuel, and then they too would flame."** What a powerful picture of the heroic leader who steps into our lives to give us opportunity and hope. We wait with rapt anticipation for those great men to show up on the world stage.

The substance of this book is threefold: great quotes, great testimonies and great biographies. Jesus said in Matthew 12:37: **"By your words you shall be justified, and by your words you shall be condemned."** The criteria for the selection of each man is, first of all, that words have come from his lips that have, in some way, honored God, or Christ, or the Bible. These men are deemed great by society for many different reasons. By some standards, many of these men have flawed character, and some might even be considered scoundrels. But deep within the recesses of the human heart, they have acknowledged, at some point in their careers, that Jehovah God controls their destiny. It is my hope that schoolchildren across the nation will read these pages and be inspired by the brief glimpses into the lives of these heroes. It is my hope that the overwhelming impact of these brave and talented men will motivate a new generation to rise above the mediocrity of the age and faithfully serve the God of all ages. The secular world would have us believe that greatness is man-made. Truly great men will continue to prove that they have been gifted for a purpose far greater than their own egos or self enrichment. They have ascended the high peaks of history because great men always bow down to a Great God.

Courtesy: National Park Service
Mt. Rushmore, South Dakota by Gutzon Borglum, 1925. 14 years in the making.
60 feet tall, 1278 acres, 400 workmen using dynamite and jackhammers.

"Lives of Great Men all remind us
We can make our lives sublime
And departing, leave behind us
Footprints on the sands of time."

Henry Wadsworth Longfellow

"I speak as a man of the world to men of the world; and I say to you, search the Scriptures! The Bible is the book of all others, to be read at all ages, and in all conditions of human life."

JOHN QUINCY ADAMS
1767 - 1848 (80 years)

"Duty is ours; the results are God's".

Adams served as the sixth PRESIDENT OF THE UNITED STATES from 1825 to 1829, and was the son of John Adams, the second President and Founding Father. He took the oath of office on a book of laws, instead of the more traditional Bible, in order to preserve the separation of church and state. In spite of this strong view of separation, he said the following: **"The highest glory of the American Revolution was this: it connected in one indissoluble bond the principles of civil government with the principles of Christianity."** Adams is regarded as one of the greatest diplomats in American history, and during his tenure as Secretary of State to James Monroe, he wrote the very important Monroe Doctrine, which officially put all other nations on notice not to try to colonize any more of the Americas or the Western Hemisphere. Adams is the only major figure in American history who knew both the Founding Fathers and Abraham Lincoln. While Adams was in office, his own father and Thomas Jefferson both died on July 4, 1826 - an ironic and fitting tribute to these great men of history. For 69 years he faithfully kept a diary, which now totals fifty volumes. The Bible was central to his concept of education. **"So great is my veneration for the Bible that the earlier my children begin to read it the more confident will be my hope that they will prove useful citizens of their country and respectable members of society."**

Look among the nations!
Observe! Be astonished! Wonder!
Because I am doing something in your days
You would not believe if you were told.
HABAKKUK 1:5

The Bible

It is impossible mentally or socially
to enslave a Bible reading people.
Horace Greeley

The Bible is a postgraduate course
in the richest library of human experience.
Herbert Hoover

If God is a reality and the soul is a reality,
and you are an immortal being,
what are you doing with your Bible shut?
Herrick Johnson

The Bible is an inexhaustible fountain of all truths.
The existence of the Bible is the greatest blessing
which humanity has ever experienced.
Immanuel Kant

All the good from the Savior of the world
is communicated through this book.
All the things desirable to man are contained in it.
Abraham Lincoln

If a man is not familiar with the Bible,
he has suffered a loss which he had better
make all possible haste to correct.
Theodore Roosevelt

"My maker was Divine Authority,
The highest wisdom, and the primal love.
Before me nothing but eternal things were made,
and I endure eternally."

DANTE ALIGHIERI
1265-1321 (56 years)

"Heaven wheels above you, displaying to you her
eternal glories, and still your eyes are on the ground."

Dante wrote "The Divine Comedy," a 14,000 line epic poem, considered to be a masterpiece of Latin literature. At the age of 35, in about the year 1300, he describes his spiritual change: **"In the middle of the journey of life I came to myself within a dark wood where the straight way was lost. A mighty flame followed a tiny spark."** He began writing his classic which tells a story of man's redemption: his relationship to God and his progression through three stages of life. Stage One is Hell (called the 'inferno'), an allegory about sin, or man's separation from God. Stage Two is Purgatory, an allegory about the virtue of living a godly life; and Stage Three is Paradise, an allegory about eternal life in Heaven with the Trinity. Dante was a pharmacist whose personal story revolved around the political wars of Italy, and his exile from his beloved Florence. Describing Hell, he said: **"Abandon hope, all ye who enter here."** Describing Purgatory, (or life on earth) he said: **"In His Will is our peace."** Describing Heaven, he said: **"At this high moment, ability failed my capacity to describe."** Perhaps best known is his quote regarding man's need for conviction. **"The darkest places in Hell are reserved for those who maintained their neutrality in times of moral crisis."** For seven hundred years, Dante has called us to accountability with God.

Eyes have not seen, Nor ears heard,
Nor entered into the heart of man,
The things which God has prepared
For them that love Him. *
1 CORINTHIANS 2:9

This is a cheerful world as I see it
From my garden under the shadow of my vines;
But if I were to ascend some high mountain
And look out over the wide lands
You know very well what I should see.
Robbers on the highways,
Pirates on the seas;
Armies fighting, cities burning;
In the amphitheaters,
Men murdered to please applauding crowds;
Selfishness and despair and cruelty
Under all roofs.

It is a bad world, my friend,
An incredibly bad world;
But I have found in the midst of it
A quiet and holy people
Who have learned a great lesson.
They have found a joy
Which is a thousand times better
Than any pleasure of our sinful lives.
They are despised and persecuted,
But they care not.
They are masters of their souls.
They have overcome the world,
These people, my friend,
Are the Christians,
And I am one of them.

CYPRIAN
4th Century Martyr

"When everything is in its place within us,
we ourselves are in equilibrium
with the whole work of God.
Deep and grave enthusiasm
for the eternal beauty and eternal order -
these surely are the foundations of wisdom."

HENRI FREDERIC AMIEL
1821-1881 (59 years)

Amiel was a Swiss philosopher and professor of Aesthetics at the Academy of Geneva. Aesthetics is one of six major fields in philosophy, and is the study of values, reflections, culture, judgment and taste. From the age of 27 until his death, Amiel wrote 17,000 pages of text that are now identified as "Journal Intime" or "Private Journal." His family were descendants from the Hugenots, French Protestants, who fled to Switzerland for religious liberty. As a teacher, Amiel said**: "The highest function of the teacher consists not so much in imparting knowledge as in stimulating the pupil to love and pursue knowledge. To know how to suggest is the art of teaching. The great artist is the simplifier."** As a philosopher, Amiel said: **"Without passion, man is a mere latent force and possibility, like the flint which awaits the shock of the iron before it can give forth its spark."** As a devout believer, Amiel said: **"Sacrifice still exists everywhere, and everywhere the elect of each generation suffer for the salvation of the rest. Sacrifice, which is the passion of great souls, has never been the law of societies. Every life is a profession of faith, and exercises an inevitable and silent influence."** Amiel understood eternal values as he said: **"It is not what he had, or even what he does which expresses the worth of a man, but what he is."**

Through Him then,
let us continually offer up
a sacrifice of praise to God,
that is, the fruit of lips
that give thanks to His name.
HEBREWS 13:15

Wisdom

Nine-tenths of wisdom consists in being wise in time.
Theodore Roosevelt

———

Guts are important. Your guts are what digest things.
But it is your brains that tell you which things to swallow
and which not to swallow.
Austin Dacey

———

I do not want the peace that passes understanding.
I want the understanding which brings peace.
Hellen Keller

———

Strategic planning is worthless,
unless there is first a strategic vision.
John Naisbitt

———

An idealist believes the short run doesn't count.
A cynic believes the long run doesn't matter.
A realist believes that what is done or left undone
in the short run determines the long run.
Sidney J. Harris

———

"To my God, a heart of flame.
To my fellow men, a heart of love.
To myself, a heart of steel."

AUGUSTINE
354-430 (76 years)

"You have created us for Thyself, O God,
and our hearts are not quiet until they rest in Thee."

Augustine is honored among Christians, both Catholic and Protestant, as one of the pivotal Church Fathers during the declining years of the Roman Empire. He was a teacher of Latin grammar who spent his early life rebelling against all things moral. At the age of 32, he experienced a dramatic conversion which finally directed his great intellect to the God of Creation. He marveled at the majesty of man when he said: **"Men go abroad to wonder at the heights of mountains, at the huge waves of the sea, at the long courses of the rivers, at the vast compass of the ocean, at the circular motions of the stars, and they pass by themselves without wondering."** Augustine became a priest and later a Bishop in the city Hippo, North Africa. His greatest works were *Confessions* and *City of God*. His doctrine of original sin influenced John Calvin and Martin Luther a thousand years later. It was his humility that defined his greatness. **"Do you wish to rise? Begin by descending. Do you plan a tower that will pierce the clouds? Do you desire to construct a vast and lofty fabric of greatness? Think first about the foundations of humility. The higher your structure is to be, the deeper must be its foundation. There is something in humility which strangely exalts the heart."** His greatest discovery was this: **"God loves each of us as if there were only one of us."**

Create in me a clean heart, O God,
And renew a steadfast spirit within me.
Do not cast me away from Your presence
And do not take Your Holy Spirit from me.
Restore to me the joy of Your salvation
And sustain me with a willing spirit.
King David, PSALM 51:10-12

"I probed the hidden depths of my soul
and wrung its pitiful secrets from it.
And when I gathered them all before the eyes of my heart,
a great storm broke within me,
bringing with it a great deluge of tears,
for I felt that I was still enslaved by my sins,
and in misery I kept crying,
"How long shall I go on saying,
tomorrow, tomorrow, tomorrow? Why not now?
Why not make an end of my ugly sins at this moment?"
I heard the inner voice of a young child say,
"take it and read it, take it and read it."
I seized the Bible and opened it,
and in silence I read the first passage
on which my eyes fell.
'Put on the Lord Jesus,
and make no provision for the flesh.'
I had no wish to read more;
for in an instant, as I came to the end of the sentence,
it was as though the light of faith
flooded into my heart,
and all the darkness of doubt was dispelled."

Augustine

To love God is the greatest romance.
To seek God is the greatest adventure.
To find God is the greatest achievement.

Augustine

"The more difficult and incredible the divine mystery is, the more honor is shown to God in believing it, and the nobler is the victory of faith."

SIR FRANCIS BACON
1561-1626 (65 years)

"Of all virtues and dignities of the mind, goodness is the greatest, being the character of the Deity; and without it, man is a busy, mischievous, wretched thing."

Bacon was an English lawyer, statesman, philosopher and scientist, who was called by Thomas Jefferson one of the three most influential men in history. He became the Attorney General of England in 1613 and was knighted (Sir) for his achievements. Bacon claimed his threefold goals were to discover truth, to serve his country, and to serve his church. He is credited with discovering the "*scientific method of inquiry,*" a process of organized objective analysis of science, still used today. Though he was an Anglican (Church of England) he showed signs of sympathy to Puritanism, attending sermons in the local Puritan chapel. Perhaps his most significant contribution was his vision for a utopian new world in North America. In his novel, *the New Atlantis*, he envisioned a land where there would be freedom of religious and political expression, greater rights for women, abolition of slavery and the elimination of debtors' prison. He played a leading role in creating the British colonies in Virginia and the Carolinas. Bacon was a devout believer who said, **"God is to be conceived as an eternally continuing Power of Thought, and is the only Essence - the Power and Cause of all Nature - the Divine Artist. Our humanity is a poor thing, except for the divinity that stirs within us."**

It is the glory of God
to conceal a matter;
but the glory of kings
is to search out a matter.
King Solomon, PROVERBS 25:2

(Bacon's favorite verse)

Quotes from Bacon

There never was found in any age of the world,
either philosophy, or sect, or religion, or law, or discipline -
which did so highly exalt the good of the community,
and increase private and particular good -
as the holy Christian faith.
Hence, it clearly appears that it was one and the same God
that gave the Christian law to men,
who also gave the laws of nature to the creature.

———

We cannot too often think,
that there is a never-sleeping eye
that reads our hearts and registers our thoughts.

———

They that deny God, destroy man's nobility.
For clearly man is of kin to the beasts by his body,
And if he be not of kin to God by his spirit,
he is a base and ignoble creature.

———

I would rather believe all the fables and myths of paganism
than to believe that this universal frame is without a Mind.

"I must live by myself alone;
but I know well that God is nearer to me than others
in my art, so I will walk fearlessly with Him."

LUDWIG van BEETHOVEN
1770 - 1827 (56 years)

"Then let us all do what is right,
strive with all our might toward the unattainable,
develop as fully as we can the gifts God has given us."

By age 7, the great Beethoven, German-born classical pianist and composer, was already performing publicly and hailed as a child prodigy. By age 25, he premiered a piano concerto in his new residence of Vienna and netted enough money for a year's living expenses. Within a year, he began to lose his hearing, likely suffering from tinnitus, a severe ringing in his ears. The cause of his malady is uncertain, but speculation was lead poisoning, typhus or auto immune disorder. He regularly immersed his head in cold water to stay awake, also a possible factor. He composed 32 piano sonatas, 16 string quartets and nine orchestral symphonies. By the age of 42 he was completely deaf, and he relied on a steel rod attached to the piano sound-board to transfer vibrations to his jaw. At the end of the premiere of his Ninth Symphony, the audience rose with a thunderous applause. Realizing that he had not heard their approval, he wept. His philosophy of music was: **"Music should strike fire from the heart of man, and bring tears from the eyes of woman."** When he died, a clap of thunder signaled his passing. He said of himself: **"There are, and will ever be, a thousand princes; but there is only one Beethoven."**

The LORD said to him,
"Who has made man's mouth?
Or who makes him mute or deaf,
or seeing or blind?
Is it not I, the LORD?
EXODUS 4:11

Music

Music speaks what cannot be expressed,
soothes the mind and gives it rest,
heals the heart and makes it whole,
flows from heaven to the soul.
Unknown

———

Music is an agreeable harmony
for the honor of God and the permissible delights of the soul.
Johann Sebastian Bach

———

The Church knew what the psalmist knew:
Music praises God. Music is well or better able
to praise him than the building of the church and all its decoration;
it is the Church's greatest ornament.
Igor Stravinsky

———

Music and rhythm find their way into the secret places of the soul.
Plato

———

Music is God's gift to man, the only art of Heaven given to earth,
the only art of earth we take to Heaven.
Walter Savage Landor

"Why is the Bible more entertaining and instructive than any other book? Is it not because it is addressed to the imagination, which is spiritual sensation, and immediately goes to the understanding or reason? The Old and New Testaments are the Great Code of Art."

WILLIAM BLAKE
1757-1827 (69 years)

"When the doors of perception are cleansed, man will see things as they truly are - infinite."

Blake was an English poet, painter and printmaker, who was called by one scholar, 'a glorious luminary, not to be classed with his contemporaries.' He invented a style of engraving, called 'relief etching,' in which he would produce poems or art with acid resistant paint on copper plates, and then etch the plates in acid to dissolve away the untreated copper. Blake believed that the spirit of man was manifest through his imagination, which was quickened by the Spirit of God. He said, **"The human mind cannot go beyond the gift of God. I myself do nothing. The Holy Spirit accomplishes all through me."** He was a Moravian whose faith taught him: **"The glory of Christianity is to conquer by forgiveness."** He spoke harshly against the Church of England, but always debated with an open mind: **"The man who never alters his opinions is like standing water, and breeds reptiles of the mind."** He bowed before the God of Creation when he said: **"To see a world in a grain of sand, and heaven in a wild flower. To hold infinity in the palms of your hand and eternity in an hour."** He was a visionary who embraced life with a passion. His philosophy was summed up when he said: **"Great things are done when men and mountains meet."**

> But the Helper, the Holy Spirit,
> whom the Father will send in My name,
> He will teach you all things,
> and bring to your remembrance
> all that I said to you.
> **Jesus, JOHN 14:26**

Forgiveness

God pardons like a mother,
who kisses the offense into everlasting forgiveness.
Henry Ward Beecher

———

The stupid neither forgive nor forget; the naive forgive and forget;
the wise forgive but do not forget.
Thomas S. Szasz

———

Forgiveness is the fragrance that the violet sheds
on the heel that has crushed it.
Mark Twain

———

Christianity, with its doctrine of humility, of forgiveness, of love,
is incompatible with the state, with its haughtiness, its violence,
its punishment and its wars.
Leo Tolstoy

———

Never does the human soul appear so strong
as when it foregoes revenge and dares to forgive an injury.
Edwin Hubbel Chapin

———

He that cannot forgive others, breaks the bridge
over which he himself must pass if he would ever reach heaven;
for everyone has need to be forgiven.
George Herbert

"I know men, and I tell you that Jesus Christ is no mere man. Between Him and every other person in the world there is no possible term of comparison. Alexander, Caesar, Charlemagne and I founded empires; but upon what did we rest the creations of our genius? Upon force. Jesus Christ alone founded his empire upon love; And at this hour millions of men would die for Him."

NAPOLEON BONAPARTE
1769-1821 (52 years)

Napoleon was born Italian, and rose in the ranks of the French army in Italy after the French Revolution. At the age of 30, he staged a coup d'état and by 35, he became the self-proclaimed Emperor of France. It was Napoleon who sold the Louisiana Purchase (14 states) to the US for 3 cents per acre. He sent France to war against every major power in Europe until he was defeated and exiled to the Island of Elba. He escaped Elba, only to be finally conquered at Waterloo. Napoleon was a bona-fide power-hungry politician who said, **"If you wish to be a success in the world, promise everything, deliver nothing."** In spite of his obsession for power, he understood that true power and authority resides, not in war, not in politics, but in the Christian faith. Of Christ he said: **"The nature of Christ's existence is mysterious, I admit; but this mystery meets the wants of man. Reject it and the world is an inexplicable riddle; believe it, and the history of our race is satisfactorily explained."** Of the Bible he said, **"The Bible is no mere book, but a Living Creature, with a power that conquers all that oppose it."** Though he showed little evidence of conforming to the image of Christ in his power laden life, nevertheless, Napoleon bowed before God's sovereignty as he said, **"There are only two forces in the world, the sword and the spirit. In the long run the sword will always be conquered by the spirit."**

For though we walk in the flesh,
we do not war according to the flesh,
for the weapons of our warfare
are not of the flesh, but divinely powerful
for the destruction of fortresses.
Paul the Apostle, 2 CORINTHIANS 10:3-4

The Desire for Power

Power tends to corrupt, and absolute power corrupts absolutely.
Lord Acton

———

We thought, because we had power, we had wisdom.
Stephen Vincent Benét

———

Nearly all men can stand adversity,
but if you want to test a man's character, give him power.
Abraham Lincoln

———

The power of man has grown in every sphere, except over himself.
Winston Churchill

———

I hope our wisdom will grow with our power,
and teach us, that the less we use our power the greater it will be.
Thomas Jefferson

———

Being powerful is like being a lady.
If you have to tell people you are, you aren't.
Margaret Thatcher

———

Use power to help people. For we are given power,
not to advance our own purposes nor to make a great show in the world,
nor a name. There is but one just use of power and it is to serve people.
George W. Bush

"First they came for the Communists,
but I was not a Communist so I did not speak out.
Then they came for the Socialists
and the Trade Unionists, but I was neither,
so I did not speak out. Then they came for the Jews,
but I was not a Jew so I did not speak out.
And when they came for me,
there was no one left to speak out for me."

DIETRICH BONHOEFFER
1906-1945 (39 years)

Dietrich Bonhoeffer was a gifted pianist who earned a doctorate in theology, taught at the University of Berlin, and was a Lutheran pastor. His father was a neurologist/ psychiatrist who had hoped Dietrich would follow in his footsteps. Perhaps that is why he said: **"In the presence of a psychiatrist I can only be a sick man; in the presence of a Christian brother, I can dare to be a sinner."** When Hitler rose to power, Dietrich voiced opposition and became a key member of the Nazi resistance movement. He was eventually banned from Berlin by the Gestapo in 1939. He was arrested in 1945 for conspiracy against Hitler and was hung in a German concentration camp just four weeks before the end of the war. Days before he died, he was quoted as saying: **"This is the end - for me the beginning of life."** His book, *The Cost of Discipleship*, has become a classic inspiration, and it begins with the following: **"Cheap grace is the mortal enemy of the church."** Of prayer he said: **"To be silent does not mean to be inactive; rather it means to breathe in the will of God, to listen attentively and be ready to obey."** The US Holocaust Memorial Museum honors his memory with his own words: **"Only he who believes is obedient, and only he who is obedient believes."**

For I consider that the
sufferings of this present time
are not worthy to be compared
with the glory that is yet
to be revealed to us.
Paul the Apostle, ROMANS 8:18

Obedience

Obedience is the fruit of faith.
Christina Rossetti

Obedience is the primary object of all sound education.
Elizabeth Missing Sewell

Obedience to lawful authority is the foundation of manly character.
Robert E. Lee

One act of obedience is better than one hundred sermons.
Dietrich Bonhoeffer

Strength was the virtue of paganism;
obedience is the virtue of Christianity.
David Hare

I am certain that obedience is the gateway
through which knowledge and love enter the mind of the child.
Anne Sullivan

"While women weep . . . and children go hungry,
I'll fight; while men go to prison. . .
And there remains one dark soul
without the light of God, I'll fight,
I'll fight to the very end!"

WILLIAM BOOTH
1829-1912 (83 years)

At the age of 13, young Booth became a pawnbroker in Nottingham, England to provide for his family after his father died. At the age of 23, he followed the call to become a fulltime evangelist in the Methodist Reform Church. For ten years, the Methodist organization kept placing him in pastoral positions, but his heart was in evangelism, so he left the Methodists and became a non-denominational preacher. He and wife Catherine began to minister to the poor through soup kitchens and in 1878, *The Salvation Army* was born. Booth understood that hungry people are primarily concerned with their physical needs. **"But what is the use of preaching the Gospel to men whose whole attention is concentrated upon a mad, desperate struggle to keep themselves alive?"** The Army was set up with military positions and military strategy, and Booth soon became known as "The General". Within his lifetime, *The Salvation Army* spread to 58 countries, and today they can be found in every corner of the earth. Booth prophesied the following: **"I consider that the chief dangers which confront the coming century will be religion without the Holy Ghost, Christianity without Christ, forgiveness without repentance, salvation without regeneration, politics without God, and heaven without hell."** Unfortunately, his prophecy rings true. He said, **"The greatness of a man's power is the measure of his surrender."**

For I was hungry,
and you gave Me something to eat;
I was thirsty,
and you gave Me something to drink;
I was a stranger,
and you invited Me in;
Jesus, MATTHEW 25:35

Compassion

Compassion is not weakness,
and concern for the unfortunate is not socialism.
Hubert H. Humphrey

––––

Kindness is the language
which the deaf can hear and the blind can see.
Mark Twain

––––

Kindness is in our power,
even when fondness is not.
Samuel Johnson

––––

When I was young, I admired clever people.
Now that I am old, I admire kind people.
Abraham Joshua Heschel

––––

Life is mostly froth and bubble,
Two things stand like stone,
Kindness in another's trouble,
Courage in your own.
Adam Lindsay Gordon

––––

The best portion of a good man's life -
his little, nameless, unremembered acts of kindness and love.
William Wordsworth

"The goal of prayer is the ear of God,
a goal that can only be reached by patient and
continuous waiting upon Him, pouring out our hearts to Him
and permitting Him to speak to us. Only by so doing can we
expect to know Him, and as we come to know Him better
we shall spend more time in His presence
and find that presence a constant and
ever-increasing delight."

E.M. BOUNDS

1835 - 1913 (78 years)

Edward Bounds became the youngest practicing attorney in the State of Missouri at the age of nineteen. Five years later, he closed his law office and became the pastor of a Methodist church. During the Civil War he was wrongly arrested by Union troops and placed in prison for 18 months. He then became a Confederate chaplain and was imprisoned again. After the war, he pastored a Methodist Episcopal church, and eventually moved to Washington, Georgia where he married, had nine children and became an itinerant evangelist. He began every morning at 4:00 am with three intense hours of prayer. He wrote 11 books on prayer, and became known as one of the great prayer warriors in history. Bounds often said: **"The church is looking for better methods. God is looking for better men."** His formula was simple: persist in prayer and wait on God. **"Our whole being must be in our praying. It is only when the whole heart is gripped with the passion of prayer that the life-giving fire descends. This is hard work, but it is God's work, and man's best labor. I think Christians fail so often to get answers to their prayers because they do not wait long enough on God. Such praying always reminds me of the little boy ringing his neighbor's doorbell, and then running away as fast as he can."**

Devote yourselves to prayer,
keeping alert in it
with an attitude of thanksgiving;
COLOSSIANS 4:2

Prayer

Do not pray for easy lives. Pray to be stronger men!
Do not pray for tasks equal to your powers.
Pray for power equal to your tasks.
Phillip Brooks

——

Pray as though everything depended on God.
Work as though everything depended on you.
Augustine

——

To be a Christian without prayer is no more possible
than to be alive without breathing.
Martin Luther King, Jr.

——

I have had prayers answered - most strangely so sometimes -
but I think our heavenly Father's lovingkindness
has been even more evident in what He has refused me.
Lewis Carroll

——

Pray often; for prayer is a shield to the soul,
a sacrifice to God, and a scourge for Satan.
John Bunyan

——

Prayer has comforted us in sorrow
and will help strengthen us for the journey ahead.
George W. Bush

**"Our humanity is trapped by moral adolescents.
We have too many men of science, too few men of God.
The world has achieved brilliance without wisdom
and power without conscience."**

General OMAR BRADLEY
1893-1981 (88 years)

**"We have grasped the mystery of the atom
and rejected the Sermon on the Mount."**

Only ten generals in U.S. history have been appointed to the war time status of General of the Army - a five star general. Bradley holds that distinction with Washington, (Revolutionary War) Grant, Sherman and Sheridan (Civil War) and Pershing, Marshall, Eisenhower, MacArthur and Henry Arnold. During the World War II Normandy invasion, he commanded 1.3 million soldiers in the 12th Army Group, the largest group ever assembled under one general. After the war, Bradley was selected as the first Chairman of the Joint Chiefs of Staff and the head of the Veterans Administration. At West Point, he played baseball on the 1914 team on which every player eventually became a general. His class of 1915 was called "the class the stars fell on," later producing 59 Generals in the Army ranks. He went on to become a math teacher at West Point before active duty. Bradley was not a tough-as-nails kind of general, however. He was known as "the soldier's general." One reporter said of him, "The thing I most admire about Omar Bradley is his gentleness. He was never known to issue an order to anybody without first saying 'Please.'" Bradley's philosophy was all about character development. **"Character is an all-inclusive thing. If a man has character, everyone has confidence in him."**

Test yourselves
to see if you are in the faith;
examine yourselves!
Or do you not recognize this about yourselves,
that Jesus Christ is in you -
unless indeed you fail the test?
Paul the Apostle, 2 CORINTHIANS 13:5

Character

Most people say that it is the intellect which makes a great scientist.
They are wrong; it is character.
Albert Einstein

––––

Character is like a tree and reputation is like a shadow.
The shadow is what we think of it; the tree is the real thing.
Abraham Lincoln

––––

There is nothing in which people more betray their character
than in what they laugh at.
Johann Wolfgang von Goethe

––––

Character is the sum and total of a person's choices.
P. B. Fitzwater

––––

There is something even more valuable to civilization than wisdom,
and that is character.
Henry Louis Mencken

––––

Reputation is what men and women think of us;
character is what God and angels know of us.
Thomas Paine

"I have a secret thought
from some things I have observed:
That God may perhaps design you
for some singular service in the world."

DAVID BRAINERD
1718-1747 (29 years)

Yale University dedicated one of its buildings (Brainerd Hall) to this young man, in spite of the fact that he was expelled in his junior year for referring to one of his tutors by saying: **"He has no more grace than this chair."** Brainerd then committed his life to mission work among the Indians of New York, New Jersey and Pennsylvania. On one occasion, a tribe was stalking him with the intention of killing him. While they observed him on his knees in prayer, a rattle snake approached, coiled to attack within inches of him, and then strangely withdrew. In amazement the Indians referred to him as a "Prophet of God" and allowed him to live. Though he had little success in converting the Indians, his greater contribution was his diary, which contained the inner thoughts of one devoted entirely to God. **"Sunday, April 25. This morning I spent about two hours in secret duties (prayer) and was enabled more than ordinarily to agonize for immortal souls. Though it was early in the morning and the sun scarcely shined at all, yet my body was quite wet with sweat."** Jonathan Edwards wrote a tribute to him, entitled *The Life and Diary of David Brainerd*. He died of tuberculosis, and has become a hero in the modern mission movement. With humble words, he said, **"We are a long time in learning that all our strength and salvation is in God."**

But even if I am being poured out
as a drink offering upon the sacrifice
and service of your faith,
I rejoice and share my joy with you all.
Paul the Apostle, PHILIPPIANS 2:17

Purpose

I determined never to stop
until I had come to the end and achieved my purpose.
David Livingstone

———

I was always told I was special,
and I was also assured that I had a gift and a purpose.
Ashley Judd

———

What mankind wants is not talent; it is purpose.
Robert Bulwer-Lytton

———

Man is not born to solve the problems of the universe,
but to find out what he has to do
within the limits of his comprehension.
Johann Wolfgang von Goethe

———

Nothing contributes so much to tranquilizing the mind
as a steady purpose - a point on which
the soul may fix its intellectual eye.
Mary Wollstonecraft

———

There is one quality which one must possess to win,
and that is definiteness of purpose,
the knowledge of what one wants,
and a burning desire to possess it.
Napoleon Hill

"God may be a matter of indifference to the evolutionists,
and 'a life beyond' may have no charm for them,
but the mass of mankind will continue
to worship their Creator, and continue to find comfort
in the promise of their Savior
who has gone to prepare a place for them."

WILLIAM JENNINGS BRYAN
1860-1925 (65 years)

Bryan still has the distinction today of being the youngest nominee for the U.S. Presidency, at age 36. He ran 3 times: in 1896, 1900 and 1908, and finally he became the Secretary of State under Woodrow Wilson. He was considered one of the greatest speakers in American history, and his populist style of government gained him the nickname, "The Great Commoner." He was credited with galvanizing the Democratic party around the principles of liberty for the common man. He is best known for his advocacy against Darwinism and Evolution, which found its ultimate drama in the 1925 Scopes "monkey trial." He prosecuted a young biology teacher who taught evolution in defiance of the *Butler Act,* Tennessee's legislation which attempted to block the teaching of anti-Christian views. Five days after the trial ended, Bryan died in Dayton, Tennessee. A Christian college bearing his name stands there now as testimony to his belief that **"All the ills from which America suffers can be traced to the teaching of evolution."** He was a man of great conviction, who stood his ground against the growing tide of secular humanism. He strongly believed, and clearly taught the following: **"The humblest citizens of all the land, when clad in the armor of a righteous cause, are stronger than all the hosts of error."**

God created man in His own image, in the image of God He created him; male and female He created them. God blessed them; and God said to them, "Be fruitful and multiply, and fill the earth, and subdue it; and rule over the fish of the sea and over the birds of the sky and over every living thing that moves on the earth."
GENESIS 1:27-28

Creation Cosmology

Astronomy leads us to a unique event,
a universe which was created out of nothing,
one with the very delicate balance needed to provide exactly
the conditions required to permit life, and one which has an underlying,
one might say, "supernatural" plan.
Arno Penzias
Nobel Prize for the 2.7K cosmic background radiation discovery

----

The intelligent layman has long suspected circular reasoning
in the use of rocks to date fossils and fossils to date rocks.
J.E. O'Rourke
American Journal of Science, 1976, 276:51

Evolution became, in a sense, a scientific religion;
almost all scientists have accepted it,
and many are prepared to bend their observations to fit with it.
H.S. Lipson
Professor of Physics, University of Manchester, UK

Evolution is a fairy tale for grownups.
This theory has helped nothing in the progress of science. It is useless.
Professor Louis Bounoure
Former President, Biological Society of Strasbourg, France

It would be very difficult to explain why the universe
should have begun in just this way (evolution),
except as an act of a God who intended to create beings like us.
Stephen Hawking
Author of _A Brief History of Time_

"Oh, God! When You scare the world with tempests,
set on fire the heavens with falling thunderbolts,
or fill all the waters of the firmament,
we forget Thee not, at the sight
of these tremendous tokens of Thy power."

WILLIAM CULLEN BRYANT
1794-1878 (83 years)

At 16 years of age, young Bryant wrote an 81 line poem that is considered to be the most profound words ever written on the subject of death. This free verse poem is *Thanatopsis*. The closing lines read as follows: **"So live, that when thy summons comes to join the innumerable caravan, which moves to that mysterious realm, where each shall take his chamber in the silent halls of death - Thou go not, like the quarry-slave at night, scourged to his dungeon, but, sustained and soothed by an unfaltering trust, approach thy grave like one who wraps the drapery of his couch about him, and lies down to pleasant dreams."** Pretty amazing for a 16 year old. Bryant was a lawyer in his early career, and later became the Editor-in-Chief, for 50 years, of the *New York Evening Post*. In 1860, using his influence and legacy as America's poet, he introduced a Presidential candidate at Cooper's Union College. That candidate was Abraham Lincoln, and that introduction was considered a turning point in Lincoln's national popularity. Bryant loved nature, and the God of nature - and his poems, "*To a Waterfowl*" and "*The Ages*," paid tribute to the sovereignty of Creator God: **"He, who, from zone to zone, guides through the boundless sky thy certain flight - In the long way that I must tread alone, will lead my steps aright."**

For you will go out with joy
And be led forth with peace;
The mountains and the hills
will break forth into shouts of joy before you,
And all the trees of the field
will clap their hands.
ISAIAH 55:12

Creation

When we see a beautiful machine, we say there is a good engineer,
And the engineer has performed a work of art;
The world is assuredly a beautiful machine,
And must therefore attribute its value to an intelligent designer.
Voltaire

———

The whole difference between construction and creation is exactly this:
a thing constructed can only be loved after it is constructed;
but a thing created is loved before it exists.
Charles Dickens

———

The created world is but a small parenthesis in eternity.
Sir Thomas Browne

———

History is a vision of God's creation on the move.
Arnold Toynbee

———

Each species is a masterpiece,
a creation assembled with extreme care and genius.
Edward O. Wilson

———

The visible mark of extraordinary wisdom and power
appear so plainly in all the works of creation.
John Locke

"I mean to live my life an obedient man - but obedient to God - subservient to the wisdom of my ancestors, and never to the authority of political truths arrived at yesterday at the voting booth."

WILLIAM F. BUCKLEY, JR.
1925 - 2008 (82 years)

"Conservatives should be adamant about the need for the reappearance of Judeo-Christianity in the public square."

Buckley is generally credited with shaping the modern conservative movement in US politics during the last half of the 20th century. He graduated from Yale with honors and spent two years as an operative for the CIA before founding *The National Review* magazine in 1955. He later hosted the political TV format *Firing Line* for 33 years, allowing him to display the intellect and sharp wit that made him such a formidable debater and opponent of liberal politicians. Born in New York City, his early years were spent in Mexico, before he was sent to Paris for formal training; thus Spanish and French were his primary languages. Even his political adversaries said of him: "He was a fount of wisdom, and he knew how to wield the language like a knight's sword." Two of his fifty books: *God and Man at Yale* and *Nearer my God* were both written to express his concern for the changing spiritual values in American culture. He argued: **"The U.S. Supreme Court is at war against religion in the public school, and the Christian faith is being replaced by another God - multiculturalism."** Newt Gingrich added, "Bill Buckley became the indispensable intellectual advocate from whose energy, intelligence, wit, and enthusiasm the best of modern conservatism drew its inspiration and encouragement."

See to it that no one takes you captive
through philosophy and empty deception,
according to the tradition of men,
according to the elementary principles
of the world, rather than according to Christ.
Paul the Apostle, COLOSSIANS 2:8

Faith

Faith is deliberate confidence in the character of God
whose ways you may not understand at the time.
Oswald Chambers

————

To one who has faith, no explanation is necessary.
To one without faith, no explanation is possible.
St. Thomas Aquinas

—————

The only faith that wears well and holds its color in all weathers,
is that which is woven of conviction.
Abraham Lincoln

————

In faith there is enough light for those who want to believe
and enough shadows to blind those who don't.
Blaise Pascal

————

Faith is the highest passion in a human being.
Many in every generation may not come that far,
but none comes further.
Soren Kierkegaard

————

Faith is different from proof; the latter is human,
the former is a gift from God.
Blaise Pascal

"I don't think you can possibly grow up
with an education in which the exposition of
the life and meaning of Jesus is central,
and NOT say that the New Testament
is the most important book in your life,
however much or little you have, in fact,
lived by it. It's the most powerful single volume
you will ever encounter."

McGEORGE BUNDY
1919-1996 (77 years)

Bundy was a Professor of Government at Harvard University. More notable was the fact that he became Dean of the Faculty of Harvard with only a bachelor's degree at the age of 34, the youngest on record. Eight years later, in 1961, he became the National Security Advisor to President John F. Kennedy, and later to President Lyndon Johnson. MacGeorge, and his older brother Bill, were the guiding influences in determining Vietnam war policy during the Kennedy and Johnson years. As a result: 60,000 Americans and 180,000 Vietnamese died in battle. In later years, Bundy publically regretted his part in escalating a war that deeply wounded the American psyche. Vietnam has become symbolic for its inability to register a clear and meaningful victory. Upon leaving politics in 1966, he became president of the Ford Foundation, known for its international projects to advance social justice and democratic values throughout the world. Bundy finished his career as Professor of History at New York University. He is best known for the infamous statement: **"Although war is evil, it is occasionally the lesser of two evils."**

For a child will be born to us,
a son will be given to us;
And the government will rest on His shoulders;
And His name will be called
Wonderful Counselor, Mighty God,
Eternal Father, Prince of Peace.
Isaiah the Prophet, ISAIAH 9:6

Power and Politics

All I want is a warm bed and a kind word and unlimited power.
Ashleigh Brilliant

There is danger from all men.
The only maxim of a free government
ought to be to trust no man living
with power to endanger the public liberty.
John Adams

The release of atom power has changed everything
except our way of thinking. The solution to this problem
lies in the heart of mankind. If only I had known,
I should have become a watchmaker.
Albert Einstein

Power is my mistress. I have worked too hard at her conquest
to allow anyone to take her away from me.
Napoleon Bonaparte

The accumulation of all powers, legislative, executive, and judiciary,
in the same hands, whether of one, a few, or many,
and whether hereditary, self-appointed, or elective -
may justly be pronounced the very definition of tyranny.
James Madison

Their insatiable lust for power is only equaled
by their incurable impotence in exercising it.
Winston Churchill

"I love to hear my Lord spoken of,
and wherever I have seen
the print of His shoe in the earth,
there have I coveted to put mine also."

JOHN BUNYAN
1628-1688 (59 years)

"When you pray, rather let your heart
be without words than your words be without heart."

Bunyan lived during a time of fierce religious persecution by the Church of England. His meager occupation was a tinker, an uneducated mender of pots and metal objects - and his early life was filled with sinfulness. He was known by his friends as "the ungodliest fellow for swearing we ever heard." He spent 3 years as a soldier during the civil war of England, caring for a wife and a blind newborn baby. At age 25 he was introduced to the grace of God and his life was changed. By the age of 30 he was preaching in small Puritan churches until arrested for preaching without a license. Several years later he was imprisoned for 11 years for making the statement: **"If you release me today, I will preach tomorrow."** While in prison he began writing a book which has become a beloved classic allegory of English literature: *The Pilgrim's Progress.* The great Puritan theologian Dr. John Owen spoke of Bunyan, "I would give all my learning to be able to preach as well as the tinker." He wrote 50 books and lived a simple life of preaching and prayer. His humble advice to us: **"Pray often; for prayer is a shield to the soul, a sacrifice to God, and a scourge for Satan. The best prayers have often more groans than words."**

But you, when you pray,
go into your inner room, close your door
and pray to your Father who is in secret,
and your Father who sees what is done
in secret will reward you.
Jesus, MATTHEW 6:6

Conviction

Every man, wherever he goes,
is encompassed by a cloud of comforting convictions,
which move with him like flies on a summer day.
Bertrand Russell

No more duty can be urged upon those
who are entering the great theater of life
than simple loyalty to their best convictions.
Edwin Hubbel Chapin

What convinces is conviction.
Lyndon B. Johnson

Follow your honest convictions and be strong.
William Makepeace Thackeray

It takes a disciplined person to listen to convictions
which are different from their own.
Dorothy Fuldman

My opinion, my conviction,
gains immensely in strength and sureness
the minute a second mind has adopted it.
Malcolm Muggeridge

"A dog barks when his master is attacked. I would be a coward if I saw that God's truth is attacked and yet would remain silent."

JOHN CALVIN
1509 - 1564 (54 years)

"There is not one blade of grass, there is no color in this world, that is not intended to make us rejoice."

Calvin was a French lawyer whose influence during the Protestant Reformation (following Luther) produced a systematic theology that still guides the doctrines of Christian thinking and practice 500 years later. His theology has become the framework for the Presbyterian church, and his doctrine of 'predestination' continues to fuel debate between two major interpretations of salvation: the sovereignty of God (Calvinism) versus the free will of man (Arminianism). Most of his local church ministry was spent in Geneva, Switzerland. His words spoke to the heart: **"Every one of us is, even from his mother's womb, a master craftsman of idols. For there is no one so great or mighty that he can avoid the misery that will rise up against him when he resists and strives against God."** On one occasion a Spanish scholar attacked Calvin's theology, forcing the civil authorities to brand him (the Spaniard) as a heretic and burn him at the stake on a pyre of his own books. Calvin's greatest work, *Institutes of The Christian Religion,* is hailed by scholars as one of the most significant writings in Christian history, in addition to his massive twenty-two volume commentary on the Bible. Calvin believed the Bible was necessary for knowing God: **"Man with all his shrewdness is as stupid about understanding (by himself) the mysteries of God, as a donkey is incapable of understanding musical harmony."**

What if God, although willing to demonstrate His wrath
and to make His power known,
endured with much patience vessels of wrath
prepared for destruction?
ROMANS 9:22

The Tulip

(John Calvin's Theology of Man's Salvation)

Total depravity.

> Man's body, soul and spirit are born in sin. Man cannot save himself.
> Romans 3:23 - "For all have sinned and fallen short of the glory of God."

Unconditional election.

> God chooses unconditionally, without man's attempt at merit.
> Ephesians 1:4 - "He chose us in Him before the foundation of the world,
> that we would be holy and blameless before Him."

Limited atonement.

> Salvation is limited to those God has chosen.
> John 10:14 - "I am the good shepherd, and I know My own and My
> own know Me, even as the Father knows Me and I know the
> Father; and I lay down My life for the sheep."

Irresistible grace.

> When God has chosen to save someone, He will.
> Romans 9:16 - "So then it does not depend on the man who wills or
> the man who runs, but on God who has mercy."

Perseverance of the saints.

> Those people God chooses cannot lose their salvation.
> John 10:28 - "And I give eternal life to them, and they will never
> perish; and no one will snatch them out of My hand."

"Multitudes sit at ease and give themselves no concern about the far greater part of their fellow sinners, who, to this day, are lost in ignorance and idolatry."

WILLIAM CAREY
1761 - 1834 (72 years)

"Expect great things from God; attempt great things for God."

By the age of 20, William Carey had taught himself Greek, Hebrew, Latin, Dutch, Italian and French. He worked for a shoemaker and often studied languages while working on the shoes. He began to sense God's calling in his life to preach the gospel in foreign cultures. An older church member said to him: "Young man, sit down; when God pleases to convert the heathen, he will do it without your aid and mine." In spite of this 'advice', his love for languages led him to India where he translated the Bible into Bengali and Sanskrit, and Carey's print shop published the Bible in 44 languages and dialects. At the age of 31, he wrote his groundbreaking missionary manifesto, *An Enquiry into the Obligations of Christians to use Means for the Conversion of the Heathens*. Two years later he and wife Dorothy and four sons set off for Calcutta. When one son died, Dorothy suffered a nervous breakdown and never completely recovered. At age 50, his print shop was consumed by fire, destroying priceless manuscripts. In spite of this setback, Carey would later become known as the "Father of Modern Missions." His advice to those who pray for the world to know Christ: **"The future is as bright as the promises of God."**

And to Him was given dominion,
glory and a kingdom, that all the peoples,
nations and men of every language
might serve Him.
The Prophet Daniel, DANIEL 7:14

The Existence of God

My dear child, you must believe in God,
despite what the clergy tells you.
Benjamin Jowett

Were there no God, we would be in this glorious world
with grateful hearts - and no one to thank.
Christina G. Rossetti

God is the universal substance in existing things.
He comprises all things. He is the fountain of all being.
In Him exists everything that is.
Seneca

God created man in His own image, says the Bible;
philosophers reverse the process: they create God in theirs.
Georg Christoph Lichtenberg

That God does not exist, I cannot deny,
That my whole being cries out for God I cannot forget.
Jean-Paul Sartre

It is natural to admit the existence of a God
as soon as one opens one's eyes.
The creation betokens the Creator.
Voltaire

"This fair Universe is in very deed the star-domed
City of God; that through every star,
through every grass-blade, and most through
every Living Soul, the glory of a present God still beams.
But Nature, which is the time-vesture of God,
reveals Him to the wise and hides Him from the foolish . . .
Is not God made visible if we will
open our minds and our eyes."

THOMAS CARLYLE
1795-1881 (85 years)

Carlyle was a Scottish author and historian who is best known for his work *The French Revolution, A History.* This book was said to be Mark Twain's favorite. After writing volume 1, his friend John Stuart Mill was editing the text when Mill's maid accidentally burned it up. Carlyle went on to write volumes 2 and 3, and then returned to his rewriting of volume 1 (what agony for a writer). Carlyle's theology went through a progressive crisis of faith, which he called the "Everlasting No" (doubt and rejection) "The Center of Indifference" (agnosticism) and finally "The Everlasting Yes." (the affirmation of things good and godly, AND the warfare against "The Everlasting No".) True faith is forced to define itself first through skepticism and then through confident conviction. In Carlyle's book, *On Heroes, Hero Worship and the Heroic in History,* he studies the great men of history, in an attempt to understand both their charisma and their legacy. He says: **"The Great Man was always as lightning out of Heaven; the rest of men waited for him like fuel, and then they too would flame."** Carlyle taught us both humility and consequence, when he said: **"Of all the acts of man, repentance is the most divine. The greatest of all faults is to be conscious of none."**

I pray that the eyes of your heart may be enlightened,
so that you will know what is the hope of His calling,
what are the riches of the glory of His inheritance in the saints,
and what is the surpassing greatness
of His power toward us who believe.
Paul the Apostle, EPHESIANS 1:18-19

Greatness

Some are born great, some achieve greatness,
and some have greatness thrust upon 'em.
William Shakespeare

____

Great men are rarely isolated mountain peaks;
they are the summits of ranges.
Thomas W. Higginson

____

If any man seeks for greatness, let him forget greatness
and ask for truth, and he will find both.
Horace Mann

____

Great men are champions and special gifts of God,
whom He gives and preserves; they do their work,
and achieve great actions, not with vain imaginations,
but by motion of God.
Martin Luther

____

A great man is one who affects the mind of his generation.
Benjamin Disraeli

____

Nothing can make a man truly great
but being truly good and partaking of God's holiness.
Matthew Henry

"When it is a question of God's almighty Spirit, never say, 'I can't'."

ANDREW CARNEGIE
1835 - 1919 (83 years)

"You're achieving God's mission for humanity and country through capitalism, but by Christianity and your own sense of patriotism, you have a duty to better mankind."

The order of the five richest men in modern history (2010) is Carnegie, Gates, Vanderbilt, Ford and Rockefeller. Carnegie was a true "rags to riches" story. He is the namesake for Carnegie Hall and Carnegie Mellon University. At his death, he had given away 4.3 billion dollars (equivalent), including the construction of 3000 libraries around the world. His goal was to gain education, then wealth, and then give it away. Young Andrew moved from Scotland and began his business career working 12 hours daily in a cotton mill for $1.20 per week. He moved to the telegraph company and then to the railroads, where his boss taught him how to invest his money. He turned his capital into Carnegie Steel in Pittsburgh, which eventually merged with J.P Morgan, forming the world's largest corporation, U.S. Steel. His philosophy of business**: "The way to become rich is to put all your eggs in one basket and then watch the basket."** His philosophy of money: **"Man does not live by bread alone. There is no class so wretched as those who possess money and nothing else. I would as soon leave my son a curse as the almighty dollar. The man who dies rich dies disgraced."**

For the love of money
is a root of all sorts of evil,
and some by longing for it
have wandered away from the faith
and pierced themselves with many griefs.
1 TIMOTHY 6:10

Generosity

Gifts should have ribbons, not strings.
Vanna Bonta

———

Real unselfishness consists in sharing the interests of others.
George Santayana

———

To wear your heart on your sleeve isn't a very good plan;
you should wear it inside, where it functions best.
Margaret Thatcher

———

O Thou who has given us so much,
mercifully grant us one thing more - a grateful heart.
George Herbert

———

There is no exercise better for the heart
than reaching down and lifting people up.
John Andrew Holmes

———

What seems to be generosity is often
no more than disguised ambition,
which overlooks a small interest
in order to secure a great one.
François de la Rochefoucauld

"When I was young, I said to God,
'God, tell me the mystery of the universe.'
But God answered, 'That knowledge is for Me alone.'
So I said, 'God, tell me the mystery of the peanut.'
Then God said, 'Well George,
that's more nearly your size.' And he told me."

GEORGE WASHINGTON CARVER
1864-1943 (79 years)

A German immigrant slave owner named Moses Carver purchased George's parents, and after the abolition of slavery, he and his wife cared for, and educated George and brother James, as their own children. George studied botany at Iowa State College and he later became a professor at Tuskeegee University for 47 years. He is best known for helping the South learn to rotate depleted cotton crops with peanuts and sweet potatoes. He created over 100 products from the peanut, including cosmetics, dyes, paints, adhesives, ink, linoleum, metal polish, shaving cream, talcum powder and wood stain. He became a good friend of Henry Ford, who built a laboratory dedicated to him in Dearborn, Michigan. A USS nuclear submarine was also named in his honor. When China's peanut imports were threatening U.S. farmers, Carver spoke to Congress, who enacted tariff legislation. They gave him a rare standing ovation. Because of his strong Christian faith, he was criticized in a 1924 New York Times article entitled, "Men of Science Never Talk That Way." Scientists and Journalists just don't learn, do they? Carver taught us, **"When you can do the common things of life in an uncommon way, you will command the attention of the world."**

To whom God willed to make known
what is the riches of the glory
of this mystery among the Gentiles,
which is Christ in you, the hope of glory.
COLOSSIANS 1:27

Nature

I love to think of nature as an unlimited broadcasting station,
through which God speaks to us every hour,
If we will only tune in.
George Washington Carver

―――

Nature is but a name for an effect
whose cause is God.
William Cowper

―――

Nature is the art of God.
Dante

―――

Nature never breaks her own laws.
Leonardo Da Vinci

―――

I contend that we have a very imperfect knowledge
of the works of nature,
till we view them as the works of God.
James McCosh

―――

Nature is an infinite sphere of which the center
is everywhere and the circumference nowhere.
Pascal

―――

We cannot command nature except by obeying her.
Francis Bacon

"The Master of Life has been good to me.
He has given me strength to face my illnesses,
and victory in the face of defeat.
He has given new purpose to live for,
new service to render and old wounds to heal.
Life and love go on, let the music play."

JOHNNY CASH
1932 - 2003 (71 years)

"I am not a Christian artist. I am an artist who is a Christian."

Johnny Cash has been called the 'philosopher / prince of American country music.' In 1999 he received the Grammy Lifetime Achievement Award. In 2004 Rolling Stone Magazine ranked him #31 on their list of the "100 Greatest Artists of all Time." He was born J.R. Cash because his parents couldn't decide on a name. The U.S. Air Force required a first name, so he became John. He was assigned to a Security Service unit as a Code Intercept Operator for Soviet Army transmissions, and was later honorably discharged at the rank of Sergeant. "The Man in Black," as he called himself, was a rebellious drug addict until finally committing his life to Christ at the age of 26. Cash understood the nature and severe consequences of sin. **"The beast in me is caged by frail and fragile bars. Sometimes I am two people. Johnny is the nice one. Cash causes all the trouble."** He later co-wrote and narrated a film about Jesus called "Gospel Road", and he appeared in Billy Graham crusades around the world. Despite his success, he never forgot the pain of rebellion against God. **"How well I have learned that there is no fence to sit on between heaven and hell."**

Do not fear those who kill the body
but are unable to kill the soul;
but rather fear Him who is able
to destroy both soul and body in hell.
Jesus the Messiah, MATTHEW 10:28

Dear Master, in whose life I see

all that I long and fail to be;

Let Thy clear light forever shine,

To shame and guide this life of mine.

Though what I dream and what I do

in my poor days are always two,

help me, oppressed by things undone,

O Thou, whose dreams and deeds were one.

JOHN HUNTER

"I find that faith in God is as natural as breathing, and I am staggered that I was so stupid as not to trust Him before."

OSWALD CHAMBERS
1874 - 1917 (43 years)

"Prayer does not fit us for the greater work; prayer is the greater work."

Chambers is the Scottish author of *My Utmost for His Highest*, the most popular Christian devotional ever written. He was educated at the Royal College of London and the University of Edinburgh as a gifted artist, but his love for art soon changed into a love for teaching the Bible. He taught in England, Japan and America, and on one trip to the US, he met his wife Biddy. As a trained stenographer, she recorded most all of his teaching. In 1911 he founded a Bible college in Clapham, England, but then suspended his teaching four years later to become a YMCA chaplain in Egypt, ministering to the troops during World War I. His wife and daughter traveled with him to Egypt, where he died two years later from appendicitis. Biddy's faithful translation of his teachings has generated 34 books by Chambers, and *My Utmost* is now published in 40 languages around the world. Chambers was a man of prayer, who said, **"The whole meaning of prayer is that we may know God. Prayer is the supreme activity of all that is noblest in our personality, and the essential nature of prayer is faith. At times God puts us through the discipline of darkness to teach us to heed Him. It is by no haphazard chance that in every age men have risen early to pray. The first thing that marks decline in spiritual life is our relationship to the early morning."**

That I may know Him
and the power of His resurrection
and the fellowship of His sufferings,
being conformed even to His death;
Paul the Apostle, PHILIPPIANS 3:10

Greatness

They're only truly great who are truly good.
George Chapman

————

There is a great man who makes every man feel small.
But the real great man is the man who makes every man feel great.
G. K. Chesterton

————

The price of greatness is responsibility.
Sir Winston Churchill

————

A contemplation of God's works,
a generous concern for the good of mankind,
and the unfeigned exercise of humility only,
denominate men great and glorious.
Joseph Addison

————

A solid and substantial greatness of soul
looks down with neglect on the censures
and applause of the multitude.
Joseph Addison

————

I've often said, the only thing standing
between me and greatness is me.
Woody Allen

"The sages and heroes of history are receding from us,
and history contracts the record of their deeds
into a narrower and narrower page.
But time has no power over the name and deeds
and words of Jesus Christ."

WILLIAM ELLERY CHANNING
1780-1842 (62 years)

Channing was the champion of the Unitarian Church movement in New England in the infancy of America. His father, Ellery Channing, was a signer of the Declaration of Independence, and his nephew was William Henry Channing, best known for his classic poem, *This is My Symphony*. The historic Unitarian Church, like Judaism, ascribed to the belief in monotheism - one God - and that one God is Jehovah God, the sovereign creator / sustainer / redeemer God of the universe. On the authority of scripture, Channing said: "**God's wisdom (the Bible) is a pledge that whatever is necessary for us, and necessary for salvation, is revealed too plainly to be mistaken.**" Channing had much to say about the soul: "**Everything here but the soul of man is a passing shadow....When shall we awake to the sublime greatness....and the glorious destinies of the immortal soul?**" Unfortunately, historic Unitarianism has now drifted into Universalism, which tolerates all religions and no longer recognizes Jehovah God and Jesus as the centerpiece of their theology. Unlike Unitarianism, evangelical Christianity continues to teach that "every knee shall bow, and every tongue shall confess that Jesus Christ is Lord, to the glory of God the Father." Monotheism will someday bow down to King Jesus.

God, after He spoke long ago to the fathers
in the prophets in many portions
and in many ways,
in these last days has spoken to us in His Son,
whom He appointed heir of all things,
through whom also He made the world.
HEBREWS 1:1-2

This is My Symphony

"To live content with small means;
to seek elegance rather than luxury,
and refinement rather than fashion;
to be worthy, not respectable,
and wealthy, not rich;
to study hard, think quietly,
talk gently, act frankly;
to listen to stars and birds,
to babes and sages, with open heart;
to bear all cheerfully, do all bravely,
await occasions, hurry never.
In a word, to let the spiritual,
unbidden and unconscious,
grow up through the common.
This is to be my symphony."

WILLIAM <u>HENRY</u> CHANNING

"The great majority of people will go on observing forms that cannot be explained; they will keep Christmas Day with Christmas gifts and Christmas benedictions; they will continue to do it; and some day suddenly wake up and discover why."

G.K. CHESTERTON
1874-1936 (62 years)

"If man is not the image of God, then he is a disease of the dust."

Author Phillip Yancey said that if he was stranded on a desert island and could choose only one book apart from the Bible, "I may well select Chesterton's own spiritual autobiography, *Orthodoxy*. Chesterton was an English author of 80 books, 200 short stories, 4000 essays and several hundred poems. He was called the "prince of paradox," and he maintained a friendly but adversarial relationship with George Bernard Shaw and Oscar Wilde. Shaw called him "a man of colossal genius." Chesterton said: **"One may understand the cosmos, but never the ego; the self is more distant than any star."** When *The Times* of England invited several eminent authors to write essays on the theme "What's Wrong with the World?" Chesterton's contribution took the form of a letter: **"Dear Sirs, I am. Sincerely yours, G. K. Chesterton."** He combined his wit with two important principles - the fallen nature of man and his own personal humility. **"When we were children we were grateful to those who filled our stockings at Christmas time. Why are we not grateful to God for filling our stockings with legs?"** His book, Everlasting Man was said to have been a major component in the conversion of C.S. Lewis. His best known quote is both simple and profound: **"Joy is the gigantic secret of the Christian."**

Now to Him who is able
to keep you from stumbling,
and to make you stand
in the presence of His glory
blameless with great joy.
JUDE 1:24

Words from Chesterton

The object of opening the mind, as of opening the mouth,
is to shut it again on something solid.

——

Christianity has not been tried and found wanting;
it has been found difficult and not tried.

——

Tolerance is the virtue of the man without convictions.

——

One may understand the cosmos, but never the ego;
the self is more distant than any star.

——

I've searched all the parks in all the cities
and found no statues of committees.

——

Courage is almost a contradiction in terms.
It means a strong desire to live, taking the form of readiness to die.

——

We call a man a bigot or a slave of dogma
because he is a thinker who has thought thoroughly and to a definite end.

——

When we really worship anything, we love not only its clearness
but its obscurity. We exult in its very invisibility.

"Christianity, rightly understood,
is identical with the highest philosophy.
The essential doctrines of Christianity are necessary
and eternal truths of reason."

SAMUEL TAYLOR COLERIDGE
1772 - 1834 (61 years)

"Christianity is not a theory or speculation,
not a philosophy of life, but a live and living process."

Coleridge was an English poet / philosopher during the era known as the Romantic period. He was a contemporary of Ralph Waldo Emerson and Thomas Carlyle, but it was his best friend William Wordsworth who helped shape his legacy as an influential writer. Though he won awards at Cambridge, he never graduated. One of his teachers deeply impacted him, causing him to write the following: **"Language is the armory of the human mind, and at once contains the trophies of its past and the weapons of its future conquests."** Perhaps his best known poem is *The Rime of the Ancient Mariner,* which give us the following original well known phrases: **"albatross around one's neck, water water everywhere-nor any drop to drink,"** and **"a sadder and wiser man."** Coleridge had a dark side - recurring depression - which led him to an addiction of opium which he never conquered. Of advice, he said this: **"Advice is like snow, the softer it falls, the longer it dwells."** Though plagued by a brilliant, yet troubled mind, his words conveyed a trust in God that transcended his problems. **"He prays best, who loves best, all things both great and small; For the dear God who loves us, He made and loves us all."**

Holding fast the faithful word
which is in accordance with the teaching,
so that he will be able both
to exhort in sound doctrine
and to refute those who contradict.
Paul the Apostle, TITUS 1:9

Slow me down, Lord!
Ease the pounding of my heart by the quieting of my mind.
Steady my hurried pace with a vision of the eternal reach of time.

Give me, amidst the confusions of my day,
The calmness of the everlasting hills.
Break the tensions of my nerves with the soothing music
Of the singing streams that live in my memory.

Help me to know the magical power of sleep;
Teach me the art of taking minute vacations,
Of slowing down to look at a flower;
To chat with an old friend or make a new one;
To pat a stray dog; to watch a spider build a web;
To smile at a child; or to read a few lines from a good book.

Remind me each day that the race is not always to the swift;
That there is more to life than increasing its speed.

Let me look upward into the branches of the towering oak
And know that it grew great and strong
Because it grew slowly and well.

Slow me down, Lord,
And inspire me to send my roots deep
Into the soil of life's enduring values
That I may grow toward the stars
Of my greater destiny.

Wilferd A. Peterson

"Where is the hope? I meet millions of people
who feel demoralized by the decay around us.
The hope that each of us has is not in who governs us,
or what laws we pass, or what great things we do as a nation.
Our hope is in the power of God
working through the hearts of people.
And that's where our hope is in this country.
And that's where our hope is in life."

CHUCK COLSON
(1931-)

Chuck Colson served as Special Counsel to President Richard Nixon and was called "the hatchet man" in the Nixon Administration from 1968-1972 because of his ruthless strategy to advance the agenda of the Nixon White House. He was famously quoted as saying, **"I'd walk over my own grandmother to re-elect Richard Nixon."**   After Nixon's Watergate scandal and resignation, Colson was convicted of obstruction of justice and spent seven months in prison. During this time in prison, Colson was given a copy of *Mere Christianity* (by C.S. Lewis) which, coupled with the influence of Christian friends and much prayer, resulted in an amazing story of his jailhouse conversion. Enemies scoffed, believing this to be a ploy of sympathy, but through the years Colson has proved to be a credible, yet humble voice of evangelical Christianity. Based on his own experience as an inmate, he later founded Prison Fellowship, an organization that has resulted in the rehabilitation of thousands of prisoners. **"The Church has been brought into the same value system as the world: fame, success, materialism and celebrity. Preoccupation with these values has perverted the church's message. We offer truth, not therapy. Don't compartmentalize your faith. God wants all of you, or none of you."**

That if you confess with your mouth Jesus as Lord,
and believe in your heart that God raised Him from the dead,
you will be saved; for with the heart a person believes,
resulting in righteousness, and with the mouth he confesses,
resulting in salvation.
ROMANS 10:9-10

Conviction

Never give in, never give in, never; never; never; never -
in nothing, great or small, large or petty - never give in -
except to convictions of honor and good sense.
Winston Churchill

I would rather live my life as if there is a God
and die to find out there isn't,
than live my life as if there isn't and die to find out there is.
Albert Camus

I have been driven many times to my knees
by the overwhelming conviction that I had nowhere to go.
My own wisdom, and that of all about me,
seemed insufficient for the day.
Abraham Lincoln

He who believes is strong; he who doubts is weak.
Strong convictions precede great actions.
Louisa May Alcott

Never, for the sake of peace and quiet,
deny your own experience or convictions.
Dag Hammarskjold

Conviction is worthless unless it is converted into conduct.
Thomas Carlyle

"It was the Lord who put into my mind
the fact that it would be possible to sail
from here to the Indies. There is no question
that the inspiration was from the Holy Spirit,
because He comforted me
with rays of marvelous inspiration
from the Holy Scriptures."

CHRISTOPHER COLUMBUS
1451-1506 (55 years)

At the age of 10, young Christoph was already traveling the seas; and at the age of 25, a ship he was sailing on was sunk by pirates and he swam six miles to shore. His brother worked for a cartographer, which may explain the confidence he had to dare an adventure that was generally considered a suicide mission. He understood the "trade winds" (actual term "tread" winds) were winds that followed a tread or track from the east in the Northern Hemisphere and from the west in the Southern Hemisphere. Following this path meant the winds would carry him on a precise track that would end in the Caribbean. Had he veered off course, the journey would have taken much longer, a sure indicator of death. Columbus made the same journey four times, following the trade winds to a historical legacy. Perhaps he lived his spiritual life like his nautical life, obeying the winds of God to carry him on a great adventure that other men mocked. He was a great navigator and also a great missionary, who challenged us: **"By prevailing over all obstacles and distractions, one may unfailingly arrive at his chosen goal or destination. No one should fear to undertake any task in the name of our Savior, if it is just and if the intention is purely for His holy service. I have found the sweetest consolation since I made it my whole purpose to enjoy His marvelous Presence."**

Eyes have not seen,
nor ears heard,
nor entered into the heart of man,
the things which God has prepared
for them that love Him. (paraphrase)
Paul the Apostle, 1 CORINTHIANS 2:9

Christ

In His life, Christ is an example, showing us how to live;
In His death, He is a sacrifice, satisfying our sins;
In His resurrection, a conqueror.
In His ascension, a king.
In His intercession, a high priest.
Martin Luther

————

Christ is the universal man, the ideal of humanity;
And it is right that He should be "crowned with many crowns,"
As each nation and each century bows to His sovereignty.
William Ralph Inge

————

If we have not bowed with Christ,
we cannot possibly live with Him.
Karl Barth

————

Take Jesus out of the perfumed cloisters of pious sentiment
And let Him walk the streets of the city.
Peter Marshal

————

Christianity is not just some sort of world view or idealist philosophy,
but has something to do with a person called Christ.
Hans Kung

————

Jesus Christ is the condescension of divinity
and the exaltation of humanity.
Phillips Brooks

"God moves in a mysterious way,
His wonders to perform;
He plants His footsteps in the sea,
And rides upon the storm."

WILLIAM COWPER
1731-1800 (68 years)

"I venerate the man whose heart is warm,
whose hands are pure, whose doctrine, and whose life
exhibit lucid proof that he is honest in the sacred cause."

To know the man William Cowper, you must first know that his name is pronounced "Cooper." He was an English poet, who was admired by William Wordsworth and acclaimed by Samuel Taylor Coleridge as "the best of modern poets." Cowper was being trained as a lawyer, but prior to the exam he experienced a depression which led friends to say he was insane. During his recuperation he was cared for by an older couple, and with their encouragement, he began writing poetry which was then set to music, later to be called hymns. Together with good friend John Newton (author of "Amazing Grace") they created the now famous collection called "Olney" Hymns. It was Cowper who first said, **"Variety's the very spice of life, that gives it all its flavor."** His best known quote helps us understand wisdom and knowledge, as he says, **"Knowledge is proud that it knows so much; wisdom is humble that it knows no more."** He was a man of prayer, who said: **"Satan trembles when he sees, the weakest saint upon his knees."** He encourages us to passionately discover ourselves, as he said: **"The only true happiness comes from squandering ourselves for a purpose."**

For this purpose also I labor,
striving according to His power,
which mightily works within me.
Paul the Apostle, COLOSSIANS 1:29

The greatest of all love
Which came from above
Was guided to planet earth
In the form of a man
Who all sin could withstand
By the plan of His lowly birth.

He came to us then, but not to intrude
He came as a humble stranger
He came for redemption
To lose, yet to gain,
And started it all in a manger.

We want to show joy, and yet to know grief
Be thankful for all that he shared
To know of the strength of the lost soul gained
And the dying heart that was spared.

Around the world in every age
The quest for hope goes on
We search for peace
That can't be found
Except in Christ alone.

GORDON LAWRENCE

**"May it please our great Author that I may demonstrate
the nature of man and his customs,
in the way I describe his figure."**

LEONARDO DA VINCI
1452-1519 (67 years)

**"I have offended God and mankind
because my work didn't reach the quality it should have."**

Perhaps the word "genius" is the only way to describe da Vinci. He was a painter, sculptor, architect, engineer, inventor, writer, musician and scientist. He was considered the archetype of the Renaissance Man, and the word "polymath" is used to describe his extraordinary talents. He was a contemporary of the great artists Rapahel and Michaelangelo. His best known works are the famous paintings of *The Lord's Supper, The Mona Lisa* and *The Vetruvian Man* (a model of man inscribed in a square and a circle, of perfect proportions). Legend has it that while a student under Verrocchio, Leonardo skillfully touched up a painting of The Baptism of Christ and his master put down his brush and never painted again. Despite his fame and talent, da Vinci was a humble man who said **"Fame alone raises herself to Heaven, but virtuous things are in favor with God."** He was known as a sparkling personality, a magnetic influence among his peers in Italy. Eventually he was contracted to live out his life at the pleasure of the King of France. With all his genius, he understood the sovereignty of God: **"I obey Thee Lord, first, because I ought to love You, and second, because only You can shorten or prolong the lives of men."** (paraphrased from Old English)

> When I consider Your heavens, the work of Your fingers,
> The moon and the stars, which You have ordained;
> What is man that You take thought of him,
> And the son of man that You care for him?
> Yet You have made him a little lower than God,
> And You crown him with glory and majesty!
> **King David, PSALM 8:3-5**

"O Lord, You give us everything, at the price of an effort."
Leonardo da Vinci

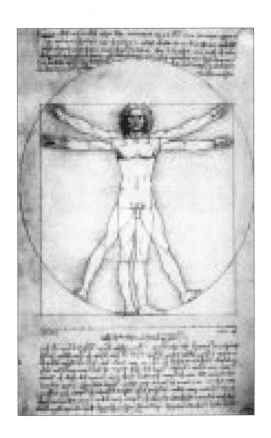

"Someday, after mastering the winds,
the waves, the tides and gravity,
we shall harness for God the energies of love,
and then, for a second time in the history of the world,
man will have discovered fire."

PIERRE TEILHARD DE CHARDIN
1881-1955 (73 years)

De Chardin, whose name is pronounced (Tey Har de Shar Dan), was a trained pale-ontologist and philosopher and priest. His best known book, *The Phenomenon of Man,* provides a broad interpretation of the cosmos and the evolution of man. To quote his friend and colleague, Julian Huxley, "evolution is nothing but matter be-come conscious of itself." That may be the best definition yet of the emptiness of the theory of evolution. As a Jesuit priest, de Chardin's writings were condemned by the Catholic Church as heresy for their rejection of the basic tenets of the Christian faith. In spite of this, he probed history and nature to understand God. He correctly under-stood the nature of man when he said: **"You are a spiritual being immersed in a human experience. You are not a human being in search of a spiritual experience. Our century is probably more religious than any other. How could it fail to be, with such problems to be solved? The only trouble is that it has not yet found a God it can adore."** His greatest concept was the "Omega Point," an idea which posed that man and nature were evolving toward a climactic point in history in which man's consciousness would eventually become one with the universe. Omega, however, is not a point, but a per-son. Jesus said, "I am the Alpha and the Omega, the beginning and the end."

"I am the Alpha and the Omega,"
says the Lord God,
"who is and who was and who is to come,
the Almighty."
King Jesus, REVELATION 1:8

Discipline

Discipline is the refining fire by which talent becomes ability.
Roy L. Smith

———

It was character that got us out of bed,
commitment that moved us into action,
and discipline that enabled us to follow through.
Zig Ziglar

———

Discipline is the bridge between goals and accomplishment.
Jim Rohn

———

He that cannot obey, cannot command.
Benjamin Franklin

———

With self-discipline most anything is possible.
Theodore Roosevelt

———

Many of life's circumstances are created by three basic choices:
the disciplines you choose to keep, the people you choose to be with;
and, the laws you choose to obey.
Charles Millhuff

———

If I want to be great
I have to win the victory over myself - self-discipline.
Harry S. Truman

"Time was, with most of us, when Christmas Day encircled all our limited world like a magic ring. . . It bound together all our home enjoyments, affections, and hopes; Everything and everyone was grouped around the Christ."

CHARLES DICKENS
1812 - 1870 (58 years)

"I will honor Christmas in my heart,
and try to keep it all the year."

Dickens ranks with Shakespeare as one of England's greatest authors. He is best known for his stories: *Oliver Twist, David Copperfield, A Tale of Two Cities, Great Expectations* and *A Christmas Carol*. His stories revolved around social reform during the Victorian era of England, and his animated characters (Ebeneezer Scrooge, Tiny Tim, Oliver Twist, Fagin) were caricatures of people he knew. His own father was put in debtor's prison, while young Charles, one of ten children, worked for pennies a week in a labor factory. He recounts that period of his life in *A Tale of Two Cities:* **"It was the best of times, it was the worst of times, it was the age of wisdom, it was the age of foolishness, it was the spring of hope, it was the winter of despair."** It was Dickens who made popular the term "Merry Christmas." For his children he wrote a book called, *The Life of Our Lord,* which begins, **"Children, I am very anxious that you should know something about the history of Jesus Christ."** He wrote: **"I love little children, and it is not a slight thing when they, who are fresh from God, love us. It is good to be children sometimes, and never better than at Christmas, when its mighty Founder was a child Himself."**

For unto you this day,
in the city of David
has been born a Savior,
who is Christ the Lord.
Angel of the Lord, LUKE 2:11

Christmas

How many observe Christ's birthday! How few, His precepts!
O! 'tis easier to keep holidays than commandments.
Benjamin Franklin

This is Christmas: not the tinsel, not the giving and receiving,
not even the carols, but the humble heart
that receives anew the wondrous gift, the Christ.
Frank McKibben

Christmas began in the heart of God.
It is complete only when it reaches the heart of man.
Unknown

He who has not Christmas in his heart
will never find it under a tree.
Charlotte Carpenter

When we were children we were grateful to those
who filled our stockings at Christmas time.
Why are we not grateful to God
for filling our stockings with legs?
G. K. Chesterton

Christmas is not a time nor a season, but a state of mind.
To cherish peace and goodwill, to be plenteous in mercy,
is to have the real spirit of Christmas.
Calvin Coolidge

"Christianity is completed Judaism, or it is nothing.
Judaism is not complete without Christianity,
and without Judaism, Christianity would not exist."

BENJAMIN DISRAELI
1804-1881 (76 years)

"The view of Jerusalem is the history of the world;
it is more, it is the history of earth and of heaven."

Benjamin was born D'Israeli (of Israel) but he dropped the apostrophe as a young man. At the age of 13, he was baptized into the Christian faith and he proudly maintained a dual allegiance all his life - Jewish heritage, Christian faith. His father was grooming him as a lawyer, but young Benjamin soon began speculating in business, only to find himself deep in debt. He began writing political novels which thrust him into the limelight of both society and politics. He soon began to champion conservative causes as a Member of Parliament, and he eventually rose to become a two-time Prime Minister of England. With a true understanding of public service he said, **"I must follow the people. Am I not their leader?"** He was a favorite of Queen Victoria, who elevated his position to that of an Earl. At his core, Disraeli was a deep thinker, eloquent writer and a devout believer. Of Christian doctrine, he said, **"The Athanasian Creed (doctrine of the Trinity) is the most splendid ecclesiastical lyric ever poured forth by the genius of man. . . Man is a being born to believe, and if no church comes forward with the title deeds of truth, he will find altars and idols in his own heart and his own imagination. . . All is mystery; but he is a slave who will not struggle to penetrate the dark veil . . . Duty cannot exist without faith."**

For there is no distinction
between Jew and Greek;
for the same Lord is Lord of all,
abounding in riches for all who call on Him;
for whoever will call on the name of the Lord will be saved.
Paul the Apostle, ROMANS 10:12-13

The Importance of Israel

For thus says the LORD of hosts,
"After glory He has sent me
against the nations which plunder you,
for he who touches you,
touches the apple of His eye."
Zechariah 2:8

The term "apple of His eye"
is a veiled reference to the cornea of the eye,
which is the outer aperture of the eyeball.
It is the most sensitive, the most delicate
and could easily be considered
the most precious part of the body
because of our total dependence on sight.
Israel is called by God Himself
the apple of His eye.

The Importance of Jerusalem

Thus says the Lord GOD,
"This is Jerusalem;
I have set her at the center of the nations,
with lands around her."
Ezekiel 5:5

The Hebrew word for center is the word 'tabor.'
This is not a geometric term. This is not a geographic term.
The word "tabor" means "navel."
Jerusalem is the "bellybutton" of the planet.

"All mankind is of one Author,
and is one volume;
when one man dies, one chapter is not
torn out of the book,
but translated into a better language."

JOHN DONNE
1572-1631 (59 years)

In an age in which Catholicism was strictly forbidden in England, Donne (pronounced Dunn) was raised Catholic and suffered political prejudice until he finally converted to the Church of England at the age of 43. When he married as a young man, his father-in-law refused to accept him, prompting the statement: "John Donne, Anne Donne, Un-Done." Despite this, the couple had 12 children. His wife died five days after giving birth to their twelfth, forcing him to spend much of his later single life attending to the children. He was a lawyer and a writer, turned Anglican Priest. His early writings were witty and satirical, but in later life he wrote much concerning death, as evidenced by the following well known verse: **"Death be not proud, though some have called thee Mighty and Dreadful, for thou art not so."** His best known words were: **"No man is an island, entire of itself...any man's death diminishes me, because I am involved in mankind; and therefore never send to know for whom the bell tolls; it tolls for thee."** But deep within the veneer of his poetry was a heart that understood the profoundness of focusing on God. He said, **"I neglect God and His Angels - for the noise of a fly, for the rattling of a coach, for the whining of a door."** He correctly understood the simple formula for living a life of meaning. **"He that fears God fears nothing else; He that sees God sees everything else."**

O death, where is your victory? O death, where is your sting?
The sting of death is sin, and the power of sin is the law;
but thanks be to God, who gives us the victory
through our Lord Jesus Christ.
Paul the Apostle, 1 CORINTHIANS 15:55-57

Death

Have the courage to live. Anyone can die.
Robert Cody

———

As a well spent day brings happy sleep,
so a life well spent brings happy death.
Leonardo da Vinci

———

Do not seek death. Death will find you.
But seek the road which makes death a fulfillment.
Dag Hammarskjold

———

Because I could not stop for death, He kindly stopped for me;
The carriage held but just ourselves and immortality.
Emily Dickinson

———

Death is no more than passing from one room into another.
But there's a difference for me, you know.
Because in that other room I shall be able to see.
Helen Keller

———

Death, so called, is a thing which makes men weep,
and yet a third of life is passed in sleep.
Lord Byron

"The most pressing question
on the problem of faith
is whether a man, as a civilized being,
can believe in the divinity of the Son of God,
Jesus Christ; for therein rests the whole of our faith."

FYODOR DOSTOYEVSKI
1821-1881 (59 years)

Dostoyevsky was a Russian novelist, considered by many to be one of Europe's greatest writers. He is best known for two books: *Crime and Punishment* and *The Brothers Karamazov.* He wrote as one who explored the human pathos of pain and suffering and despair; and for this reason, he is considered to be a major influence in 20th century existentialism. He earned the right to speak of despair. He was born with epilepsy and he spent five years as a young man in a Siberian prison because of his anti-government idealism: **"In summer, intolerable closeness; in winter, unendurable cold. All the floors were rotten, and filth so thick one could slip and fall. We were packed like herrings in a barrel."** In spite of the bleakness of Russian society, where government tried hard to replace religion and morality, he transcended his despair with deep conviction. Psalm 42:5 teaches us that despair is sometimes a human condition that becomes a catalyst to our faith. **"Science, which has become a great power in the last century, has analyzed everything divinely handed down to us in the holy books. After this cruel analysis, the learned of this world have nothing left of all that was sacred. But they have only analyzed the parts and overlooked the whole, and indeed their blindness is marvelous."**

Why are you in despair, O my soul?
And why have you become disturbed
within me? Hope in God,
for I shall again praise Him
for the help of His presence.
PSALM 42:5

I asked God for strength that I might achieve.
I was made weak that I might learn humbly to obey.
I asked for health that I might do greater things.
I was given infirmity that I might do better things.
I asked for riches that I might be happy.
I was given poverty that I might be wise.
I asked for power that I might have the praise of men.
I was given weakness that I might feel the need of God.
I asked for all things that I might enjoy life.
I was given life that I might enjoy all things.
I got nothing that I asked for,
but everything I hoped for.
Almost despite myself,
my unspoken prayers were answered.
I am, among all men, most richly blessed.

Unknown Confederate Soldier

"The great question of our time is not
communism versus individualism,
not Europe versus American,
nor East versus West -
It is whether man can bear to live without God."

WILL DURANT
1885-1981 (96 years)

Durant is best known for his Pulitzer Prize winning 11 volume, *A History of Civilization,* which he co-authored with his wife, Ariel. In 1977, President Gerald Ford awarded him the highest honor given to a US civilian, The Presidential Medal of Freedom. While working on his Ph.D at Columbia University Durant taught lessons at a local Presbyterian Church that later became the foundation for his life's work. Durant was a philosopher who sought to understand the comprehensive scope of human history. In humility, he said: **"Sixty years ago I knew everything; now I know nothing; education is a progressive discovery of our own ignorance. Woe to him who teaches men faster than they can learn."** Perhaps his greatest observation was not insight into progress, but rather insight into destruction, as he said, **"A great civilization is not conquered from without until it has destroyed itself within."** Perhaps more important to him than his literary achievement was his partnership with his wife Ariel. He wrote, **"The love we have in our youth is superficial compared to the love that an old man has for his old wife."** He and Ariel died within 2 weeks of each other, at the age of 96. He loved to say, **"Never mind your happiness; do your duty. . . And seek, beneath the universal strife, the hidden harmony of all things."**

The God who made the world and all things in it,
since He is Lord of heaven and earth,
does not dwell in temples made with hands;
nor is He served by human hands, as though He needed anything,
since He Himself gives to all people life and breath and all things;
Paul the Apostle, ACTS 17:24-25

The March of History

Life must be lived forward,
but it can only be understood backward.
Søren Kierkegaard

———

And history becomes legend and legend becomes history.
J. Cocteau

———

History is the record of encounters
between character and circumstance.
Donald Creighton

———

The past is always a rebuke to the present.
Robert Penn Warren

———

A country without a memory is a country of madmen.
George Santayana

———

If you would understand anything,
observe its beginning and its development.
Aristotle

———

The deepest, the only theme of human history,
compared to which all others are of subordinate importance,
is the conflict of skepticism with faith.
Johann Wolfgang von Goethe

"Men have a great deal of pleasure
in human knowledge, in studies of natural things;
but this is nothing compared to that joy which arises
from divine light shining into the soul."

JONATHAN EDWARDS
1703 - 1758 (54 years)

"Of all the knowledge that we can ever obtain,
the knowledge of God, and the knowledge of
ourselves, are the most important."

Jonathan Edwards was the president of The College of New Jersey (later Princeton University) at the time of his death, caused from a smallpox inoculation. He became the namesake of Jonathan Edwards College, one of the twelve residential colleges of Yale University. He was a scholar and a theologian, but primarily, he was an eloquent preacher to the Northampton, Massachusetts church that he pastored. He became a catalyst of The First Great Awakening (1730-1755), a revival movement that saw thousands of people in the 13 colonies profess Christ. Edwards is best known for his sermon (at the age of 38) entitled "Sinners in the Hands of an Angry God." It is reported that he read the sermon, which still brought people to tears and repentance: **"Your wickedness makes you, as it were, heavy as lead, and to tend downwards with great weight and pressure towards hell; and if God should let you go, you would immediately sink and swiftly descend and plunge into the bottomless gulf . . . and all your righteousness would have no more influence to uphold you and keep you out of hell, than a spider's web would have to stop a falling rock."**

And they said
to the mountains and to the rocks,
"Fall on us and hide us
from the presence of Him
who sits on the throne,
and from the wrath of the Lamb;
REVELATION 6:16

Repentance

If you have sinned, do not lie down without repentance;
for the lack of repentance after one has sinned
makes the heart yet harder and harder.
John Bunyan

———

Repentance is a grace of God's Spirit
whereby a sinner is inwardly humbled and visibly reformed.
Thomas J. Watson

———

Some often repent, yet never reform;
they resemble a man traveling in a dangerous path,
who frequently starts and stops, but never turns back.
Bonnell Thornton

———

Of all acts of man repentance is the most divine.
The greatest of all faults is to be conscious of none.
Thomas Carlyle

———

Confess yourself to heaven:
Repent what's past; avoid what is to come.
William Shakespeare

"My religion consists of a humble admiration
for the superior Spirit
who reveals Himself in the slight details
that we are able to perceive
with our frail and feeble minds."

ALBERT EINSTEIN
1879-1955 (76 years)

Everything about Einstein was an enigma. He was born Jewish, raised in a Catholic school, suffered childhood speech difficulties, yet learned Euclidian geometry and infinitesimal calculus at the age of 12. He moved from Germany to Italy to Switzerland, and took a job processing new inventions at the Patent Office. He moved to Princeton, New Jersey as Hitler began to condemn the Jews of Europe. Eventually he introduced the world to his famous "theory of relativity." Einstein, who struggled with organized religion, nevertheless said, **"Science without religion is lame, religion without science is blind. A legitimate conflict between science and religion cannot exist."** Einstein was a Zionist, one who believed strongly in the rebirth of Israel and was asked to be the president of Israel in 1952. Einstein's favorite word was "mystery." His motivation in life was to understand the mysteries of God. **"The most beautiful thing we can experience is the mysterious. It is the source of all true art and all science. He to whom this emotion is a stranger - who can no longer pause to wonder and stand rapt in awe - is as good as dead; his eyes are closed."** For Einstein, God was always the source of science and wonder: **"I want to know God's thoughts; the rest are just details."** His passion to understand God should be ours as well.

But we speak God's wisdom in a mystery,
the hidden wisdom which God predestined before the ages to our glory;
the wisdom which none of the rulers
of this age has understood;
for if they had understood it
they would not have crucified the Lord of glory;
Paul the Apostle, 1 CORINTHIANS 2:7-8

Mystery

The final mystery is oneself.
Oscar Wilde

––––

Mystery creates wonder and wonder
is the basis of man's desire to understand.
Neil Armstrong

––––

Mystery is another name for our ignorance;
if we were omniscient, all would be perfectly plain.
Tryon Edwards

––––

When I was young, I said to God, 'God, tell me the mystery
of the universe.' But God answered, 'that knowledge is for me alone.'
So I said, 'God, tell me the mystery of the peanut.'
Then God said, 'Well, George, that's more nearly your size.'
And He told me.
George Washington Carver

––––

The workings of the human heart are the profoundest mystery
of the universe. One moment they make us despair of our kind,
and the next we see in them the reflection of the divine image.
Charles W. Chesnutt

––––

It began in mystery, and it will end in mystery,
but what a savage and beautiful country lies in between.
Diane Ackerman

"From this day forward, the millions of our school children
will daily proclaim in every city and town, every village
and rural school house, the dedication of our nation
and our people to the Almighty."

General DWIGHT DAVID EISENHOWER
1890 - 1969 (78 years)

Eisenhower (whose name means "iron worker") was a five star Army General, and was named the Supreme Commander of Allied Forces in Europe during World War II. Though tactical warfare was his expertise, he said: **"I hate war as only a soldier who has lived it can, and as one who has seen its brutality, its futility and its stupidity."** After the war, his popularity as a war hero made him the president of Columbia University, and later he became the 34th President of the United States. He was a man of strong principle who said: **"The supreme quality for leadership is unquestionably integrity. Without it, no real success is possible."** As a Republican President for two terms, he enlarged the Social Security program, launched the space program and began the interstate highway system. He overthrew the government of Iran and introduced the Civil Rights Act of 1957. Eisenhower is best known for adding the words "under God" to the Pledge of Allegiance in 1954, and adopting "In God We Trust" as the motto of the United States. With conviction he said: **"A people that values its privileges above its principles soon loses both. I have one yardstick by which I test every major problem, and that yardstick is: Is it good for America?"**

Blessed is the nation
whose God is the LORD,
The people whom He has chosen
for His own inheritance.
PSALM 33:12

(Eisenhower's Inaugural Verse)

Integrity

Have the courage to say no. Have the courage to face the truth.
Do the right thing because it is right.
These are the magic keys to living your life with integrity.
W. Clement Stone

——

It's not what we eat but what we digest that makes us strong;
not what we gain but what we save that makes us rich;
not what we read but what we remember that makes us learned;
and not what we profess but what we practice that gives us integrity.
Francis Bacon

——

One of the truest tests of integrity
is its blunt refusal to be compromised.
Chinua Achebe

——

In times like these, men should utter nothing for which they
would not be willingly responsible, through time and in eternity.
Abraham Lincoln

——

Integrity has no need of rules.
Albert Camus

——

The man who cannot endure to have his errors and shortcomings
brought to the surface and made known, but tries to hide them,
is unfit to walk the highway of truth.
James Allen

"Father, make me a crisis man.
Bring those I contact to a decision.
Let me not be a milepost on a single road.
Make me a fork that men must turn
one way or another on facing Christ in me."

JIM ELLIOT
1927-1956 (28 years)

It was Tertullian, a 2nd century Christian writer who said, "The blood of the martyrs is the seed of the Church." It would seem a great waste of humanity for a gifted young Wheaton graduate to travel to Equador as a missionary, only to be killed by the very people he was trying to help. Yet this was the legacy of the 28 year old Jim Elliot. He and four other men began a friendly dialogue - including food, gifts and airplane rides - with the Huaorani Indians (also known as the Aucas). They were deceived by one of the Indians, named George, and consequently murdered. The amazing conclusion to this tragedy is that these men (Jim Elliot, Ed McCully, Roger Youderian, Pete Fleming and Nate Saint) became models for missionary zeal and sacrifice. They did not die in vain. Other missionaries began to share their faith with the Indians in Equador, and many natives were led to Christ. Jim's own wife and daughter, Elisabeth and Valerie, returned years later, in a spirit of forgiveness, to minister to the same Indians. Jim's faith was contagious. He said: **"Too often we attempt to work for God to the limits of our incompetence, rather than to the limit of God's omnipotence."** He is best known for the following statement, which epitomizes the missionary's heart: **"He is no fool who gives what he cannot keep to gain what he cannot lose."**

Most important, I count all things to be loss
in view of the surpassing value
of knowing Christ Jesus my Lord,
for whom I have suffered the loss of all things,
and count them but rubbish
so that I may gain Christ.
Paul the Apostle, PHILIPPIANS 3:8

102

Sacrifice

Sacrifice, which is the passion of great souls,
has never been the law of societies.
Henri Frederic Amiel

———

Sacrifice still exists everywhere,
and everywhere the elect of each generation
suffers for the salvation of the rest.
Henri Frederic Amiel

———

Those things which are precious are saved only by sacrifice.
David Kenyon Webster

———

If Jesus Christ be God and died for me,
then no sacrifice can be too great for me to make for Him.
C. T. Studd

———

I have nothing to offer but blood, toil, tears, and sweat.
Sir Winston Churchill

———

I regret that I have but one life to give for my country.
Nathan Hale

———

It is not what we take up, but what we give up, that makes us rich.
Henry Ward Beecher

"All I have seen teaches me to trust the Creator for all I have not seen. Nature is too thin a screen; the glory of the omnipresent God bursts through everywhere. Never lose an opportunity of seeing anything beautiful, for beauty is God's handwriting."

RALPH WALDO EMERSON
1803 - 1882 (78 years)

"God enters by a private door into every individual."

Emerson was an American philosopher and poet who gave prominence to an intellectual elitism known as Transcendentalism. His father was a Unitarian minister in a day when the Bible was still considered to be an authoritative source. Emerson entered Harvard University at the age of 14, and upon graduation decided to be known as "Waldo." At the age of 26, he became an Associate Pastor of Second Church, Boston, but by the age of 34, his brand of religion was rejected as liberal even by Harvard's standards. His best friend was Henry David Thoreau, another Transcendentalist, who believed that God was revealed equally through all religions. Emerson was a great intellectual as well as a great orator, but he suffered in old age, ironically, from a mental disease called Aphasia. This malady prevented the patient from being able to speak or write at the same time. He sought after God, but the spirit of the age prohibited him from enjoying a simple, orthodox faith. He said: **"A person will worship something, have no doubt about that. We may think our tribute is paid in secret in the dark recesses of our hearts, but it will be found out. That which dominates our imaginations and our thoughts will determine our lives and our character."**

For while I was passing through
and examining the objects of your worship,
I also found an altar with this inscription,
'TO AN UNKNOWN GOD.'
Therefore what you worship in ignorance,
this I proclaim to you.
Paul the Apostle, ACTS 17:23

Words from Emerson

If the stars should appear but one night
every thousand years, how man would marvel and stare.

Never lose an opportunity of seeing anything that is beautiful;
for beauty, which is God's handwriting, is a wayside sacrament.

If a man writes a better book, preaches a better sermon,
or makes a better mouse-trap than his neighbor,
the world will make a beaten path to his door.

It is easy in the world to live after the world's opinion,
it is easy in solitude to live after your own;
but the great man is he who, in the midst of the world,
keeps with perfect sweetness the independence of solitude.

There is properly no history; only biography.
All history is but the lengthened shadow of a great man.
The first thing a great person does
is make us realize the insignificance of circumstance.

Truth is the property of no individual but is the treasure of all men.

Great men are they who see that the spiritual
is stronger than any material force.

"Speculations? I have none. I am resting on certainties. . . We ought to value the privilege of knowing God's truth far beyond anything we can have in this world."

MICHAEL FARADAY
1791-1867

"A Christian finds his guide in the Word of God, and commits the keeping of his soul into the hands of God. "

Perhaps the summary tribute that could be spoken of Michael Faraday was that Albert Einstein kept a photograph of Faraday on his study wall, alongside pictures of Isaac Newton and James Clerk Maxwell. Faraday was a chemist and a physicist at the Royal Institution of Great Britain, and his main contributions were the discovery of electro-magnetic induction, leading to the development of the electric motor. The Faraday Constant (magnitude of electricity per mole of electrons) is dedicated to him. The term "physicist" was a newly coined identity which Faraday rejected. **"It is both to my mouth and ears so awkward that I think I shall never use it. The equivalent of three separate sounds of "I" in one word is too much."** In chemistry, he invented an early form of what would later become the Bunsen burner, and he discovered benzene and the metallurgical process called electrolysis. Faraday was a lifelong member in the Sandemanian Church, a Protestant church in Scotland which adhered strictly to first century Christian principles and practices. He was an elder who preached regularly in his church. In one of his messages he said: **"The Bible, and it alone, with nothing added to it nor taken away from it by man, is the sole and sufficient guide for each individual, at all times and in all circumstances."** English author Aldous Huxley said of him: "Even if I could be Shakespeare I think that I should still choose to be Faraday."

Make your ear attentive to wisdom, Incline your heart to understanding;
For if you cry for discernment, Lift your voice for understanding;
If you seek her as silver And search for her as for hidden treasures; Then
you will discern the fear of the LORD And discover the knowledge of God.
King Solomon, PROVERBS 2:2-4

The Joy of Discovery

Man cannot discover new oceans
unless he has the courage to lose sight of the shore.
Andre Gide

———

Discovery consists in seeing what everyone else has seen
and thinking what no one else has thought.
Albert Szent-Gyorgyi

———

The real voyage of discovery consists not in seeking new landscapes
but in having new eyes.
Marcel Proust

———

The greatest discovery of my generation
is that a human being can alter his life by altering his attitudes.
William James

———

The process of scientific discovery is, in effect,
a continual flight from wonder.
Albert Einstein

———

One of the greatest discoveries a man makes, one of his greatest surprises,
is to find he can do what he was afraid he could not.
Henry Ford

———

**"Tell God all that is in your heart -
as one unloads one's heart,
its pleasures, and its pains, to a dear friend.
Blessed are they who attain to such familiar,
unreserved intercourse with God."**

FRANCOIS FENELON
1651 - 1715 (63 years)

**"Oh, how seldom the soul is silent,
in order that God may speak."**

King Louis the XIV (fourteenth) of France appointed Fenelon to be tutor and mentor to the grandson of the King. François Fénelon was a Catholic theologian, poet and writer, who succeeded in molding the rebellious young man into a man of character. Fenelon wrote the book, *The Adventures of Telemachus*, as a guide for training the young Duke. The book, however, was a thinly veiled attack on the French monarchy, which eventually cost Fenelon his prestigious position. He said: **"When kings interfere in matters of religion, they enslave instead of protect."** In Ulysses's book *The Iliad and the Odyssey*, Mentor was the teacher of Telemachus, the son of Ulysses. Fenelon is also known today as one of the disciples of "Quietism," a philosophy of monastic withdrawal from the world which supposedly leads to absolute peace and perfection with God. A life of simplicity and withdrawal is good only when God leads the individual to such a life. It should not become a social standard. Fenelon's words on prayer continue to challenge us to greater communion with God: **"Let us pray to God that He would root out of our hearts every thing of our own planting, and set there, with His own hands, the tree of life, bearing all manner of fruits."**

Blessed are those who wash their robes,
so that they may have the right
to the tree of life,
and may enter by the gates
into the city.
REVELATION 22:14

THE ANVIL

Last eve I paused beside a blacksmith's door,
And heard the anvil ring the vesper chime;
Then looking in, I saw upon the floor,
Old hammers worn with beating years of time.
"How many anvils have you had," said I,
"To wear and batter all these hammers so?"
"Just one," said he, and then, with twinkling eye,
"The anvil wears the hammers out, you know."
"And so," I thought, "The Anvil of God's Word
For ages skeptic blows have beat upon,
Yet, though the noise of falling blows was heard,
The Anvil is unharmed, the hammers gone."
ATTRIBUTED TO JOHN CLIFFORD

———-

Who drives the horses of the sun
Shall lord them but a day
Better the lowly deed were done
And kept the humble way.

The dust shall hide the sword of fame
The rust shall hide the crown.
Aye, none shall nail so high his name
Time will not tear it down.

The happiest heart that ever beat
Was in some quiet breast
That found the common daylight sweet
And left to heaven the rest.
JOHN VANCE CHENEY

"I don't even think about a retirement program
because I'm working for the Lord, for the Almighty.
And even though the Lord's pay isn't very high,
His retirement program is, you might say,
out of this world."

GEORGE FOREMAN
1949 -

"Sure the fight was fixed. I fixed it with a right hand."

Foreman is a two-time World Heavyweight Boxing Champion who has the distinction of regaining his title 20 years later at the age of 45. As an amateur he was undefeated in 27 bouts and then won the 1968 Olympic gold medal before turning pro. His greatest victories were against Joe Frasier and Ken Norton, and his greatest losses (on points) were to Muhammed Ali and Evander Holyfield. He ranks #9 among the 100 best boxers and his record is 76 wins and 5 losses. **"When I was a kid in Houston, we were so poor we couldn't afford the last two letters, so we called ourselves 'po'."** Foreman admits he has become more famous for the George Foreman Grill than he was in his boxing career. He has ten children, and the five boys are all named George. **"I called them all George because I was worried that when I was older I might suffer from memory loss."** After his second defeat he had a life-changing experience by accepting Christ as the "new manager" of his life. With a new sense of purpose, he continued to fight until achieving his second title, while also pastoring a church in downtown Houston. He wrote the book *God in My Corner* to portray his spiritual transformation, and he wrote the book *Going the Second Smile* to portray the lovable side of this fierce fighting machine. To his congregation he says: **"The knowledge of God and the spirit of giving is the only true gift that can be passed from generation to generation."**

Blessed is the man who walks not in the counsel of the ungodly,
nor stand in the path of sinners,
nor sits in the seat of scoffers!
But his delight is in the law of the LORD,
and in His law he meditates day and night.
King David, PSALM 1:1-2 (George's Favorite Verse)

IF

If you can keep your head when all about you
Are losing theirs and blaming it on you;
If you can trust yourself when all men doubt you,
But make allowance for their doubting too;
If you can wait and not be tired by waiting,
Or, being lied about, don't deal in lies,
Or, being hated, don't give way to hating,
And yet don't look too good, nor talk too wise;
If you can dream - and not make dreams your master;
If you can think - and not make thoughts your aim;
If you can meet with triumph and disaster
And treat those two imposters just the same;
If you can bear to hear the truth you've spoken
Twisted by knaves to make a trap for fools,
Or watch the things you gave your life to, broken,
And stoop and build 'em up with wornout tools;
If you can make one heap of all your winnings
And risk it on one turn of pitch-and-toss,
And lose, and start again at your beginnings
And never breathe a word about your loss;
If you can force your heart and nerve and sinew
To serve your turn long after they are gone,
And so hold on when there is nothing in you
Except the Will which says to them: "Hold on."
If you can talk with crowds and keep your virtue,
Or walk with kings - nor lose the common touch;
If neither foes nor loving friends can hurt you;
If all men count with you, but none too much;
If you can fill the unforgiving minute
With sixty seconds' worth of distance run -
Yours is the Earth and everything that's in it,
And - which is more - you'll be a Man, my son!

RUDYARD KIPLING

"He who shall introduce into public affairs
the principles of primitive Christianity
will change the face of the world."

BENJAMIN FRANKLIN
1706-1790 (84 years)

"The longer I live, the more convincing proofs I see
of this truth — that God governs in the affairs of men."

Franklin has been referred to as "the only President of the United States who was not President of the United States." He was a "Founding Father" who has been called a "polymath," a lofty equivalent for a "Renaissance Man", or one who is so skilled at so many disciplines as to be hailed as a genius. Franklin was foremost a scientist and inventor (electricity, optics, sound, etc.) whose vast writings on values, common sense and politics launched a career that made him an international personality and beloved statesman. He is the only man to sign all four of the founding U.S. documents of liberty. His proposal for the Great Seal of the U.S. was a picture of Moses, the Israelites and the Pillar of Fire, with the inscription, **"Rebellion to tyrants is obedience to God."** He was raised a Puritan, briefly attended a Presbyterian church and supported the publication of George Whitefield's sermons on the front page of his Gazette, thereby contributing greatly to the spiritual revival in the United States, known as The Great Awakening. Of the founding of the United States he said: **"We have been assured in the Sacred Writings, that 'except the Lord build the house they labor in vain who build it.' I firmly believe this."**

Delight yourself
in the ways of the Lord
and He will give you
the desires of your heart.
King David, PSALM 37:4

Poor Richard's Almanac

No man e'er was glorious,
who was not laborious.

Would you live with ease?
Do what you ought,
and not what you please.

Look before,
or you'll find yourself behind.

There's many witty men
whose brains can't fill their bellies.

Fish and visitors stink in three days.

'Tis easy to see, hard to foresee.

God helps those that help themselves.

He that cannot obey, cannot command.

God heals, and the doctor takes the fees.

Humility makes great men twice honorable.

Creditors have better memories than debtors.

Take this remark from Richard poor and lame,
Whate'er's begun in anger ends in shame.

He that can have patience, can have what he will.

Poverty wants some things, luxury many things, avarice all things.

Early to bed and early to rise, makes a man healthy, wealthy and wise.

Here comes the Orator! with his flood of words, and his drop of reason.

"With his countrymen indifferent to their own condition, where else could Washington turn, but to his God."

ARNOLD FRIBERG
1913 - 2010 (97 years)

"We trust that this painting communicates the urgent need for prayer, in guiding the people and the leaders of the United States of America."

Arnold Friberg is an American artist best known for his painting of George Washington during the winter of 1777-1778 in "The Prayer at Valley Forge." Born to parents of Scandinavian descent, young Arnold began cartooning at age seven. After high school he attended the Chicago Academy of Fine Arts, followed by the Grand Central School of Art in New York City, where one of his fellow students was Norman Rockwell. He was later commissioned to paint over 300 pictures of the Royal Canadian Mounted Police, and to date, he is the only honorary member of the "Mounties" who is an American citizen. When World War II began he was offered the rank of captain to draw recruitment posters, but he chose instead to serve in the 86th infantry division, both in Europe and the Pacific. After the war, he was recruited by Hollywood's famous director, Cecil B. Demille, to paint promotional artwork for the upcoming movie production called "The Ten Commandments." In order to provide realism for "The Prayer at Valley Forge," he traveled there in the dead of winter, sketching and photographing until his fingers were numb. Artistic interpretation of Scripture was the highest and most sacred privilege to Mr. Friburg, who expresses his passion: **"Art is always at its best when serving a cause greater than the artist."**

For whatever is born of God
overcomes the world;
and this is the victory
that has overcome the world - our faith.
John the Apostle, 1 JOHN 5:4

Freedom

It is by the fortune of God that,
in this country, we have three benefits:
freedom of speech, freedom of thought,
and the wisdom never to use either.
Mark Twain

Freedom is the recognition that no single person,
no single authority or government, has a monopoly on the truth;
but that every individual life is infinitely precious,
that every one of us put in this world
has been put there for a reason and has something to offer.
Ronald Reagan

The cost of freedom is always high,
but Americans have always paid it.
And one path we shall never choose,
and that is the path of surrender, or submission.
John Fitzgerald Kennedy

Freedom of religion, freedom of the press,
freedom of person under the protection of the habeas corpus;
and trial by juries impartially selected - these principles
form the bright constellation which has gone before us.
Thomas Jefferson

We, and all others who believe in freedom as deeply as we do,
would rather die on our feet than live on our knees.
Franklin D. Roosevelt

"I do not feel obliged to believe
that the same God who has endowed us
with sense, reason and intellect
has intended us to forego their use."

GALILEO (di Vincenzo Bonaiuti de') **GALILEI**
1564-1642 (77 years)

"Mathematics is the language in which
God has written the universe."

We call Galileo by his first name because his full Italian name is too long to attempt. He is considered by Einstein and Hawking to be the father of astronomy, physics and modern science. From Copernicus, a generation earlier, he learned the theory that the earth rotated around the sun, contrary to the teaching of the Roman Church. Based on research with his newly redesigned telescope, Galileo proved his theory while studying Venus. The Church authorities condemned him as a heretic because Psalm 96:10, Ecclesiastes 1:5) and sentenced him to house arrest until his death ten years later. He argued, **"It is surely harmful to souls to make it a heresy to believe what is proved. The Bible shows the way to go to heaven, not the way the heavens go."** A hundred years later, the Church recanted when overwhelming evidence was established. With all his profoundness, Galileo made the following observation: **"The sun, with all those planets revolving around it and dependent on it, can still ripen a bunch of grapes as if it had nothing else in the universe to do."** He was a man of faith, whose life was made miserable by heavy-handed authorities. He said, **"I've loved the stars too fondly to be fearful of the night."**

Say among the nations,
"The LORD reigns;
Indeed, the world is firmly established,
it will not be moved;
He will judge the peoples with equity."
PSALM 96:10

The Mind of Galileo

I have never met a man so ignorant
that I couldn't learn something from him.
Galileo Galilei

———

You cannot teach a man anything;
you can only help him discover it in himself.
Galileo Galilei

———

In questions of science, the authority of a thousand
is not worth the humble reasoning of a single individual.
Galileo Galilei

———

And who can doubt that it will lead to the worst disorders
when minds created free by God are compelled
to submit slavishly to an outside will? . . . These are the novelties
which are apt to bring about the ruin of commonwealths
and the subversion of the state.
Galileo Galilei

———

Facts which at first seem improbable will, even on scant explanation,
drop the cloak which has hidden them
and stand forth in naked and simple beauty.
Galileo Galilei

———

Nature is relentless and unchangeable,
and it is indifferent as to whether its hidden reasons and actions
are understandable to man or not.
Galileo Galilei

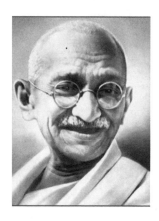

"I like your Christ, I do not like your Christians.
Your Christians are so unlike your Christ.
If Christians would really live according
to the teachings of Christ, as found in the Bible,
all of India would be Christian today."

MOHANDAS GANDHI
1869 - 1948 (78 years)

The title "Mahatma" was given to Gandhi, which means "Great Soul." He is also re-ferred to as "Bapu", which means "father." He is known today as India's "father of the nation" for leading India toward independence from the British in 1947. Trained in London as a lawyer, he spent 21 years in South Africa developing a reputation as an advocate for non-violent resistance to racial injustice. On one occasion, while traveling on a South African train, he was moved from a first class seat to third class, while holding a first class ticket. When he returned to India, he led the Indian Nation-al Congress to peacefully rally for India's independence. In 1999, he was Time Mag-azine's runner up to Albert Einstein as the "Person of the Century." All of India's cur-rency bears the picture of this quiet, humble, yet powerful influence. One of the weapons he used against both followers and adversaries was the act of fasting. Though he embraced all religions, his language was peppered with biblical terms such as grace and faith, divine providence and Creator God. **"Our life is a long and arduous quest after Truth. But for my faith in God, I should have been a raving maniac - Before the throne of the Almighty, man will be judged, not by his acts but by his inten-tions. For God alone reads our hearts."** Hopefully his quest for truth led him to bow be-fore the one true God.

For you shall not worship any other god,
for the LORD, whose name is Jealous,
is a jealous God.
EXODUS 34:14

The Quest for Truth

Truth is a gem that is found at a great depth;
whilst on the surface of this world,
all things are weighed by the false scale of custom.
Lord Byron

———

Peace if possible, truth at all costs.
Martin Luther

———

I will be as harsh as truth, and uncompromising as justice.
I am in earnest, I will not equivocate, I will not excuse,
I will not retreat a single inch, and I WILL be heard.
William Lloyd Garrison

———

Truth is often eclipsed but never extinguished.
Titus Livy

———

Beyond a doubt truth bears the same relation to falsehood
as light to darkness.
Leonardo da Vinci

———

Truth is so obscure in these times, and falsehood so established,
that, unless we love the truth, we cannot know it.
Blaise Pascal

———

Whatever satisfies the soul is truth.
Walt Whitman

"Talk about the questions of the day,
There is but one question, and that is the Gospel.
It is the impregnable rock of Holy Scripture.
It can and will correct everything that needs correcting."

WILLIAM E. GLADSTONE
1809-1898 (87 years)

"Of one thing I am, and always have been, convinced -
it is not by the State that man can be regenerated."

Great Britain called him the G.O.M. (Grand Old Man). Gladstone was Prime Minister of England for four tenures, and he was a Liberal Party statesman who may have been best known for fighting battles to cut taxes and improve the budget and economy of Great Britain. His philosophy was: **"All the world over, I will back the masses against the classes."** He was a gifted orator who turned finance meetings into pep rallies. One MP (Member of Parliament) exclaimed: "He made finance and figures exciting, and succeeded in constructing budget speeches epic in form and performance. . . By universal consent it was one of the grandest displays and most able financial statements ever heard in the House of Commons." Gladstone wanted reform so badly that he was known for wandering the streets at night to salvage prostitutes and find them gainful employment. For exercise, until the age of 81, he chopped down trees at the age of 85, he bequeathed his collection of 32,000 books to a local library, using a wheelbarrow himself to transport them a quarter mile to their new home. At his funeral, two future kings, Edward VII and George V, humbled themselves as pallbearers for their servant leader.

Blessed is the nation
whose God is the LORD -
the people whom He has chosen
for His own inheritance.
PSALM 33:12

Desiderata

(Latin for "Things Desired")

Go placidly amid the noise and the haste,
and remember what peace there may be in silence.
As far as possible, without surrender, be on good terms with all persons.
Speak your truth quietly and clearly; and listen to others,
even to the dull and the ignorant; they too have their story.
Avoid loud and aggressive persons; they are vexatious to the spirit.
If you compare yourself with others, you may become vain or bitter,
for always there will be greater and lesser persons than yourself.
Enjoy your achievements as well as your plans.
Keep interested in your own career, however humble;
it is a real possession in the changing fortunes of time.
Exercise caution in your business affairs, for the world is full of trickery.
But let this not blind you to what virtue there is;
many persons strive for high ideals,
and everywhere life is full of heroism.

Be yourself. Especially do not feign affection. Neither be cynical about love,
for in the face of all aridity and disenchantment, it is as perennial as the grass.
Take kindly the counsel of the years, gracefully surrendering the things of youth.
Nurture strength of spirit to shield you in sudden misfortune.
But do not distress yourself with dark imaginings.
Many fears are born of fatigue and loneliness.
Beyond a wholesome discipline, be gentle with yourself.
You are a child of the universe, no less than the trees and the stars;
you have a right to be here.
And whether or not it is clear to you,
no doubt the universe is unfolding as it should.
Therefore be at peace with God, whatever you conceive Him to be.
And whatever your labors and aspirations,
in the noisy confusion of life,
keep peace in your soul.
With all its sham, drudgery, and broken dreams,
it is still a beautiful world.
Be cheerful. Strive to be happy.

MAX EHRMANN

"Surely, God on high has not refused
to give us enough wisdom to find ways
to bring an improvement in relations
between the two great nations on earth."

MIKHAIL GORBACHEV
1931 -

"The story of St. Francis fascinates me,
and has played a fundamental role in my life.
It was through St. Francis that I arrived at the Church."

Gorbachev was elected the General Secretary of the Soviet Union in 1985. Under the influence of Ronald Reagan and Margaret Thatcher of Great Britain, Gorbachev began to introduce sweeping reforms in the Soviet Union that were known as "glasnost" (openness). The result was an emphasis on: 1) freedom of speech 2) private ownership of business 3) free elections and 4) reduced government control. In 1989 The Berlin Wall (which personified communism) was destroyed. In 1990 Gorbachev was awarded the Nobel Peace Prize for his efforts to promote reform. But in 1991, the Soviet states began to go independent, and the USSR collapsed from economic weakness and political revolution. Ironically, Mr. Gorbachev had introduced western style democratic change, and the country could not survive the new freedom. Gorbachev's faith was questioned within political circles, but his words seem to express his inner desire to serve the God of freedom. Of his destiny, he said: **"I don't know how many years God will be giving me, or what His plans are."**

'For I know the plans that I have for you,'
declares the LORD,
'plans for welfare and not for calamity,
to give you a future and a hope.'
JEREMIAH 29:11

Freedom

The secret of happiness is freedom.
The secret of freedom is courage.
Thucydides

────

While we are free to choose our actions,
we are not free to choose the consequences of our actions.
Stephen R. Covey

────

Those who desire to give up freedom in order to gain security
will not have, nor do they deserve, either one.
Benjamin Franklin

────

Everything that is really great and inspiring
is created by the individual who can labor in freedom.
Albert Einstein

────

Freedom is never more than one generation away from extinction.
Ronald Reagan

────

Freedom is the oxygen of the soul.
Moshe Dayan

"The men who followed Christ were unique in their generation. They turned the world upside down because their hearts had been turned right side up. The world has never been the same."

BILLY GRAHAM
1918 -

"Being a Christian is more than just an instantaneous conversion. It is a daily process whereby you grow to be more and more like Christ."

Billy Graham became the youngest person at age 30 to serve as a college president during his tenure at Northwestern College in Minnesota. In 1949 he launched a large tent revival crusade in Los Angeles that catapulted him to national recognition, and in 1991, he spoke to 250,000 people in New York's Central Park. For over 50 years, he has preached a simple gospel message of salvation through faith in Jesus Christ, reaching an estimated 2.2 billion people globally through radio, television and stadium crusades. His message is bold and uncompromising: **"Courage is contagious. When a brave man takes a stand, the spines of others are often stiffened."** He was a personal counsel to eleven U.S. Presidents, from Truman to G. W. Bush, and he ranks #7 on Gallup's list of "The World's Most Admired People" in the 21st Century. Early in his career, a fellow evangelist accused Billy of setting religion back 100 years. His response: **"I did indeed want to set religion back, not just 100 years but 1,900 years, to the Book of Acts, when first century followers of Christ were accused of turning the Roman Empire upside down."** He often speaks about the believers' eternal home in heaven. Referring to his own longing to see Christ, he said, **"I look forward to seeing Christ and bowing before Him in praise and gratitude . . . for using me on this earth, by His grace - just as I am."**

We proclaim Him,
admonishing every man
and teaching every man with all wisdom,
so that we may present every man
complete in Christ.
Paul the Apostle, COLOSSIANS 1:28

One Solitary Life

Here is a man who was born in an obscure village,
the child of a peasant woman. He grew up in another village.
He worked in a carpenter shop until He was thirty.
Then for three years He was an itinerant preacher.
He never owned a home. He never wrote a book.
He never held an office. He never had a family.
He never went to college. He never put His foot inside a big city.
He never traveled two hundred miles from the place He was born.
He never did one of the things that usually accompany greatness.
He had no credentials but Himself...
While still a young man, the tide of popular opinion
turned against Him. His friends ran away.
One of them denied Him. He was turned over to His enemies.
He went through the mockery of a trial.
He was nailed upon a cross between two thieves.
While He was dying His executioners gambled
for the only piece of property He had on earth – His coat.
When He was dead, He was laid in a borrowed grave
through the pity of a friend.
Nineteen long centuries have come and gone,
and today He is a centerpiece of the human race
and leader of the column of progress.
I am far within the mark when I say that
all the armies that ever marched,
all the navies that were ever built,
all the parliaments that ever sat,
and all the kings that ever reigned, put together,
have not affected the life of man upon this earth
as powerfully as that one solitary life.

James Allen Francis

**"Hold fast to the Bible. To the influence of this Book
we are indebted for all the progress made in true civilization.
The Bible is the sheer anchor of our liberties.
Write its principles upon your heart,
and practice them in your lives."**

ULYSSES S. GRANT
1822-1885 (63 years)

U.S. Grant was the 18th President of the U.S., and the face on our $50 bill. He rose to fame as the Union General who defeated Confederate General Robert E. Lee during the Civil War. Military historians say that he rivaled Napoleon as a tactical leader on the battlefield. His actual name was Hiram Ulysses, but during his training at the U.S. Military Academy, he adopted "Ulysses S." His army buddies said the U.S. stood for "Uncle Sam", but later they said it stood for "Unconditional Surrender." Oddly enough, after his first 14 years of military service, he abruptly quit and became a farmer, bill collector and leather salesman. When the Civil War began, he reenlisted and was soon appointed a General by Abraham Lincoln. The Battle of Vicksburg became a turning point in the war due to Grant's strategies. He said, **"In every battle there comes a time when both sides consider themselves beaten - then he who continues the attack wins."** After the war, Grant became a two-term president who fought battles to strengthen a war-torn economy. Preserving the morality and character of the nation was equally important as he said, **"Leave the matter of religion to the family altar, the church, and the private school, supported entirely by private contributions. Keep the church and state forever separate."**

I have fought the good fight, I have finished the course,
I have kept the faith; in the future there is laid up for me
the crown of righteousness, which the Lord, the righteous Judge,
will award to me on that day; and not only to me,
but also to all who have loved His appearing.
Paul the Apostle, 2 TIMOTHY 4:7-8

The Touch of the Masters Hand

'Twas battered and scarred, and the auctioneer
Thought it scarcely worth his while
To waste much time on the old violin,
But he held it up with a smile.
"What am I bidden, good folks," he cried,
"Who'll start the bidding for me?
A dollar, a dollar - now who'll make it two _
Two dollars, and who'll make it three?
Three dollars once, three dollars twice,
Going for three. . . but no!

From the room far back a gray-haired man
Came forward and picked up the bow;
Then wiping the dust from the old violin,
And tightening up the strings,
He played a melody, pure and sweet,
As sweet as an angel sings.
The music ceased and the auctioneer
With a voice that was quiet and low,
Said: "What am I bidden for the old violin?"
And he held it up with the bow.

"A thousand dollars - and who'll make it two?
Two thousand - and who'll make it three?
Three thousand once, three thousand twice
And going - and gone," said he.
The people cheered, but some of them cried,
"We do not quite understand -
What changed its worth?" The man replied:
"The touch of the master's hand."

And many a man with life out of tune,
And battered and torn with sin,
Is auctioned cheap to a thoughtless crowd.
Much like the old violin.
A "mess of pottage," a glass of wine,
A game and he travels on,
He's going once, and going twice -
He's going - and almost gone!
But the MASTER comes, and the foolish crowd,
Never can quite understand,
The worth of a soul, and the change that's wrought
By the touch of the MASTER'S hand.
MYRA B. WELCH

"It is impossible, mentally or socially, to enslave a Bible reading people. The principles of the Bible are the groundwork of human freedom."

HORACE GREELEY
1811-1872 (61 years)

Greeley is best remembered for one simple admonition: **"Go west, young man, go west."** He founded the New York Tribune during the 1840's and became known as the greatest newspaper editor in the world. The Tribune established a reputation of good taste, high moral standards, and intellectual appeal. Greeley had a keen ability for framing each page to appeal to the reader. He was a crusader for the working class of society. He fought against the railroad industry and mounted a major journalistic campaign against slavery. He was always seen in public, even in summer, with a full length topcoat, carrying an umbrella. Greeley was part of the briefly known "Whig Party," united against excessive power in the Executive branch. The Whigs eventually became Republicans, but in 1872 Greeley became a third party candidate in the newly formed Liberal Republican Party. He lost in a landslide, but worse, his wife died immediately after the election and his partner took control of the Tribune. Greeley went into depression and he died before the electoral college voted. He offers wisdom for every man seeking success: **"Fame is a vapor, popularity an accident, and riches take wings. Only one thing endures and that is character."**

For all that is in the world,
the lust of the flesh
and the lust of the eyes
and the boastful pride of life,
is not from the Father,
but is from the world.
1 JOHN 2:16

Character

A good character is the best tombstone.
Those who loved you and were helped by you
will remember you when forget-me-nots have withered.
Carve your name on hearts, not on marble.
Charles H. Spurgeon

———

Character, not circumstances, make the man.
Booker T. Washington

———

I have a dream that my four little children will one day live in a nation
where they will not be judged by the color of their skin
but by the content of their character.
Martin Luther King, Jr.

———

The proper time to influence the character of a child
is about a hundred years before he is born.
Dean Inge

———

It is well for the world that in most of us, by the age of thirty,
the character has been set like plaster, and will never soften again.
William James

———

Thoughts lead on to purpose, purpose leads on to actions,
actions form habits, habits decide character,
and character fixes our destiny.
Tryon Edwards

"I repent of ever having recorded one single song,
and ever having performed one concert,
if my music, and more importantly, my life,
has not provoked you into greater Godliness,
and to sell out more completely to Jesus."

KEITH GREEN
1953-1982 (29 years)

Keith Green was a drug addict musician, whose life was dramatically changed when he and his Jewish wife Melody found meaning in their lives through Jesus Christ. Keith wrote 40 songs by the age of eleven, and he played Kurt Von Trapp in a theatrical production of "The Sound of Music." He had a five-year contract with Decca Records, and he appeared on numerous TV shows as a child pop artist. Keith died in a plane crash at the age of 29. His style was passionate. His music was lively and captivating. Some of his best songs were "Your Love Broke Through," "You Put This Love In My Heart," and "Asleep In The Light." Since his death, Keith has amassed a worldwide following dedicated to his music and his uncompromising legacy.

Lyrics from "Your Love Broke Through"
"Like a foolish dreamer, trying to build a highway to the sky
All my hopes would come tumbling down, and I never knew just why.
Until today, when You pulled away the clouds
that hung like curtains on my eyes.
Well I've been blind all these wasted years and I thought I was so wise,
But then You took me by surprise"

The Spirit of the Lord is upon me, because he anointed me
to preach the gospel to the poor. He has sent me to proclaim
release to the captives, and recovery of sight to the blind,
to set free those who are oppressed,
to proclaim the favorable year of the Lord.
Jesus the Messiah, LUKE 4:18-19

Truth

We seek the truth and will endure the consequences.
Charles Seymour

A lie gets halfway around the world
before the truth has a chance to get its pants on.
Winston Churchill

Truth is not only violated by falsehood;
it may be equally outraged by silence.
Henri Frederic Amiel

In order that all men may be taught to speak the truth,
it is necessary that all likewise should learn to hear it.
Samuel Johnson

Of course it's the same old story.
Truth usually is the same old story.
Margaret Thatcher

A truth that's told, even with bad intent
beats all the lies you can invent.
William Blake

I believe that in the end truth will conquer.
John Wycliffe

"God does not die on the day that we cease to
believe in a personal deity. But we die on the day
when our lives cease to be illumined
by the steady radiance, renewed daily,
of a wonder, the Source of which
is beyond all reason."

DAG HAMMARSKJOLD
1905-1961 (56 years)

John F. Kennedy said of Hammarskjold, "I realize I am a small man in comparison to him. He was the greatest statesman of our century. Hammarskjold was the second Secretary General of the United Nations. He died at the age of 56, while on a trip to Zambia to settle international conflict. It was rumored for years that his plane was sabotaged. Hammarskjold was a Swedish diplomat whose family had served the Swedish crown since the 17th century. He is the only person in history to receive the Nobel Peace Prize posthumously. He wrote one book, entitled *Markings,* and he has been described by history as a Christian mystic, in the ranks of Thomas a Kempis, Thomas Merton, Blaise Pascal, William Blake and A.W. Tozer. Christian mysticism is described as men who are known by their conviction, their deep commitment to prayer and their desire to follow the pure tenets of the Christian faith. On the subject of prayer, Hammarskjold said**: "Your cravings as a human animal do not become a prayer just because it is God whom you ask to attend to them."** He said of the Christian faith, **"The longest journey is the journey inwards."** We could learn much from this great, but humble man, whose life was characterized by this self styled declaration of his purpose in life. **"If only I may grow: firmer, simpler, quieter, warmer."**

Just as He chose us in Him before the foundation of the world,
that we would be holy and blameless before Him.
In love, He predestined us to adoption
as sons through Jesus Christ to Himself,
according to the kind intention of His will . . .
Paul the Apostle, EPHESIANS 1:4-5

Markings

From generations of soldiers and government officials on my fathers side,
I inherited a belief that no life was more satisfactory
than one of selfless service to your country - or humanity.
This service required a sacrifice of all personal interests,
but likewise the courage to stand up unflinchingly for your convictions.

———

That God should have time for you, you seem to take
as much for granted as that you cannot have time for Him.

———

When all your strength ought to be focused into one
pencil of light pointing up through the darkness,
you allow it to be dissipated in a moss fire
where nothing is consumed but all life is suffocated.

———

On the bookshelf of life, God is a useful work of reference,
always at hand but seldom consulted.

———

The "men of the hour," the self assured who strut about among us
In the jingling harness of their success and importance,
how can you let yourself be irritated by them.
Let them enjoy their triumph - on the level to which it belongs.

———

The most dangerous of all moral dilemmas, when we are obliged
to conceal truth in order to help the truth to be victorious.

———

If even dying is to be a social function, then please,
grant me the favor of sneaking out on tiptoes without disturbing the party.

"The Spirit of Liberty is the spirit of Him who,
nearly two thousand years ago,
taught mankind that lesson
it has never learned, but never quite forgotten:
that there is a kingdom
where the least shall be heard
and considered side by side with the greatest."

Judge LEARNED HAND
1872 - 1961 (91 years)

Learned (pronounced Larned) Hand was a U.S. District Court Judge in New York and better known as the Senior Justice for the U.S. Court of Appeals for the Second Circuit. Hand has been quoted more often than any other lower-court judge by legal scholars and by the Supreme Court of the United States. He is best known for saying: **"Liberty lies in the hearts of men and women; when it dies there, no constitution, no law, no court can save it."** Hand was one of the youngest judges ever appointed to the Court of Appeals. Born into perhaps "the most distinguished legal family in northern New York" he graduated from Harvard and practiced law for a brief time, but he admitted, **"I was never any good as a lawyer."** Though he possessed a true innate legal insight, it was his eloquence when writing judicial opinions (4000 in his career) that made him famous. Though politics prevented him from reaching the Supreme Court, he is referred to, even today, as: "unquestionably the first among American judges." In an attempt to always remain impartial, he once described himself as **"a conservative among liberals, and a liberal among conservatives."**

But let justice roll down like waters
and righteousness like
an ever-flowing stream.
AMOS 5:24

Liberty

Whoever would overthrow the liberty of a nation
must begin by subduing the freeness of speech.
Benjamin Franklin

———

It is seldom that liberty of any kind is lost all at once.
David Hume

———

The preservation of the sacred fire of liberty and the destiny of the
republican model of government are justly considered...
And staked on the experiment entrusted
to the hands of the American people.
George Washington

———

There is danger from all men.
The only maxim of a free government
ought to be to trust no man living
with power to endanger the public liberty.
John Adams

———

The condition upon which God hath given liberty to man
is eternal vigilance...
John Philpot Curran

———

Is life so dear, or peace so sweet,
as to be purchased at the price of chains or slavery?
Forbid it, Almighty God! I know not what course others may take
but as for me; give me liberty or give me death!
Patrick Henry

"I think I did see all Heaven before me
and the great God Himself.
Whether I was in my body or out of my body
as I wrote it, (Handel's Messiah)
I know not. God knows."

GEORGE FRIDERIC HANDEL
1685-1759 (74 years)

The Hallelujah Chorus is the dramatic conclusion from Handel's "Messiah", and is considered to be the greatest choral masterpiece in all history. Handel was born in Germany, trained in Italy, and finally settled in England. As a boy, his father strictly favored the study of law over music, and young Handel hid a harpsichord in the attic to practice privately. His music has been played at every British coronation for 250 years. Beethoven said of him: "He is the greatest composer that ever lived. I would uncover my head and kneel before his tomb." Mozart said of him, "Handel understands effect better than any of us - when he chooses, he strikes like a thunderbolt." Bach said of him, "Handel is the only person I would wish to see before I die, and the only person I would wish to be, were I not Bach." Upon hearing the Hallelujah Chorus, Joseph Haydn is said to have wept like a child and exclaimed: "He is the master of us all." In spite of suffering a stroke and losing an eye, Handel continued to inspire his audiences. It was King George II of England who began the tradition of standing in honor of the Hallelujah Chorus. Upon being complimented of his noble entertainment for the royal family, Handel said, **"I should be sorry if I only entertained them; I wished to make them better."**

Then I heard something like the voice of a great multitude
and like the sound of many waters
and like the sound of mighty peals of thunder, saying,
"Hallelujah! For the Lord our God, the Almighty, reigns.
John the Apostle, REVELATION 19:6

Heaven

Heaven - the treasury of everlasting life.
William Shakespeare

———

Aim at heaven and you will get earth thrown in.
Aim at earth and you get neither.
C. S. Lewis

———

Earth's crammed with heaven,
And every common bush afire with God;
And only he who sees, takes off his shoes;
The rest sit round it and pluck blackberries.
Elizabeth Barrett Browning

———

The doctrine of the Kingdom of Heaven,
which was the main teaching of Jesus,
is certainly one of the most revolutionary doctrines
that ever stirred and changed human thought.
H. G. Wells

———

What can be more foolish than to think
that all this rare fabric of heaven and earth could come by chance,
when all the skill of art is not able to make an oyster!
Anatole France

———

Heaven wheels above you, displaying to you her eternal glories,
and still your eyes are on the ground.
Dante Alighieri

"Civilization today reminds me of an ape with a blowtorch
playing in a room full of dynamite.
It looks like the monkeys operate the zoo,
and the inmates are taking over the asylum."

VANCE HAVNER

1901– 1986 (84 years)

"The Kingdom of God is no place for a man
with his face pointed one way and his feet the other.
God is not taking people to heaven backwards."

Dr. Vance Havner has been called the "Dean of America's Revival Preachers." Born in Jugtown, North Carolina, he began preaching when he was 12 years old. The author of 38 books, Havner has become one of the most quoted preachers in modern history. Regarding politics, he once said, **"America was built, not by politicians running for something; but by statesman standing for something."** During a hospital stay while in his seventies, Vance was told by Billy Graham, "You can't go home just yet. We preachers need more sermon material!" Many of the church's best known quotes have originated from this humble, homespun pastor who turned one-liners into sermons. **"The church is supposed to be a hospital for sinners, not a museum for saints. - Some preachers ought to put more fire into their sermons, or more sermons into the fire - Too many churches start at eleven o'clock sharp, and end at twelve o'clock dull - The church is so subnormal that if it ever got back to the New Testament normal it would seem to be abnormal. - Plenty of church members are shaky about what they believe, while not many are shaken by what they believe."** Billy Graham once said of him, "I do not know of any man in my generation who has stirred revival fires in the hearts of so many people throughout the nation as has Vance Havner."

But to this one I will look,
declares the LORD.
To him who is humble and contrite of spirit,
and who trembles at My word.
ISAIAH 66:2

The Wit and Wisdom of Vance Havner

Plenty of church members are shaky about what they believe,
while not many are shaken by what they believe.

———-

To some, Christianity is an argument.
To many, it is a performance. To a few, it is an experience.

———-

God's Word is not obsolete. It is absolute.

———-

America was built, not by politicians running for something,
but by statesman standing for something.

———-

We are suffering today
from a species of Christianity today
as dry as dust,
as cold as ice,
as pale as a corpse,
and as dead as King Tut.
We are suffering today,
not from a lack of correct heads,
but from a lack of consumed hearts.

———-

I came to Christ as a country boy.
I did not understand all about the plan of salvation.
One does not have to understand it; one has only to stand on it.
I do not understand all about electricity,
But I do not intend to sit around in the dark till I do.

"Our Creator would never have made such lovely days,
and have given us the deep hearts to enjoy them,
above and beyond all thought,
unless we were meant to be immortal."

NATHANIEL HAWTHORNE
1804-1864 (59 years)

Hawthorne is best known for his novels, *The Scarlett Letter* and *The House of Seven Gables.* He was born in Salem, Massachusetts, and his great, great grandfather was a judge during the Salem witch trials. The family name at that time was spelled HATHORNE, but because of his disdain for the family identity he re-spelled his name HAWTHORNE. His novels were identified as dark Romanticism because of his tendency to develop stories that portrayed the sinful, guilty and evil side of human nature. His Puritan background trained him to understand man's fallen nature, when he said: **"What other dungeon is so dark as one's own heart! What jailer so inexorable as one's self!"** For a brief time he and his wife lived in a transcendentalist community, but he rejected this idealism when he said: **"Eager souls. . . may propose to refashion the world in accordance with their dreams; but evil remains, and so long as it lurks in the secret places of the heart, utopia is only the shadow of a dream."** Hawthorne lived a simple, reclusive life as an author with his faithful wife, Sophia. His writings usually reflected deep spiritual pondering. **"If we would know what heaven is, let us retire into the depths of our own spirits, and we shall find it there among holy thoughts and feelings."**

For since the creation of the world,
His invisible attributes, His eternal power
and divine nature, have been clearly seen,
being understood through what has been made,
so that they are without excuse.
Paul the Apostle, ROMANS 1:20

Humility

God sends no one away empty
except those who are full
of themselves.
Dwight L Moody

Always remember there are two kinds of people in the world.
Those who come into the room and say, "Well, here I am."
And those who come in and say, "Ah, there you are."
Frederick L. Collins

The first test of a truly great man is humility.
John Ruskin

Do you wish to rise? Begin by descending.
Do you plan a tower that will pierce the clouds?
Do you desire to construct a vast and lofty fabric of greatness?
Think first about the foundations of humility.
The higher your structure is to be, the deeper must be its foundation.
There is something in humility which strangely exalts the heart.
Augustine

Man was created on the sixth day so he wouldn't be boastful,
Since he came after the flea in the order of creation.
The Haggadah

"Whenever I think of God I can only conceive of Him
as a Being infinitely GREAT and infinitely GOOD.
This last quality of the divine nature inspires me
with such confidence and joy that I could have written even
a song of pity in a cheerful tempo."

JOSEPH HAYDN
1732-1809 (77 years)

Haydn was an Austrian composer best known as the Father of the Symphony and the Father of the String Quartet. He was a friend of Mozart and a teacher to Beethoven. At the age of six, his parents sent him to live with a music teacher, but during his early life, with both parents and teacher, he ate so little that he remembers always being hungry, perhaps attributing to his small stature. His young choirboy voice came to the attention of villagers, and he soon moved to Vienna (for the next nine years) to sing at St. Stephen's Cathedral. When his voice changed he was immediately dismissed and put out on the streets. Until the age of 25 he was a musical entrepreneur, and finally he gained attention from a local Baron who employed him as a Kappelmeister (music director). More than any other composer, Haydn was known for introducing humor into his compositions. His notoriety caught the attention of the wealthiest family in the Austrian empire, where he was employed for the next 30 years. His advice: **"Young people can learn from my example that 'something can come from nothing.' What I have become is the result of my hard efforts."**

But by the grace of God I am what I am,
and His grace toward me did not prove vain;
but I labored even more than all of them,
yet not I, but the grace of God with me.
Paul the Apostle, 1 CORINTHIANS 15:10

The Passion of the Heart

There is a road from the eye to heart
that does not go through the intellect.
G. K. Chesterton

——

The workings of the human heart are the profoundest mystery
of the universe. One moment they make us despair of our kind,
and the next we see in them the reflection of the divine image.
Charles W. Chesnutt

——

He is greatest whose strength carries up the most hearts
by the attraction of his own.
Henry Ward Beecher

——

Many find their heart when they have lost their head.
Friedrich Nietzsche

——

It has pleased God that divine truth
should not enter the heart through the understanding,
but the understanding through the heart.
Blaise Pascal

——

Two things are bad for the heart -
running up stairs and running down people.
Bernard M. Baruch

"The ground of our hope is Christ in the world,
But the evidence of our hope is Christ in the heart."

MATTHEW HENRY
1662 - 1714 (51 years)

"In all God's providences, it is good to compare
His word and His works together; for we shall find
a beautiful harmony between them,
and that they mutually illustrate each other."

Matthew Henry was born in the very year (1662) that The Church of England legis-lated The Act of Uniformity, stating that preaching, prayer and the sacraments had to conform to the practice of the state church. The Puritans, who were called "non-comformists," believed in being led by Scripture and the Spirit to worship in free-dom. Henry's pastor father, was part of the "Puritan Ejection," forcing him and his family into exile. Young Henry was not allowed to go to Oxford or Cambridge be-cause of his faith. He became a Presbyterian pastor, and his six volume *Commentary on the Bible* became a primary source of influence for George Whitefield and John Wesley in The Great Awakening. Henry's devotional insight into Scripture is considered to be one of the purest sources today of biblical exegesis. Spurgeon said, "If a man can purchase but very few books, my first advice to him would be, let him purchase the very best - Matthew Henry's Commentary." Henry said of prayer: **"We cannot do without God; and God will not do without us. Though we cannot by our prayers give God any information, yet we must by our prayers give Him honor."**

Blessing and glory and wisdom
and thanksgiving and honor
and power and might,
be to our God forever and ever. Amen.
The Angels of Heaven, REVELATION 7:12

144

The Ground of Our Hope

Almost 2000 years ago today,
The stone against His grave was rolled away.
And in the blinding darkness of the tomb
He rose and shattered there the grief and gloom
Within the hearts of those who worshipped Him.
Although that day and time have now grown dim
One message through the ages has been hurled.
His love is hope and light for all the world.

And as the dawn of Easter fills the skies
We too, with Him, in Spirit must arise.
For even underneath us in the earth
There is a faithful promise of rebirth.
If there's a stone against your heart today,
Look up to Him, and it will roll away.
John Van Brakle

—

My most cherished possession I wish to leave you
is my faith in Jesus Christ.
For with Him and nothing else you can be happy.
But without Him and with all else you'll never be happy.
Patrick Henry

—

All that is best in the civilization of today
is the fruit of Christ's appearance among men.
Daniel Webster

—

"It cannot be emphasized too strongly or too often that this great nation was founded, not by religionists, but by Christians; not on religions - but on the gospel of Jesus Christ!"

PATRICK HENRY
1736-1799 (63 years)

Patrick Henry was a courageous soldier and patriot in the American Revolution. He is considered one of the Founding Fathers of our country, and he later became the Governor of Virginia. Henry was married twice. His first wife, Sarah, gave him six children. His second wife, Dorothea, gave him eleven more children. A little known fact about this great man was that his first wife had suffered a mental illness that rendered her mad. She was confined to the basement and lovingly cared for her until her death. At the age of 39, Patrick Henry stood before the House of Burgesses on March 23, 1775, at St. John's Church in Richmond, Virginia, and uttered those now famous words which inspired war against the British forces.

**"Is life so dear or peace so sweet
as to be purchased at the price of chains and slavery?
Forbid it, Almighty God!
I know not what course others may take,
but as for me, give me liberty, or give me death!"**

Perhaps there was pain in his voice as he spoke of chains and slavery. Perhaps those words, which now echo through our history, were a veiled reference to his loving wife, who spent four years in mental torment. She died in 1776, as husband Patrick gave birth to a country.

> But whenever a person turns to the Lord,
> the veil is taken away.
> Now the Lord is the Spirit,
> and where the Spirit of the Lord is,
> there is liberty.
> **2 CORINTHIANS 3:16-17**

Patriotism

Patriotism is supporting your country all the time,
and your government when it deserves it.
Mark Twain

————

Patriotism is easy to understand in America;
it means looking out for yourself by looking out for your country.
Calvin Coolidge

————

Patriotism is not short, frenzied outbursts of emotion,
but the tranquil and steady dedication of a lifetime.
Adlai E. Stevenson

————

A nation reveals itself not only by the men it produces
but also by the men it honors, the men it remembers.
John Fitzgerald Kennedy

————

My affections were first for my own country,
then, generally, for all mankind.
Thomas Jefferson

————

I only regret that I have but one life to give for my country.
Nathan Hale

————

A patriot must always be ready
to defend his country against his government.
Edward Abbey

"The days of the Messiah will occur when the Jews
return to Palestine. This King who arises will have
the seat of his rule in Zion. His fame will be even greater
than that of King Solomon. Because of His consummate justice,
the nations will obey him. God Himself
will destroy anyone who rises up against Him."

THEODOR HERTZL
1860-1904 (44 years)

On May 14, 1948, the United Nations acknowledged the right of the Jews to establish the nation/state of Israel. After 2500 years of domination by foreign nations,
they had finally returned home to their "promised land." The catalyst of this dramatic
event was Theodor Hertzl, who began The Zionist Movement fifty years earlier.
Trained as a lawyer in Austria, he traveled to France and witnessed the brutal exe-
cution of a Jewish soldier in the French army, accused of being a German spy. He
saw firsthand the bigotry that we call today "anti-Semitism." He turned his attention
from the legal profession and became a journalist, a means by which he could gain
the attention of the world. He wrote the book, *The Jewish State*, as a call to Jews
everywhere to nationalize and secure a homeland. The Zionist movement was born,
and Hertzl carried the banner until his death eight years later. He believed that God
had ordained Zionism to fulfill scripture: **"God would not have sustained the Jewish people for so long if it had not been designated some destiny in human history. It is true that
we aspire to our ancient land. But what we want in that ancient land is a new blossoming
of the Jewish spirit."** His best known quote: **"If you will it, it is no dream."**

Oh, that the salvation of Israel
would come out of Zion!
When the LORD restores His captive people,
Jacob will rejoice, Israel will be glad.
King David, PSALM 14:7

The Legacy of the Jew

If the statistics are right,
the Jews constitute but one percent of the human race.
It suggests a nebulous dim puff of star dust
lost in the blaze of the Milky Way.
Properly the Jew ought hardly to be heard of,
but he is heard of, has always been heard of.
He is as prominent on the planet as any other people,
and his commercial importance is extravagantly out of proportion
to the smallness of his bulk. His contributions
to the world's list of great names in literature, science, art, music,
finance, medicine, and abstruse learning
are also away out of proportion to the weakness of his numbers.
He has made a marvelous fight in the world,
in all the ages; and has done it with his hands tied behind him.
He could be vain of himself, and be excused for it.
The Egyptian, the Babylonian, and the Persian rose,
filled the planet with sound and splendor,
then faded to dream-stuff and passed away;
the Greek and the Roman followed, and made a vast noise,
and they are gone; other peoples have sprung up
and held their torch high for a time, but it burned out,
and they sit in twilight now, or have vanished.
The Jew saw them all, beat them all,
and is now what he always was, exhibiting no decadence,
no infirmities of age, no weakening of his parts,
no slowing of his energies, no dulling of his alert and aggressive mind.
All things are mortal but the Jew; all other forces pass, but he remains.
What is the secret of his immortality?

MARK TWAIN

"To call the Bible a great book is an understatement.
It is, quite simply, the cornerstone
of Western Civilization."

CHARLETON HESTON
1923-2008 (84 years)

"You who inherit the heavy privilege
to serve in freedom's name.
You must brace for battle surely to come."

Charleton Heston was an ACTOR, but more than that, he was a CRUSADER. After serving in World War II, he began his career as a Shakesperean actor in New York. With several supporting roles under his belt, he was cast to play the part of Moses in the epic film "The Ten Commandments." He was soon cast for the leading role in the epic film, "Ben Hur," which earned an unprecedented eleven Oscar awards. He became an iconic figure in the film industry and the eventual president of the Screen Actors Guild. He used his influence to crusade with conviction for causes he considered just. In 1963 he marched against segregation with Martin Luther King Jr, and he fought for gun control after the Kennedy assassination. By the 1980's, Heston changed his politics from liberal to conservative causes. With the same conviction he denounced the culture war as being waged **by a generation of media, educators, entertainers and politicians.** In his seventies, he opposed abortion, and he became the outspoken president of the National Rifle Association, defending Second Amendment rights. President George W. Bush awarded him the Presidential Medal of Freedom. With conviction, Heston said **"Political correctness is tyranny with manners."**

Now I urge you, brethren,
keep your eye on those
who cause dissensions and hindrances
contrary to the teaching which you learned,
and turn away from them.
Paul the Apostle, ROMANS 16:17

The Ten Commandments

Exodus 20: 1-17
I am the LORD your God,
who brought you out of the land of Egypt,
out of the house of slavery.

1. You shall have no other gods before Me.

2. You shall not make for yourself an idol, or any likeness of what is in heaven above or on the earth beneath or in the water under the earth.
You shall not worship them or serve them; for I, the LORD your God, am a jealous God.

3. You shall not take the name of the LORD your God in vain, for the LORD will not leave him unpunished who takes His name in vain.

4. Remember the sabbath day, to keep it holy; "for in six days the LORD made the heavens and the earth, the sea and all that is in them, and rested on the seventh day; therefore the LORD blessed the sabbath day and made it holy.

5. Honor your father and your mother, that your days may be prolonged in the land which the LORD your God gives you.

6. You shall not murder.

7. You shall not commit adultery.

8. You shall not steal.

9. You shall not bear false witness against your neighbor.

10. You shall not covet your neighbor's house; you shall not covet your neighbor's wife or his male servant or his female servant or his ox or his donkey or anything that belongs to your neighbor.

"Most people are willing to take the Sermon on the Mount
as a flag to sail under,
but few will use it as a rudder to steer by."

OLIVER WENDELL HOLMES, SR.
1809-1894 (85 years)

Two great men, father and son. OWH, Sr. was a doctor, author and poet. OWH, Jr. was a U.S. Supreme Court justice. The elder Holmes was a professor of medicine at Harvard, and the originator of the word "anesthesia." He was a member of the "Fireside Poets," which included well known author-poets: Longfellow, Bryant, Lowell, and Whittier. He was an entertaining speaker who said, **"Speak clearly, if you speak at all; carve every word before you let it fall."** The younger Holmes was appointed by Theodore Roosevelt to the U.S. Supreme Court in 1902, and was voted to the bench unanimously in a rare exhibit of nonpartisan affirmation. In his 30 years as a justice, he became known as the "The Great Dissenter," a term assigned to those who stood against the popular tide of the majority in Supreme Court Decisions, in a brave act of conviction. Conviction to stand on principle is a rare commodity in our world. The true test of conviction is searching your heart to find out where you draw the line - not in public where you carefully shape your reputation, but in private, where your soul exposes its weakness before the eyes of an all-seeing God.

"The greatest act of faith
is when a man understands
he is not God."

OLIVER WENDELL HOLMES, JR.
(1841-1935) (94 years)

But I say to you, love your enemies
and pray for those who persecute you,
so that you may be sons of your Father
who is in heaven; for He causes His sun
to rise on the evil and the good,
and sends rain on the righteous and the unrighteous.
Jesus the Messiah, MATTHEW 5:44-45

Excerpt from

The Sermon on the Mount

Matthew 5:1–18

When Jesus saw the crowds, He went up on the mountain;
and after He sat down, His disciples came to Him.
He opened His mouth and began to teach them, saying,
Blessed are the poor in spirit, for theirs is the kingdom of heaven.
Blessed are those who mourn, for they shall be comforted.
Blessed are the gentle, for they shall inherit the earth.
Blessed are those who hunger and thirst for righteousness,
for they shall be satisfied.
Blessed are the merciful, for they shall receive mercy.
Blessed are the pure in heart, for they shall see God.
Blessed are the peacemakers,
for they shall be called sons of God.
Blessed are those who have been persecuted for righteousness,
for theirs is the kingdom of heaven.
Blessed are you when people insult you and persecute you,
and falsely say all kinds of evil against you because of Me.
Rejoice and be glad, for your reward in heaven is great;
for in the same way they persecuted
the prophets who were before you.
You are the salt of the earth; but if the salt has become tasteless,
how can it be made salty again? It is no longer good for anything,
except to be thrown out and trampled under foot by men.
You are the light of the world.
A city set on a hill cannot be hidden;
nor does anyone light a lamp and put it under a basket
but on the lampstand, and it gives light to all who are in the house.
Let your light shine before men in such a way
that they may see your good works,
and glorify your Father who is in heaven.

"The whole inspiration of our civilization springs from the teachings and the lessons of the prophets. To read the Bible for these fundamentals is a necessity of American life."

HERBERT HOOVER

1874 - 1964 (90 years)

"The Bible is a postgraduate course in the richest library of human experience."

Herbert Hoover, the 31st President of the United States, was a no-nonsense, get the job done, mining engineer who began his public service by helping 9 million starving Europeans with food relief during World War I. During the Harding administration, he became the Secretary of Commerce, and is reputed to be the best Commerce Secretary in U.S. History. Having been an engineer and businessman, he aggressively sought ways to eliminate waste and increase efficiency in business and industry. Calvin Coolidge called him Wonder Boy for his reputation to solve problems. Elected as President in 1928, nine months later the country suffered The Great Depression. Unemployment rose to 24% and 5,000 banks failed. In spite of his reputation for fixing things, he was unable to turn the economy around in four years. His reputation was damaged and he suffered the despise of the nation, but he later served Presidents Truman and Eisenhower in efforts to make the growing government more effective. He was a man of ideals who believed in his country but was disappointed in his government. His only hope was in the next generation, as he proclaimed: **"The glory of the nation rests in the character of her men. And character comes from boyhood. Thus every boy is a challenge to his elders."**

I thank Christ Jesus our Lord,
who has strengthened me,
because He considered me faithful,
putting me into service.
Paul the Apostle, I TIMOTHY 1:12

Character

Be more concerned with your character than your reputation,
because your character is what you really are,
while your reputation is merely what others think you are.
John Wooden

Weakness of attitude becomes weakness of character.
Albert Einstein

Character develops itself in the stream of life.
Johann Wolfgang von Goethe

People do not seem to realize
that their opinion of the world is also a confession of character.
Ralph Waldo Emerson

Character is doing the right thing when nobody's looking.
There are too many people who think
that the only thing that's right is to get by,
and the only thing that's wrong is to get caught.
J.C. Watts

Talents are best nurtured in solitude,
but character is best formed in the stormy billows of the world.
Johann Wolfgang von Goethe

"The spectacle of a nation praying
is more awe inspiring
than the explosion of an atomic bomb.
Prayer is man's greatest means of tapping
the infinite resources of God."

J. EDGAR HOOVER
1895-1972 (77 years)

"A child who has been taught to respect the laws of
God will have little difficulty respecting the laws of men."

Hoover became the first Director of the FBI, the Federal Bureau of Investigation, from 1935 to 1972, a total of 37 years. From 1924 to 1935 (11 years prior) he directed the FBI's predecessor, the Bureau of Investigation. Because of the controversial nature of Hoover's lengthy term of administration, the tenure of the FBI Chief is now limited to ten years. His agency did battle over the years with gangsters such as John Dillinger and Al Capone, with subversive groups such as the Communist Party and the American Nazi Party, and with racial hate groups, such as the Black Panthers and the Ku Klux Klan. He continually did battle with the U.S. Justice Department to use subversive tactics to counter the guerilla tactics of the enemy. For this reason, he was surrounded by controversy, rumors, threats and slander. Three U.S. Presidents talked of firing him, but backed down because of his support in Congress. He was a controversial figure, whose life is still subject to questions regarding his character and his lifestyle. Nevertheless, he goes on record as bowing down before a sovereign God. After a lifetime of fighting crime, he concludes: **"The cure for crime is not the electric chair, but the high chair."**

I tell you that in the same way,
there will be more joy in heaven
over one sinner who repents
than over ninety-nine righteous persons
who need no repentance.
Jesus, LUKE 15:7

Discipline

Discipline doesn't break a child's spirit half as often
as the lack of it breaks a parent's heart.
Anonymous

———

There is a certain combination
of anarchy and discipline in the way I work.
Robert de Niro

———

Discipline is simply the art of making the soldiers
fear their officers more than the enemy.
Claude Adrien Helvetius

———

Without discipline the Army would just be a bunch of guys
wearing the same color clothing.
Frank Burns

———

The secret of discipline is motivation.
When a man is sufficiently motivated,
discipline will take care of itself.
Sir Alexander Paterson

———

Apply your heart to discipline
And your ears to words of knowledge.
Proverbs 23:12

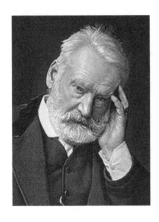

"England has two books,
one which she has made,
and one which made her.
Shakespeare and the Bible."

VICTOR HUGO

1802-1885 (82 years)

Victor Hugo was a French poet and novelist during the era of Napoleon, best known to the world for two novels - *The Hunchback of Notre Dame* and his great work on social justice called *Les Miserables*. This book, which is 1200 pages in length, took 17 years to write. His novels and poems have not only captured the imagination of many generations, but his stories have inspired over a thousand musical compositions. The shortest correspondence in history was when he wrote to his publisher, inquiring about *Les Mis*. He inquired, "?". His publisher wrote back "!". In addition to writing and painting, Hugo became a strong advocate against the many injustices of the French government. This prompted his best known quote: **"No army can withstand the strength of an idea whose time has come."** When Napoleon III finally abolished the French constitution, Hugo went into self exile on an island, writing for 19 years. At the time of his death, he was hailed as a national hero, and two million men marched in his funeral procession. Hugo was known as a man of prayer, who said: **"There are times in a man's life when, regardless of the attitude of the body, the soul is on its knees in prayer."**

Be anxious for nothing,
but in everything,
by prayer and supplication,
with thanksgiving,
let your requests be made known to God.
Paul the Apostle, PHILIPPIANS 4:6

"Winter is on my head,
but eternal spring is in my heart.
The nearer I approach the end,
the plainer I hear around me the immortal symphony
of the world to come.
For half a century, I have been writing
my thoughts in prose and verse;
but I feel that I have not said
one thousandth part of what is in me.
When I have gone down to the grave
I shall have ended my day's work.
But another day will begin the next morning.
Life closes in the twilight but opens with the dawn."

Victor Hugo

"My religious belief teaches me to feel as safe in battle as in bed. God has fixed the time for my death."

General STONEWALL JACKSON
1824 - 1863 (39 years)

"Be content and resigned to God's will.
Duty is ours; consequences are God's."

Thomas Jonathan Jackson graduated 17 of 59 at the U.S. Military Academy at West Point. He taught philosophy and artillery at the Virginia Military Institute (VMI), where his military insight continues even today. He is famous for saying: **"When war does come, my advice is to draw the sword and throw away the scabbard."** Military historians consider him to be one of the most gifted tactical commanders in U.S. history. Five years before the Civil War, he organized and taught a Sunday School class to the local black community in his own Presbyterian Church. Jackson's face appeared on the Confederate $500 bill, and his image (with Davis and Lee) was carved on the granite face of Stone Mountain, Georgia - the size of 3 football fields, 12 feet deep. In the Battle of Chancellorsville, Virginia, Jackson won because he silently descended on the Union army after dark. Ironically, when returning to his own camp, silently after dark, he was surprised by "friendly fire," lost an arm to amputation and died 8 days later from pneumonia. His final words were: **"It is the Lord's Day; my wish is fulfilled. I have always desired to die on Sunday. Let us cross over the river and rest under the shade of the trees."**

I was in the Spirit on the Lord's day,
and I heard behind me a loud voice
like the sound of a trumpet.
John the Apostle, REVELATION 1:10

The Final Curtain Call

The fear of death follows from the fear of life.
A man who lives fully is prepared to die at any time.
Mark Twain

The idea is to die young as late as possible.
Ashley Montagu

While I thought that I was learning how to live,
I have been learning how to die.
Leonardo Da Vinci

Death is a distant rumor to the young.
Andrew A. Rooney

The day which we fear as our last is but the birthday of eternity.
Seneca

Our death is not an end if we can live on in our children
and the younger generation. For they are us,
our bodies are only wilted leaves on the tree of life.
Albert Einstein

Death is caused by swallowing small amounts
of saliva over a long period of time.
Attributed to George Carlin

"I have carefully and regularly perused these Holy Scriptures, and am of the opinion that the volume, independent of its divine origin, contains more true sublimity, more exquisite beauty, pure morality, more important history, and finer strains of poetry and eloquence, than could be collected within the same compass from all other books - whatever age or language they may have been written."

WILLIAM JAMES
1842 - 1910 (68 years)

William James was a Harvard professor of medicine, philosophy and psychology, who is best known for his two-volume, 1200-page text *Principles of Psychology*. He never took a course or read a book about psychology until he began teaching the subject. Perhaps that speaks of the brilliance of James - or maybe it speaks of the emptiness of modern psychology. He is considered today the 14th most eminent psychologist of the 20th century. He spoke of human potential when he said: **"Compared to what we ought to be, we are half awake."** Born into a wealthy family who traveled frequently to Europe, his primary languages were German and French. His book, *Varieties of Religious Experience,* considered faith to be a valid quest for truth, but his concept of God fell short of acknowledging God as a personal and relational God. He said: **"The God whom science recognizes must be a God of universal laws exclusively. He cannot accommodate His processes to the convenience of individuals."** James bowed his knee to God, but he failed to fully enjoy the fact that God is our Father and we are His children.

Eyes have not seen, nor ears heard,
nor entered into the heart of man,
the things that God has prepared
for them that love Him.
1 CORINTHIANS 2:9

Religion

Religion is to do right. It is to love, it is to serve,
it is to think, it is to be humble.
Ralph Waldo Emerson

———

Those who say religion has nothing to do with politics
do not know what religion is.
Mahatma Gandhi

———

Many have quarreled about religion that never practiced it.
Benjamin Franklin

———

I have ... a terrible need ... shall I say the word? ... of religion.
Then I go out at night and paint the stars.
Vincent van Gogh

———

Science investigates, religion interprets.
Science gives man knowledge which is power;
religion gives man wisdom which is control.
Martin Luther King, Jr.

———

My feeling is religious insofar as I am imbued
with the consciousness of the insufficiency of the human mind
to understand more deeply the harmony of the Universe
which we try to formulate as 'laws of nature.'
Albert Einstein

———

"Providence has given our people
the choice of their rulers, and it is the duty,
as well as privilege and interest,
of a Christian nation to select
and prefer Christians
for their rulers."

JOHN JAY
1745 - 1829 (83 years)

In the book *Seven Who Shaped Our Destiny*, author Richard Morris identifies the seven key Founding Fathers of the United States as: Benjamin Franklin, George Washington, John Adams, Thomas Jefferson, John Jay, James Madison, and Alexander Hamilton. Jay was President of the Continental Congress in 1778 and chosen by George Washington as the first Chief Justice of the U.S. Supreme Court. Later he became the Governor of New York, a position that allowed him to promote legislation leading to the abolition of slavery. After he campaigned against slavery for 22 years, in 1799 the state of New York passed a bill guaranteeing that all slaves would be free over a gradual period ending on July 4, 1827. It was this driving force that finally led to the emancipation of all slaves in 1861. Jay was even known for buying slaves with his own money, and then setting them free. He co-authored *The Federalist Papers* with Alexander Hamilton and James Madison, a work that is still considered today to be a major interpreter of the U.S. Constitution. In 1821, he was elected the president of the American Bible Society. Today, the **John Jay Institute for Faith, Society and Law** exists for the purpose of training and preparing leaders of American public life to be men and women of virtue, wisdom, and justice.

It was for freedom that Christ set us free;
therefore keep standing firm
and do not be subject again
to a yoke of slavery.
Paul the Apostle, GALATIANS 5:1

Worship

Men are idolaters and want something to look at and kiss and hug,
or throw themselves down before;
they always did, they always will;
and if you don't make it of wood
you must make it of words.
Oliver Wendell Holmes

———

The worship of God is not a rule of safety;
It is an adventure of the spirit,
A flight after the unattainable.
Alfred North Whitehead

———

I have in my heart a small, shy plant called reverence;
that I cultivate every week by worshipping with the people of God.
Oliver Wendell Holmes

———

God is to be praised with the voice,
and the heart should follow after in holy exultation.
Charles Spurgeon

———

Worship is the missing jewel of the evangelical church.
A.W. Tozer

———

As worship begins in holy expectancy, it ends in holy obedience.
Richard Foster

———

"Had the doctrines of Jesus been preached always
as pure as they came from His lips,
the whole civilized world
would now have been Christians."

THOMAS JEFFERSON
1743 - 1826 (83 years)

"I tremble for my country when I reflect that God is just;
that His justice cannot sleep forever."

Thomas Jefferson is often cited as the greatest of American Presidents. He was George Washington's first Secretary of State, and the third President. It was he who established the Military Academy at West Point, founded the University of Virginia and is best known as the creator of the Declaration of Independence. He is called a polymath, one who is so skilled at so many things as to be revered as a genius. The American Institute of Architects identifies Jefferson's timeless design of the University of Virginia campus as the most significant work of architecture in America. In 1807, he signed a bill abolishing the slave trade. When President John F. Kennedy welcomed 49 Nobel Prize winners to the White House he said, "I think this is the most extraordinary collection of talent and of human knowledge that has ever been gathered together at the White House – with the possible exception of when Thomas Jefferson dined alone." His face is immortalized on Mount Rushmore. Jefferson said: **"Great times call forth great leaders."** He said this about religion and government: **"The reason that Christianity is the best friend of government is because Christianity is the only religion that changes the heart."**

But one who looks intently at the perfect law,
the law of liberty, and abides by it,
not having become a forgetful hearer
but an effectual doer,
this man will be blessed in what he does.
James Brother of Jesus, JAMES 1:25

Excerpt from

The Declaration of Independence

When, in the course of human events,
it becomes necessary for one people
to dissolve the political bands
which have connected them with another;
and to assume among the powers of the earth,
the separate and equal station
to which the laws of nature and of nature's God entitle them,
a decent respect to the opinions of mankind
requires that they should declare the causes
which impel them to the separation.

We hold these truths to be self-evident,
that all men are created equal,
that they are endowed by their Creator
with certain unalienable rights,
that among these are life, liberty and the pursuit of Happiness.
That to secure these rights,
governments are instituted among Men,
deriving their just powers from the consent of the governed,
That whenever any form of government
becomes destructive of these ends,
it is the right of the people to alter or to abolish it,
and to institute new government,
laying its foundation on such principles
and organizing its powers in such form,
as to them shall seem most likely
to effect their safety and happiness . . .

And for the support of this declaration,
with a firm reliance on the protection of Divine Providence,
we mutually pledge to each other
our lives, our fortunes, and our sacred honor.

"In the pure, strong hours of the morning,
when the soul of the day is at its best,
lean upon the window sill of God, and look into His face,
and get your marching orders for the day.
Then go out into the day with the sense
of a Hand upon your shoulder."

E. STANLEY JONES
1884 - 1973 (88 years)

Jones left Baltimore, Maryland and the comforts of the United States to become a Methodist Episcopal missionary to India. He began to teach the Dalits, one of the lower castes, and he gained the attention of the academic and political community. He became a personal friend of Gandhi and Nehru, and it was Jones' biography of Gandhi that convinced Martin Luther King to embrace non-violent means of social change. He became an ambassador of peace, and was nominated for a Nobel Peace Prize when called upon to broker peace between Japan and the United States. In Japan, he is referred to as the "Apostle of Peace." He wrote twenty-six books, of which the best known is *The Christ of the Indian Road*. In the subtle memoirs of the Indian National Congress, during the critical days of India's independence movement, Stanley Jones was quietly in the background, influencing the leaders toward reconciliation. His words had great influence: **"If reconciliation is God's chief business, it is ours - between man and God, between man and himself, and between man and man."**

Now all these things are from God,
who reconciled us to Himself through Christ
and gave us the ministry of reconciliation.
2 CORINTHIANS 5:18

Honor

Show me the man you honor,
and I will know what kind of man you are.
Thomas Carlyle

———

Success without honor is an unseasoned dish;
it will satisfy your hunger, but it won't taste good.
Joe Paterno

———

Any person of honor chooses rather
to lose his honor than to lose his conscience.
Michel de Montaigne

———

Better to die ten thousand deaths than wound my honor.
Joseph Addison

———

When your mission is to restore honor and integrity to the White House,
you've got to be willing to use any means necessary.
Paul Begala, Democratic Political Strategist

———

We laugh at honor and are shocked to find traitors in our midst.
C.S. Lewis

———

Nobody can acquire honor by doing what is wrong.
Thomas Jefferson

"Two things fill the mind with ever new and increasing wonder and awe, the more often and the more seriously I reflect upon them: the starry heavens above me and the moral law within me."

IMMANUEL KANT
1724-1804 (79 years)

"The Bible is an inexhaustible fountain of all truths. The existence of the Bible is the greatest blessing which humanity has ever experienced."

Kant was a German philosopher who became the Professor of Metaphysics and Logic at the University of Konigsberg in what is now a Russian city. The University was renamed Immanuel Kant University in 2005 because of his vast contribution to western philosophy. For eleven years he withdrew from the public, in order to write his 800 page "magnum opus" called *The Critique of Pure Reason.* After learning Hebrew as a young man, he changed the first letter of his name from "E" to "I," which means "God with us." Much of his work centered around his quest for understanding God, the soul and freedom, though his conclusions were steeped in language that obscured the simple truths of knowing the God of Creation. Kant lived by a noble code of ethics: **"By a lie, a man annihilates his dignity as a man. From such crooked wood as that which man is made of, nothing straight can be fashioned."** Regarding his lifelong study of metaphysics and the meaning of life, he said: **"Metaphysics is a dark ocean without shores or lighthouse, strewn with many a philosophic wreck."** His response to the human condition was to live a noble life: **"It is not necessary that while I live I live happily; but it is necessary that so long as I live I should live honorably. Do what is right, though the world may perish."**

Come now, and let us reason together, says the LORD:
though your sins be as scarlet, they shall be as white as snow;
though they be red like crimson, they shall be as wool.
ISAIAH 1:18

Honor

If it be a sin to covet honor, I am the most offending soul.
William Shakespeare

If honor be your clothing, the suit will last a lifetime;
but if clothing be your honor, it will soon be worn threadbare.
William Arnot

Those who give, hoping to be rewarded with honor,
are not giving, they are bargaining.
Philo Judaeus

All honor to him who shall win the prize,
The world has cried for a thousand years;
But to him who tries and fails and dies,
I give great honor and glory and tears.
Joaquin Mille

Honor is like an island, rugged and without shores;
once we have left it, we can never return.
Nicholas Boileau

Who sows virtue reaps honor.
Leonardo da Vinci

"At the Day of Judgment we shall not be asked what we have read, but rather, what we have done."

THOMAS A KEMPIS
1380 - 1471 (91 years)

"Without the Way, there is no going,
Without the Truth, there is no knowing,
Without the Life, there is no living."

Thomas was born in Kempen, Germany - thus he became Thomas of Kempen, later shortened to Thomas a Kempis. His actual last name was Hamerken, which means "the hammer." At the age of 26, Thomas followed his brother John into the Mount St. Agnes Monastery. He was ordained a priest seven years later, and, as was the custom of monastic monks, he was trained to copy the Latin version of the Bible - letter for letter, word for word, page by page, chapter by chapter. In his lifetime, he didn't just read the Bible - he copied it four times! As a young boy, Thomas encountered the Brethren of the Common Life, and was deeply moved by their devotion to purity and simplicity. Thomas later wrote: **"Purity and simplicity are the two wings with which man soars above the earth and all temporary nature."** He is best known for *The Imitation of Christ*, a book that has become a devotional classic through the centuries. Thomas lived a simple life and he spoke much about the importance of faith: **"Faith is required of thee - not loftiness of intellect, nor deepness in the mysteries of God."** The faith of Thomas echoes through time, 600 years later.

And without faith
it is impossible to please Him,
for he who comes to God must believe
that He is, and that He is a rewarder
of those who seek Him.
HEBREWS 11:6

Simplicity

Simplicity is the ultimate sophistication.
Leonardo da Vinci

———

Everything should be made as simple as possible, but not simpler.
Albert Einstein

———

There is no greatness
where there is not simplicity, goodness, and truth.
Leo Tolstoy

———

A vocabulary of truth and simplicity
will be of service throughout your life.
Winston Churchill

———

In character, in manner, in style, in all things,
the supreme excellence is simplicity.
Henry Wadsworth Longfellow

———

As you simplify your life, the laws of the universe will be simpler;
solitude will not be solitude, poverty will not be poverty,
weakness will not be weakness.
Henry David Thoreau

———

Nothing is true, but that which is simple.
Johann Wolfgang von Goethe

The same revolutionary beliefs
for which our forebearers fought,
are still at issue around the globe —
the belief that the rights of man come,
not from the generosity of the state,
but from the hand of God.

JOHN FITZGERALD KENNEDY
1917 - 1963 (46 years)

Kennedy rose to fame during WWII as the Naval commander of the PT-109 torpedo boat. Rammed by a Japanese destroyer, he inspired his troops to survival and valiantly saved one of his crew members, receiving numerous awards, including The Purple Heart. When asked how he earned these heroic metals: he humbly joked: **"It was involuntary. They sank my boat."** He became a U.S. Representative, then a Senator before his election as the 35th President of the U.S. in 1960. In 1955 he wrote the book *"Profiles in Courage"* which made him the only President to receive a Pulitzer award. His presidency was best known for confronting Russian Premier Khrushchev in the Cold War standoff which pitted western democracy against communism, drawing its climax in the Cuban Missile Crisis. He personified both strength and wisdom when he said: **"those who make peaceful revolution impossible, will make violent revolution inevitable."** In his short tenure of three years he set our course for the moon, negotiated a nuclear test ban treaty and encouraged the Civil Rights Act (of 1964). Struck down by an assassin's bullet, the nation mourned the loss of this leader who promoted freedom around the world. He inspired us when he said: **"With a good conscience our only sure reward, with history the final judge of our deeds, let us go forth to lead the land we love, asking His blessing and His help, but knowing that here on earth God's work must truly be our own."**

To loosen the bonds of wickedness, To undo the bands of the yoke.
To let the oppressed go free, and break every yoke.
ISAIAH 58:6 (From Kennedy's Inaugural Address)

<u>The Words of Kennedy</u>

A man may die, nations may rise and fall, but an idea lives on.

———

A nation that is afraid to let its people judge the truth and falsehood
in an open market is a nation that is afraid of its people.

———

Let every nation know, whether it wishes us well or ill,
that we shall pay any price, bear any burden, meet any hardship,
support any friend, oppose any foe,
to assure the survival and the success of liberty.

———

Mothers all want their sons to grow up to be President,
but they don't want them to become politicians in the process.

———

The great enemy of the truth is very often not the lie -
deliberate, contrived and dishonest -
but the myth, persistent, persuasive and unrealistic.

———

And so, my fellow Americans, ask not what your country can do for you;
ask what you can do for your country.

———

I am certain that after the dust of centuries has passed over our cities,
we too will be remembered, not for victories or defeats in battle or in politics,
but for our contribution to the human spirit.

"Faith is the highest passion in a human being. Many in every generation may not come that far, but none comes further."

SOREN KIERKEGAARD
1813-1855 (42 Years)

"Personality is only ripe when a man has made the truth his own."

Kierkegaard was a philosopher and theologian who earned a Ph.D. at the University of Copenhagen in his native Denmark. He is known today as the *Father of Existentialism,* though he personally never used the term, and might not even agree with its interpretation today. Its origin came from his statement: **"The thing is to find a truth which is true for me, to find the idea for which I can live and die."** Interpreters drew the idea of a subjective truth which cannot be quantified, and therefore leads to despair. Soren popularized the phrase: **"Life can only be understood backwards; but it must be lived forwards."** His reference to faith in Christ became known as a "leap of faith." His criticism of the state church, the Church of Denmark, has been confused with his personal faith. He said: **"A great man is one that can develop convictions in solitude and carry them out in a crowd."** One of the images associated with Kierkegaard is the mysterious "mask:" **"Do you not know that there comes a midnight hour when every one has to throw off his mask?"** His life was lived as one who loved God and wrestled to understand Him. In his closing journals he wrote: **"I never forget how God helps me, and it is therefore my last wish that everything may be to His honor."**

Now faith is the assurance of things hoped for, the conviction
of things not seen. For by it the men of old gained approval.
By faith we understand that the worlds were prepared
by the word of God, so that what is seen was not made
out of things which are visible.
HEBREWS 11:1-3

Truth

The pursuit of truth and beauty is a sphere of activity
in which we are permitted to remain children all our lives.
Albert Einstein

——

Truth has nothing to do with the number of people it convinces.
Paul Claudel

——

Power is not sufficient evidence of truth.
Samuel Johnson

——

A lie travels round the world,
while Truth is putting on her boots.
Charles H. Spurgeon

——

The great enemy of the truth is very often not the lie -
deliberate, contrived and dishonest -
but the myth - persistent, persuasive and unrealistic.
John Fitzgerald Kennedy

——

Truth is mighty and will prevail.
There is nothing wrong with this, except that it ain't so.
Mark Twain

——

The love of truth has its reward in heaven and even on earth.
Friedrich Nietzsche

"God of our fathers, known of old,
Beneath whose awful Hand we hold
Lord God of Hosts, be with us yet,
Lest we forget - lest we forget!"

RUDYARD KIPLING
1865 - 1936 (70 years)

"God could not be everywhere,
and therefore he made mothers."

In the early 20th Century, there was no author, better read or better loved, than Rudyard Kipling. Born in British India, Kipling drew from his childhood in Mumbai (formerly Bombay) when he wrote the classic children's work: *The Jungle Book*. Author Henry James said of him: "Kipling strikes me personally as the most complete man of genius that I have ever known." In 1907, he became the youngest recipient of the coveted Nobel Prize in Literature, even though Oxford University refused him a scholarship on the grounds that he "lacked the academic ability." His faith was unorthodox, despite many Biblical references. In his short story, *The Church That Was At Antioch,* Kipling revealed disdain for the established church when he said: "His own disciples shall wound Him worst of all." Voted the favorite poem of the British Empire "If," Kipling's monumental poem of inspiration. **"If you can fill the unforgiving minute with sixty seconds' worth of distance run, yours is the earth and everything that's in it, and which is more - you'll be a man, my son!"**

Immediately Jesus stretched out His hand
and took hold of him,
and said to him,
"You of little faith, why did you doubt?"
MATTHEW 14:31

L'Envoi

When Earth's last picture is painted, and the tubes are twisted and dried,
When the oldest colors have faded, and the youngest critic has died,
We shall rest, and, faith, we shall need it-lie down for an aeon or two,
'Til the Master of All Good Workmen shall set us to work anew!

And those that were good will be happy: they shall sit in a golden chair;
They shall splash at a ten-league canvas with brushes of comets' hair;
They shall find real saints to draw from-Magdalene, Peter and Paul;
They shall work for an age at a sitting and never be tired at all!

And only the Master shall praise us, and only the Master shall blame;
And no one shall work for money, and no one shall work for fame,
but each for the joy of the working, and each, in his separate star,
Shall draw the thing as he sees it for the God of things as they are!

Rudyard Kipling

"When principles that run against your deepest convictions begin to win the day, then battle is your calling, and peace has become sin; you must, at the price of dearest peace, lay your convictions bare before friend and enemy, with all the fire of your faith."

ABRAHAM KUYPER
1837 - 1920 (83 years)

Abraham Kuyper was the Prime Minister of the Netherlands in 1901 and was so popular that he became known as "the bellringer of the common people." His career began as a minister in the Dutch Reformed Church, which was a state controlled institution. He founded the Reformed Church of the Netherlands and his influence in the United States touched the lives of notables such as Frances Shaeffer and Chuck Colson. The Reformed Bible College in Grand Rapids, Michigan has now become Kuyper College. Even greater than his influence in the Netherlands was his impact on South African policies of equity. His words convey a true thirst for God: **"It is not your idea, not your understanding, not your thinking, not your reasoning, not even your profession of faith, that here can quench the thirst. The homesickness goes out after God Himself. It is not the name of God but God Himself whom your soul desires and cannot do without."** In a world which speaks freely of the sovereignty of nations and individuals, Kuyper alone seemed to understand the true meaning of sovereignty: **"In the total expanse of human life there is not a single square inch of which the Christ, who alone is sovereign, does not declare, 'That is mine!'"**

As the deer pants
for the water brooks,
So my soul pants for You, O God.
My soul thirsts for God,
For the Living God.
PSALM 42:1-2

Courage

Courage is the thing.
All goes, if courage goes.
J. M. Barrie

———

Promise me you'll always remember:
You're braver than you believe,
and stronger than you seem,
and smarter than you think.
Christopher Robin to Winne the Pooh

———

Courage without conscience is a wild beast.
R. G. Ingersoll

———

Courage doesn't always roar.
Sometimes courage is the quiet voice
at the end of the day saying,
"I will try again tomorrow."
Mary Anne Radmacher

———

A great leader's courage to fulfill his vision
comes from passion, not position.
John C. Maxwell

"To live a disciplined life and to accept the result of
that discipline as the will of God -
that is the mark of a man."

TOM LANDRY
1924 - 2000 (75 years)

"A team that has character doesn't need stimulation."

Landry was the legendary coach of the Dallas Cowboys football team for 29 seasons. He won 2 Super Bowl championships and still holds the record for 20 consecutive winning seasons in the NFL. Landry was an Industrial Engineering major at the University of Texas where he played until becoming a bomber pilot in World War II. After returning to play six seasons for the New York Giants, he then became the defensive coordinator opposite Vince Lombardi, who was the offensive coordinator. Landry is generally considered one of the greatest coaches in football history due to his ability to create innovative new strategies for offense and defense. He developed the now popular 4-3 Defense, The Flex Defense and the "preshift formation," which means the formation continues to stand and shift in order to analyze and rattle the offense. His "Doomsday Defense" helped the Cowboys rise to the third most wins in NFL history. The substance of Landry, however, was not football, but faith. He said: **"When you accept Christ, He becomes first in your life. It's this priority that gives me peace."** Landry's faith as a Christian was respected by players and coaches alike. His influence in the Fellowship of Christian Athletes made him a hero to young men looking for a role model. Landry taught his men: **"When you win a game, you have to teach. When you lose a game, you have to learn."**

It is for discipline that you endure;
God deals with you as with sons;
for what son is there
whom his father does not discipline?
HEBREWS 12:7

Discipline

We must all suffer from one of two pains:
the pain of discipline or the pain of regret.
The difference is discipline weighs ounces while regret weighs tons.
Jim Rohn

―――

Without discipline, there's no life at all.
Katharine Hepburn

―――

Discipline is wisdom and vice versa.
M. Scott Peck

Discipline must be a habit so ingrained that it is stronger
than the excitement of the goal or the fear of failure.
Gary Ryan Blair

―――

Self-respect is the fruit of discipline;
the sense of dignity grows with the ability to say no to oneself.
Abraham J. Heschel

―――

Man must be disciplined, for he is by nature raw and wild.
Immanuel Kant

―――

If we do not discipline ourselves the world will do it for us.
William Feather

"The Bible is a book in comparison with which all others in my eyes are of minor importance; and which, in all my perplexities and distresses, has never failed to give me light and strength."

ROBERT E. LEE
1807-1870 (63 years)

"My whole trust is in God, and I am ready for whatever He may ordain. My chief concern is to try to be a humble, earnest Christian."

Lee was an outstanding engineering student in his class at the U.S. Military Academy. He went on to serve in the Army Corps of Engineers for 25 years, including a three year position as the head of West Point. He was then asked to lead the Army's 2nd Cavalry division. Seven years later, as the Civil War began, Lincoln asked him to lead the Union troops, but he declined. He then accepted a position in the Confederate army, serving his native Virginia. 620,000 dead men later, General Lee surrendered to General Grant at Appomattox. Though he fought for the South, his conscience struggled with the injustice of slavery. He wrote to his wife: **"In this enlightened age, there are few I believe, but what will acknowledge that slavery as an institution is a moral & political evil in any country."** Admired by both sides after the war, he is referred to today as the "Marble Man," an inference to his flawless character. An excerpt from those who honor him says: **"He was a foe without hate; a soldier without cruelty; he was Caesar without ambition, and Napoleon without selfishness."**

But I see a different law
in the members of my body,
waging war against the law of my mind
and making me a prisoner of the law
of sin which is in my members.
Paul the Apostle, ROMANS 7:23

Innocence

The greater our innocence,
the greater our strength and the swifter our victory.
Mahatma Gandhi

———

Innocence dwells with wisdom, but never with ignorance.
William Blake

———

The knowledge that makes us
cherish innocence makes innocence unattainable.
Irving Howe

———

Virtue, dear friend, needs no defense.
The surest guard is innocence.
Horace

———

A man writes to throw off the poison
which he has accumulated because of his false way of life.
He is trying to recapture his innocence.
Henry Miller

———

That's what it takes to be a hero, a little gem of innocence
inside you that makes you want to believe
that there still exists a right and wrong,
that decency will somehow triumph in the end.
Lise Hand

"There are two kinds of people;
Those who say to God, 'Thy will be done."
And those to whom God says,
'All right, then, have it your way.'"

C.S. LEWIS
1898 - 1963 (64 years)

Clive Staples Lewis was an Irish Professor of Medieval and Renaissance English at both Oxford and Cambridge Universities. As a student he received the highest academic award, called a "triple first," excelling in Greek and Latin literature, Ancient History and English. Early in life, Lewis was an avowed atheist who dabbled in the occult. He became a Christian at age 33 due to the influence of his good friend J.R.R. Tolkein, the author of *Lord of the Rings.* Prior to his faith, he describes himself as one who was **"angry at God for not existing."** When faced with the reality of the Christian gospel, he admits resisting as one who was **"kicking, struggling and resentful - looking in every direction for a chance to escape."** Lewis is perhaps best known for two of his thirty-five books: *Mere Christianity*, which was voted "Best Book of the Twentieth Century" by Christianity Today Magazine in 2000, and the seven-part children's series, *The Chronicles of Narnia*, which has sold over 100 million copies in 41 languages. In the story, *The Lion, the Witch, and the Wardrobe*, Lewis used animals to portray a fantasy-like picture of the battle of good and evil. Lewis made profound theology very simple: **"Christianity, if false, is of no importance, and if true, of infinite importance. The only thing it cannot be is moderately important."**

I have been crucified with Christ; and it is no longer I who live,
but Christ lives in me; and the life which I now live in the flesh
I live by faith in the Son of God,
who loved me and gave Himself up for me.
Paul the Apostle, GALATIANS 2:20

Excerpt from

Mere Christianity

I am trying here to prevent anyone saying
the really foolish thing that people often say about Him:

They say, "I'm ready to accept Jesus as a great moral teacher,
but I don't accept His claim to be God."

That is the one thing we must not say.
A man who was merely a man and said
the sort of things Jesus said would not be a great moral teacher.
He would either be a lunatic —
on the level with the man who says he is a poached egg —
or else he would be the Devil of Hell.
You must make your choice.
Either this man was, and is, the Son of God,
or else a madman or something worse.
You can shut Him up for a fool,
you can spit at Him and kill Him as a demon,
or you can fall at His feet and call Him Lord and God,
but let us not come with any patronizing nonsense
about His being a great human teacher.
He has not left that open to us. He did not intend to.

C.S. Lewis

**"I believe God made me for a purpose,
but he also made me fast.
And when I run I feel His pleasure."**

ERIC LIDDELL
1902 - 1945 (43 years)

**"The secret of my success over the 400 meter
is that I run the first 200 meter as fast as I can. Then,
for the second 200 meter, with God's help, I run faster."**

The Scotsman newspaper voted Eric Liddell (rhymes with fiddle) as the most popular athlete in Scotland's history. Known as "the flying Scotsman", his story was made into a movie called "Chariots of Fire." Eric spent his first five years in China, the son of Protestant missionaries. At age six, his parents placed him in Elthan College, a boarding house in England, where, in later years, he developed into a formidable athlete (rugby, cricket, track). His headmaster described him as being "entirely without vanity." He graduated from Edinburgh University with a BA in Science while also playing for the Scottish National Rugby Union. In the 1924 Olympics, Eric withdrew from the 100 meter race (his best event) because of his Christian conviction NOT to compete on Sunday. He ran the 200m and 400m instead, winning the gold and bronze medals, and setting a new world record. Before the race, his competitor, the American Jackson Schultz, handed him a verse, which he carried in his hand. It read: "Those who honor me, I will honor." (I Samuel 2:30) He later served as a missionary to China for 18 years, and died in a Chinese prison camp, just 5 months before World War II was over. He lived as an athlete and died as a servant hero. His philosophy was: **"We are all missionaries. Wherever we go, we either bring people nearer to Christ, or we repel them from Christ."**

They who wait on the LORD
will renew their strength;
They will mount up with wings like eagles,
They will run and not get tired,
They will walk and not become weary.
Isaiah the Prophet, ISAIAH 40:31

Humility

Always remember there are two kinds of people in the world.
Those who come into the room and say, "Well, here I am."
And those who come in and say, "Ah, there you are."
Frederick L. Collins

———

Be aware that a halo has to fall only a few inches to be a noose.
Dan McKinnon.

———

He that shall humble himself shall be exalted.
Matthew 23:12

———

What makes humility so desirable is the marvelous thing it does to us;
it creates in us a capacity for the closest possible intimacy with God.
Monica Baldwin

———

If I have seen further than others,
it is by standing upon the shoulders of giants.
Isaac Newton

"I can see how it might be possible for a man to look down upon the earth and be an atheist, but I cannot conceive how he could look up into the heavens and say there is no God."

ABRAHAM LINCOLN
(1809-1865) 56 years

"That the Almighty does make use of human agencies and directly intervenes in human affairs is one of the plainest statements in the Bible."

By the time Abraham Lincoln took office as the 16th President of the United States, seven states, from South Carolina to Texas, had seceded from the Union as a reaction to Lincoln's desire to abolish slavery. Three more states would follow. Never before had a President faced such pressure. Lincoln quoted the Bible when he said, "a house divided against itself cannot stand." Favoring national unity over states' rights, the Civil War cost the nation 620,000 lives. Standing on conviction that few men have known, Lincoln, the first Republican President, explained by saying, **"Be sure you put your feet in the right place, then stand firm. My concern is not whether God is on our side; my greatest concern is to be on God's side, for God is always right."** The slaves were freed, and Reconstruction marked an era of rebuilding the nation. With only 18 months of formal education, Lincoln rose to the rank of the wisest and noblest of national leaders. He gave his life for a cause he believed just, and he modeled for us a humble confidence that can only be explained by godly principles: **"All the good from the Savior of the world is communicated through this Book. All the things desirable to man are contained in it."** In simple words, Lincoln defined for us a great work ethic: **"I will prepare, and then perhaps my chance will come."**

For our gospel did not come to you
in word only, but also in power
and in the Holy Spirit with full conviction;
just as you know what kind of men
we proved to be among you for your sake.
Paul the Apostle, I THESSALONIANS 1:5

The Gettysburg Address

Four score and seven years ago
our fathers brought forth on this continent,
a new nation, conceived in liberty,
and dedicated to the proposition
that all men are created equal.

Now we are engaged in a great civil war,
testing whether that nation, or any nation so conceived
and so dedicated, can long endure.
We are met on a great battlefield of that war.
We have come to dedicate a portion of that field,
as a final resting place for those who here gave their lives
that this nation might live.
It is altogether fitting and proper that we should do this.
But, in a larger sense, we can not dedicate - we can not consecrate -
we can not hallow this ground.
The brave men, living and dead, who struggled here,
have consecrated it, far above our poor power to add or detract.

The world will little note, nor long remember what we say here,
but it can never forget what they did here.
It is for us the living, rather, to be dedicated here
to the unfinished work which they who fought here
have thus far so nobly advanced.

It is rather for us to be here dedicated
to the great task remaining before us -
that from these honored dead we take increased devotion
to that cause for which they gave the last full measure of devotion -
that we here highly resolve that these dead shall not have died in vain.
That this nation, under God, shall have a new birth of freedom -
and that government of the people, by the people,
for the people, shall not perish from the earth.

"It was not the outer grandeur of the Roman
but the inner simplicity of the Christian
that lived on through the ages."

CHARLES AUGUSTUS LINDBERGH
1902-1974 (72 years)

"God made life simple. It is man who complicates it."

At the age of 25, Lindbergh became an overnight success in 1927 when he flew 33 hours from New York to Paris non-stop in the plane that he dubbed *"The Spirit of St. Louis."* After training from the U.S. Army Air Service, Lieutenant Lindberg became a U.S. Postal Air Mail pilot. Twice he parachuted from a downed plane, and then faithfully retrieved and delivered the mail. On his historic trans-Atlantic arrival in Paris - 150,000 Frenchman cheered his arrival. As a newly acclaimed celebrity, he visited every state in the U.S. and logged 1,200 miles in parades. Due to a relative's heart disease, he invented the glass perfusion pump, an instrument that led to the eventual design of the artificial heart. Because of his celebrity status, his first born son was abducted and killed in what was then called, "the crime of the century." He later moved his family to Europe to avoid notoriety. After Pearl Harbor, he returned to the US to fly 50 combat missons during World War II. In his book, *WE,* he described a spiritual bond with his plane. The real meaning behind *WE* is the presence of a loving God who guides us during dark hours of solitude. Lindberg puts in perspective the beauty of solitude when he wrote: **"In wilderness I sense the miracle of life, and behind it our scientific accomplishments fade to trivia."**

The pride of man will be humbled
And the loftiness of men will be abased;
And the LORD alone will be exalted in that day.
ISAIAH 2:17

Solitude

Conversation enriches the understanding,
but solitude is the school of genius.
Edward Gibbon

——

Language has created the word loneliness
to express the pain of being alone,
and the word solitude
to express the glory of being alone.
Paul Tillich

——

I have never found a companion
that was as comfortable as solitude.
Henry David Thoreau

——

Talent is best nurtured in solitude.
Johann Wolfgang von Goethe

——

In solitude - where we are least alone.
Lord Byron

——

The best thinking has been born in solitude.
Thomas Edison

——

In the world, a man lives in his own age;
in solitude he lives in all ages.
William Matthews

"If you have men who will only come
if they know there is a good road,
I don't want them.
I want men who will come
if there is no road at all."

DAVID LIVINGSTONE
1813-1873 (60 years)

RAW DETERMINATION AND DARING PERSISTENCE may best describe the life of David Livingstone. He ranks as one of the great explorers in modern history. He was one of the first westerners to travel across Africa, and he was the first white face to see "the smoke that thunders," otherwise known as Victoria Falls. He named it after the current Queen of England. His quest was to find the source of the Nile, and in the process he discovered many natural wonders, now logged into science journals. His first career was that of a medical missionary for 17 years, living in Central Africa and sharing the gospel with the village natives. During this time he was mauled by a lion, a wound that handicapped him the rest of his life. In spite of this he said, **"Without Christ, not one step; with Him, anywhere!"** He spent the next 36 years traveling the African continent, suffering pneumonia, tropic ulcers, dysentery and malaria. When he died, his heart was cut out and buried under a tree in Zambia. His body was carried a thousand miles by his loyal servants, in order to ship the body back to England to be buried among England's noblest in Westminster Abbey. He became a legendary hero, best known for this statement: **"I determined never to stop until I had come to the end, and achieved my purpose."**

I have been on frequent journeys, in dangers from rivers,
dangers from robbers, dangers from my countrymen,
dangers from the Gentiles, dangers in the city,
dangers in the wilderness, dangers on the sea,
dangers among false brethren; I have been in labor and hardship,
through many sleepless nights, in hunger and thirst,
often without food, in cold and exposure.
The Apostle Paul, 2 CORINTHIANS 11:26-27

Courage

Courage is contagious. When a brave man takes a stand,
the spines of others are often stiffened.
Billy Graham

———

It is the character of a brave and resolute man
not to be ruffled by adversity and not to desert his post.
Marcus Tullius Cicero

———

We are face to face with our destiny,
and we must meet it with a high and resolute courage.
For us is the life of action, of strenuous performance of duty;
let us live in the harness, striving mightily;
let us rather run the risk of wearing out than rusting out.
Theodore Roosevelt

———

Courage is grace under pressure.
Ernest Hemingway

———

The courage we desire and prize
is not the courage to die decently, but to live manfully.
Thomas Carlyle

———

In the world you will have trouble; but take courage,
for I have overcome the world.
Jesus Christ

"The Bible is one of the greatest blessings
bestowed by God on the children of men.
It has God for its author; salvation for its end,
and truth without any mixture for its matter."

JOHN LOCKE
1632-1704 (age 72)

"To love truth for truth's sake is the principal part
of human perfection in this world,
and the seed-plot of all other virtues."

John Locke was a British philosopher and physician who developed many of the ideas of societal liberty, property and authority that contributed to the US Constitution and Declaration of Independence. Thomas Jefferson considered Locke, with Bacon and Newton, to be three of the greatest men in history for their contribution to the physical and moral sciences. It was Locke who popularized the idea of the "tabula rosa," meaning that man at birth is a "blank slate," waiting to be molded by society. Perhaps that is why he said, **"Parents wonder why the streams are bitter, when they themselves have poisoned the fountain."** Locke carefully used reason to establish a path which leads to irrefutable truth." He said, **"It is one thing to show a man that he is in error, and another to put him in possession of truth."** His book, *An Essay Concerning Human Understanding,* has been used to establish principles of public education and counseling. He said, **"The discipline of desire is the background of character."** He understood that wisdom could only be obtained by influence: **"To give a man full knowledge of morality, I would send him to no other book than the New Testament."**

For the LORD gives wisdom;
From His mouth come knowledge and understanding.
He stores up sound wisdom for the upright;
He is a shield to those who walk in integrity,
guarding the paths of justice,
And He preserves the way of His godly ones.
PROVERBS 2:6-8

Wisdom

It is characteristic of wisdom not to do desperate things.
Henry David Thoreau

———

Science is organized knowledge. Wisdom is organized life.
Immanuel Kant

———

Wise men talk because they have something to say;
Fools talk because they have to say something.
Plato

———

The perfection of wisdom, and the end of true philosophy
is to proportion our wants to our possessions
and our ambitions to our capacities;
then we will be a happy and a virtuous people.
Mark Twain

———

It's so simple to be wise.
Just think of something stupid to say and then don't say it.
Sam Levenson

———

We thought, because we had power, we had wisdom.
Steven Vincent Benet

———

Knowledge is proud that it knows so much;
Wisdom is humble that it knows no more.
William Cowper

"I propose that God should be openly and audibly
invoked at the United Nations . . .
I do so in the conviction that we cannot make
the United Nations into a successful instrument
of God's peace without God's help -
and that with His help we cannot fail."

HENRY CABOT LODGE, Jr.
1902 - 1985 (82 years)

Lodge was the U.S. Ambassador to the United Nations for seven years, longer than any one else in U.N. history. He was a Lieutenant Colonel in World War II, and served as a three-term Republican US Senator from Massachusetts. Ironically, his grandfather, Henry Cabot Lodge, Sr., ran against John F. Kennedy's grandfather for the Senate in 1916, and won. Then he (Cabot, Jr.) ran against John F. Kennedy for the same Senate seat in 1952 and lost. Later, Henry Jr.'s son, George Cabot, ran against Ted Kennedy for the same Senate seat in 1962, and lost. Finally, Lodge ran as a Vice Presidential candidate in 1960 and lost to the newly elected John F. Kennedy. Kennedy then appointed him to the post of U.S. Ambassador to Vietnam and the Vatican. Lodge had suggested that Viet Nam become a protectorate of the United States, or else face severe military involvement. He was ignored, and the Viet Nam war cost the U.S. many lives. Cabot said: **"The essential purpose of the United Nations is to keep peace. Everything it does to prevent World War III is good. Everything which does not further that goal is superfluous."**

Pursue peace with all men,
and the sanctification
without which, no one will see the Lord.
HEBREWS 12:14

Peace

When the darkness of dismay comes,
endure until it is over,
because out of it will come
that following of Jesus which is an unspeakable joy.
Oswald Chambers

———

We must wait for God, long, meekly,
in the wind and wet, in the thunder and lightning,
in the cold and the dark.
Wait, and He will come.
He never comes to those who do not wait.
Frederick W. Faber

———

God takes life's broken pieces
and gives us unbroken peace.
Wilbert Donald Gough

———

I live for those who love me, for those who know me true.
For the Heaven that smiles above me, and awaits my spirit too.
For the cause that lacks assistance, for the wrong that needs resistance,
For the future in the distance and the good that I can do.
George Linnaeus Banks

"Think of only three things:
your God, your family and the Green Bay Packers -
in that order."

VINCE LOMBARDI
1913 - 1970 (57 years)

"Perfection is not attainable, but if we chase perfection
we can catch excellence."

Perhaps the greatest tribute to Vince Lombardi was the renaming of the Superbowl Trophy to call it the Vince Lombardi Trophy. Young Vince had intentions of studying to be a Catholic priest before playing football at Fordham University and becoming one of the "Seven Blocks of Granite" - the name given to the legendary offensive line. For several years he taught high school Latin, chemistry and physics, until taking a position as the offensive coordinator for the New York Giants (opposite Tom Landry who was the DC for the team). At age 45, he took the position of Head Coach for the Green Bay Packers, and led the team to an unmatched three consecutive NFL championships and later, two Super Bowl titles. Lombardi was so popular that Republican Richard Nixon considered asking him (a Kennedy Democrat) to run as the Vice Presidential nominee in 1968. His players loved him as coach and motivator. In his book *Running to Daylight*, Lombardi was often quoted as saying: **"I firmly believe that any man's finest hour, the greatest fulfillment of all that he holds dear, is that moment when he has worked his heart out in a good cause and lies exhausted on the field of battle - VICTORIOUS."**

Don't you know that those who run in a race
all run, but only one receives the prize?
Run in such a way that you may win.
1 CORINTHIANS 9:24

Perfection

Trifles make perfection, but perfection is no trifle.
Michelangelo

This is the very perfection of a man,
to find out his own imperfections.
Saint Augustine

Perfectionism is the voice of the oppressor.
Anne Lamott

The true work of art is but a shadow of the divine perfection.
Michelangelo

To improve is to change; to be perfect is to change often.
Winston Churchill

What is once well done is done forever.
Henry David Thoreau

When you aim for perfection, you discover it's a moving target.
Geoffrey F. Fisher

"Lives of great men all remind us,
we can make our lives sublime;
and, departing, leave behind us,
footprints on the sands of time."

HENRY WADSWORTH LONGFELLOW
1807-1882 (75 years)

"Glorious indeed is the world of God around us,
but more glorious is the world of God within us."

Longfellow was an American poet, the most popular of his generation. He was a Harvard professor of Modern Languages for 20 years and gained mastery of at least ten languages: English, French, Italian, Spanish, German, Dutch, Danish, Swedish, Finnish and Icelandic. He was well known for translating Dante's *Divine Comedy*, and his best known poems were "Paul Revere's Ride", "The Village Blacksmith" and "The Song of Hiawatha." His second wife, Frances, died when a candle caught her dress on fire. Henry was badly burned when trying to save her. His face was severely scarred, which accounts for the beard, which became his signature look. During the Civil War, he penned these words: **"I heard the bells on Christmas Day, Their old, familiar carols play, And wild and sweet The words repeat, Of peace on earth, goodwill to men!"** Longfellow spoke of man's eternal nature when he said, **"Life is real! Life is earnest! and the grave is not its goal; dust thou art; to dust returnest, was not spoken of the soul."** He reminded us of the sovereignty of God, when he said, **"At first laying down, as a fact fundamental, that nothing with God can be accidental."** Of the Sabbath, he said, **"Day of the Lord, as all our days should be."** His benediction in life: **"Hail to the King of Bethlehem."**

For I am convinced that neither death, nor life, nor angels,
nor principalities, nor things present, nor things to come,
nor powers, nor height, nor depth, nor any other created thing,
will be able to separate us from the love of God,
which is in Christ Jesus our Lord.
Paul the Apostle, ROMANS 8:38-39

The Soul of Man

The soul is placed in the body like a rough diamond,
and must be polished, or the luster of it will never appear.
Daniel Defoe

———

Whatever satisfies the soul is truth.
Walt Whitman

———

Every moment and every event of every man's life on earth
plants something in his soul.
Thomas Merton

———

I put my heart and my soul into my work,
and have lost my mind in the process.
Vincent van Gogh

———

The soul that sees beauty may sometimes walk alone.
Johann Wolfgang von Goethe

———

The human soul has still greater need of the ideal
than of the real. It is by the real that we exist;
it is by the ideal that we live.
Victor Hugo

"God creates out of nothing.
Therefore until a man is nothing,
God can make nothing out of him."

MARTIN LUTHER
1483-1546 (62 years)

It is hard to imagine having the courage to stand against the prevailing religious institution of its day, the Roman Catholic Church, and dare to call the Papal system corrupt. Luther was a Catholic priest, a monk and university professor with a Doctorate of Theology. At the age of 34 he boldly nailed 95 Theses (doctrinal statements) to the door of the Wittenburg Church, in order to challenge the practice of selling salvation as a fund-raising practice. It was his conviction that salvation occurred as a free gift from God, through a simple act of faith. Within two months his writings had spread throughout Europe and sparked a grass roots resistance known as The Protestant Reformation. He fought for reform for several years until finally confronted at the Diet of Worms conference in a "repent or suffer" proposition. He responded, **"I am bound by the Scriptures I have quoted and my conscience is captive to the Word of God. I cannot and will not retract anything, since it is neither safe nor right to go against conscience. May God help me. Amen."** He was branded a heretic, excommunicated from the Church, declared an outlaw, and was WANTED DEAD OR ALIVE. He lived on to found the Lutheran Church and adopted new biblical standards. He changed the world system. He spoke with conviction when he said: **"Every man must do two things alone; he must do his own believing and his own dying."**

For I am not ashamed of the gospel, for it is the power of God for salvation
to everyone who believes, to the Jew first and also to the Greek.
For in it the righteousness of God is revealed from faith to faith;
as it is written, "But the righteous man shall live by faith."
Paul the Apostle, ROMANS 1:16-17

Courage

Courage is going from failure to failure without losing enthusiasm.
Winston Churchill

———

Courage is doing what you're afraid to do.
There can be no courage unless you're scared.
Eddie V. Rickenbacker

———

People don't follow titles, they follow courage.
William Wells Brown

———

You will find as you grow older that courage
is the rarest of all qualities to be found in public life.
Benjamin Disraeli

———

Have courage for the great sorrows of life and patience for the small ones;
and when you have laboriously accomplished your daily task,
go to sleep in peace. God is awake.
Victor Hugo

———

Without courage all virtues lose their meaning.
Winston Churchill

———

"The world is in a constant conspiracy
against the brave.
It's the age old struggle.
The roar of the crowd on the one side,
and the voice of your conscience on the other."

GENERAL DOUGLAS MACARTHUR
1880-1964 (84 years)

MacArthur began his career in the Army Corps of Engineers and later transferred into Infantry. He served during World War I, II and the Korean War, and he became not only the Army Chief of Staff, but also one of only five men promoted to the post "General of the Army." He was Field Marshal of the Philippines when Japan attacked the US. When Japan surrendered, he became the Supreme Commander of the Allied Powers in Japan, effectively making him the leader of all decisions from 1945 to 1948. It was MacArthur and his staff that helped Japan 1) rebuild the infrastructure 2) become a democratic government 3) reduce the powers of the Emperor 4) draft a new constitution and 5) become a strong industrial economy. MacArthur lead UN Forces against the aggression of North Korea in 1950. MacArthur understood that warfare was both physical and spiritual when he said: **"It must be of the Spirit if we are to save the flesh."** He loved the Army, he loved the sound of the bugle and guns, but he loved his family more. Perhaps his lasting legacy was this statement: **"It is my hope that, when I am gone, my son will remember me, not from the battle field, but in the home, repeating with him our simple daily prayer, 'Our Father Who Art in Heaven.' "**

For our struggle is not against flesh and blood,
but against spiritual rulers and powers, against the world forces
of this darkness, against the spiritual forces
of wickedness in the heavenly places.
Paul the Apostle, EPHESIANS 6:12

The Lords Prayer

Pray, then, in this way:
Our Father who is in heaven,
Hallowed be Your name.
Your kingdom come. Your will be done,
On earth as it is in heaven.
Give us this day our daily bread.
And forgive us our debts,
as we also have forgiven our debtors.
And do not lead us into temptation,
but deliver us from evil.
For Yours is the kingdom and the power
and the glory forever. Amen.

Matthew 6:9-13

"We have staked the whole of all our political
institutions upon the capacity of mankind
for self-government, upon the capacity
of each and all of us to govern ourselves,
to control ourselves,
to sustain ourselves according to
The Ten Commandments of God."

JAMES MADISON
1751-1836

Most Americans have no idea that the U.S. currency includes a $5,000 bill (with Madison's picture), nor that there is also a $100,000 bill. Madison was the fourth President of the United States, a Founding Father, and is generally considered to be the author of the U.S. Constitution and the accompanying Bill of Rights. He was the Secretary of State to President Thomas Jefferson, and was instrumental in negotiating the Louisiana Purchase which effectively doubled the size of the United States. He was a co-author of *The Federalist Papers,* a series of 85 articles which continue today to give brilliant interpretation to the meaning and intent of the U.S. Constitution. Madison wrote *The Federalist Papers* with Alexander Hamilton (Secretary of the Treasury) and John Jay (the first Chief Justice). Hamilton later became known as a Federalist, one who sought for a strong, centralized government. Madison fought against it, as he is quoted: **"In framing a government which is to be administered by men over men you must first enable the government to control the governed; and in the next place oblige it to control itself."** Later as President, he favored a larger government. Perhaps Madison personified for modern Americans the dilemma, the tension we feel between wanting a large, powerful, expensive government, or wanting a smaller government which favors personal responsibility and the authority of the states to control the destiny of its citizens. We continue Madison's battle today.

Therefore it is necessary to be in subjection, not only because of wrath,
but also for conscience' sake. For because of this you also pay taxes,
for rulers are servants of God, devoting themselves to this very thing.
ROMANS 13:5-6

Governing the Government

The democracy will cease to exist when you take away from those
who are willing to work and give to those who would not.
Thomas Jefferson

———

Hold on, my friends, to the Constitution and to the Republic for which it stands.
Miracles do not cluster, and what has happened once in 6000 years,
may not happen again. Hold on to the Constitution, for if the American Constitution
should fail, there will be anarchy throughout the world.
Daniel Webster

———

The state is the coldest of all cold monsters. Coldly it lies, too;
and this lie creeps from its mouth; 'I, the state, am the people.'
Friedrich Nietzsche

———

When you have an efficient government, you have a dictatorship.
Harry Truman

———

It is dangerous to be right when the government is wrong.
Voltaire

———

No man's life, liberty, or property is safe while the legislature is in session.
Mark Twain

**"Behold this truth in a simple creed
Enough for all the roads we go.
In love is all the law we need.
In Christ is all the God we know."**

EDWIN MARKHAM
1852-1940 (87 years)

Edwin Markham was an American poet, author and educator. During his early literary career, he served as a school principal and county superintendent in California. He rose to fame with the poem, "Man with a Hoe," modeled after the painting of the same name by French painter Jean Francois Millet. His words reflected the agony in the picture, the agony of toil and hardship as a result of "the curse" in Genesis 3:17-19. **"Bowed by the weight of centuries, he leans upon his hoe and gazes on the ground; The emptiness of ages in his face, and on his back the burden of the world. Whose breath blew out the light within this brain?"** He was honored by two Presidents, Hoover and Roosevelt, and his birthday was a local school holiday in Staten Island, NY, where he lived. The children would bring flowers to cover his lawn. His other famous poem was "Lincoln, Man of the People." His poetry framed for us words of wisdom regarding suffering and perseverance: **"For all your days prepare, and meet them ever alike. When you are the anvil, bear - when you are the hammer, strike."** Regarding the challenges of personal failure, he encouraged us to turn our losses into strengths as he admonished: **"Defeat may serve as well as victory to shake the soul and let the glory out."**

He is the image of the invisible God, the firstborn of all creation.
For by Him all things were created, both in the heavens and on earth,
visible and invisible, whether thrones or dominions
or rulers or authorities, all things have been created
through Him and for Him.
COLOSSIANS 1:15-16

Excerpt from

The Man with the Hoe

Bowed by the weight of centuries he leans
Upon his hoe and gazes on the ground,
The emptiness of ages in his face,
And on his back, the burden of the world.
Who made him dead to rapture and despair,
A thing that grieves not and that never hopes,
Stolid and stunned, a brother to the ox?
Who loosened and let down this brutal jaw?
Whose was the hand that slanted back this brow?
Whose breath blew out the light within this brain?

Is this the thing the Lord God made and gave
To have dominion over sea and land;
To trace the stars and search the heavens for power;
To feel the passion of Eternity?

Edwin Markham

"Today's Christians are too often like deep sea divers, encased in suits designed for many fathoms deep, marching bravely forth to pull the plugs out of bathtubs."

PETER MARSHALL
1902 - 1949 (46 years)

"Man cannot comprehend infinity. Yet the crumb of our pity comes from the loaf of God's compassion. The milk of human kindness comes from the dairies of God's love."

Dr. Peter Marshall was the Scottish-born chaplain for the United States Senate, while he also served as the Pastor of the New York Avenue Presbyterian Church in Washington, D.C. After his untimely death at the age of 46, his wife Catherine wrote his biography titled *A Man Called Peter,* which was later turned into a film by the same name. Catherine went on to write a total of 20 books, and son Peter John Marshall followed his father into ministry, graduating from Yale and Princeton Seminary. Thanks to wife Catherine, Dr. Marshall's sermons have become famous: "Mr. Jones, Meet the Master," "By Invitation of Jesus," and "Keeper of the Springs" have all become classic messages of timeless truth, uniquely delivered by a humble spokesman for the Christian faith. Sometimes God uses a premature death to call our attention to the short but shining brilliance of a man's life. Peter Marshall's prayers still echo through the decades as a call to obedience: **"Lord, where we are wrong, make us willing to change; where we are right, make us easy to live with."**

But when you give a reception,
invite the poor, the crippled, the lame,
the blind, and you will be blessed,
since they do not have the means
to repay you; for you will be repaid
at the resurrection of the righteous.
Jesus, LUKE 14:13-14

Infinity

To see a world in a grain of sand and heaven in a wild flower
Hold infinity in the palms of your hand and eternity in an hour.
William Blake

———

The soul is truly an image of the infinity of God,
and no words can do justice to its grandeur.
William Ellery Channing

———

A billion stars go spinning through the night,
blazing high above your head.
But in you is the presence that will be,
when all the stars are dead.
Rainer Maria Rilke

———

Two things are infinite: the universe and human stupidity;
and I'm not sure about the universe.
Albert Einstein

———

Our minds are finite, and yet even in these circumstances of finitude
we are surrounded by possibilities that are infinite,
and the purpose of life is to grasp as much as we can out of that infinitude.
Alfred North Whitehead

———

Silently one by one, in the infinite meadows of heaven,
Blossomed the lovely stars, the forget-me-nots of the angels.
Henry Wadsworth Longfellow

"The end of learning is to know God,
and out of that knowledge,
to love Him and imitate Him"

JOHN MILTON
1606-1674 (58 years)

John Milton is often called "England's greatest author," an honor that places him in the ranks of William Shakespeare. Perhaps Milton can best be understood by knowing that his own father (also John) was expelled permanently from his home by grandfather Richard Milton, when he was found reading an English version of the Bible. John, the father, therefore rejected the heavy-handed authority of the Roman Church, and also the one-state-religion in the Church of England. He became a Protestant, and a Puritan, one committed to the basic tenets of the Protestant Church today. Young John followed his dad. Young Milton was reputed to have command of at least seven languages (Latin, Greek, Hebrew, French, Spanish, Italian, English) His best known work was *Paradise Lost,* an epic story of Adam and Eve, the love of God the Father, the treachery of Satan, and the heroic rescue of the human race by Jesus, the Son. Written in twelve volumes, in a massive body of 11,000 lines, Milton was blind (in his 50's) when he began this incredible work of literature. Milton spoke eloquently of death when he said, **"Death is the golden key that opens the palace of eternity."** He also gave us a wonderful interpretation of the life which rejects the appetites of the flesh. **"He who reigns within himself, and rules his passions, desires and fears is more than a king."**

And we know that God causes
all things to work together
for good to those who love God,
to those who are called
according to His purpose.
ROMANS 8:28

Paradise

If a man could pass through Paradise in a dream,
and have a flower presented to him as a pledge
that his soul had really been there,
and if he found that flower in his hand when he awake -
Aye, what then?
Samuel Taylor Coleridge

———

Be such a man, and live such a life, that if every man were such as you,
and every life a life like yours, this earth would be God's Paradise.
Phillip Brooks

———

Love is a portion of the soul itself, and it is of the same nature
as the celestial breathing of the atmosphere of paradise.
Victor Hugo

———

Verily I say unto thee,
Today shalt thou be with me in paradise.
Jesus

———

"The world has yet to see what God can do
with one man fully consecrated to Him.
By the grace of God, I will be that man."

DWIGHT L. MOODY
1837 - 1899 (62 years)

"I have more trouble with D.L. Moody
than with any other man I ever met."

Perhaps no other INDIVIDUAL has become such an INSTITUTION as this man. The Moody Press, Moody Broadcasting Network, Moody Church and Moody Bible Institute have created a worldwide impact from their base in Chicago, Illinois. As a young shoe salesman, Moody applied for church membership at age 18, and was denied membership for an entire year. His teacher later said: "I can truly say that I have seen few persons whose minds were spiritually darker than was his." By age 23, he started a street mission and was teaching the Bible to hundreds of people. Even President Lincoln came to hear him. By age 38 he drew crowds of up to 20,000, hungry to hear Moody preach the gospel message of Jesus. Moody said: **"Prayer does not mean that I bring God down to my thoughts and my purposes, and bend His government according to my foolish notions. Prayer means that I am raised up in union and design with Him; and I enter into <u>His counsel</u> and carry out <u>His purpose</u>. The Christian on his knees sees more than the philosopher on tiptoe. Next to the might of God, the serene beauty of a holy life is the most powerful influence of good in all the world. God doesn't seek for golden vessels, and does not ask for silver ones, but He must have clean ones."**

Not by might
nor by power,
but by My Spirit,
says the LORD of hosts.
ZECHARIAH 4:6

Devotion

This, and this alone, is Christianity,
a universal holiness in every part of life,
a heavenly wisdom in all our actions,
not conforming to the spirit and temper of the world
but turning all worldly enjoyments
into means of piety and devotion to God.
William Law

———

True strength lies in submission which permits one to dedicate his life,
through devotion, to something beyond himself.
Henry Mille

———

Perpetual devotion to what a man calls his business,
is only to be sustained by perpetual neglect of many other things.
Robert Louis Stevenson

———

All is holy where devotion kneels.
Oliver Wendell Holmes, Sr.

———

The highest flights of charity, devotion, trust, patience and bravery,
to which the wings of human nature have spread themselves,
have been flown for religious ideals.
William James

———

Devotion, when it does not lie under the check of reason,
is apt to degenerate into enthusiasm.
Joseph Addison

"The greatest artists, philosophers and,
until quite recent times, scientists,
through the Christian centuries, . . . have all believed
that the New Testament promise of eternal life is valid,
and that the great drama of the Incarnation,
which embodies it, is indeed
the master-drama of our existence."

MALCOLM MUGGERIDGE
1903-1990 (87 years)

Muggeridge was a journalist and author from England, who traveled to India, Egypt and Russia in search of socialism and communism as a way of life. He was a self-proclaimed agnostic, and his style of writing in his early years was irreverent and satirical. In 1955, he wrote an article entitled, "Does England Really Need a Queen?" On the one hand, he fell from grace in social and political circles. On the other hand, he became widely acclaimed as a broadcaster who was a hard-hitting interviewer and a source of objectivity and conviction, one that stood against the tide of popular opinion. He liked to say: **"Never forget that only dead fish swim with the stream."** In the late 60's, his convictions finally found meaning when he acknowledged the reality of Christ in his life. **"Every happening, great and small, is a parable whereby God speaks to us, and the art of life is to get the message. . . If the greatest of all, Incarnate God, chooses to be the servant of all, who would wish to be the master?. . . It has been said that when human beings stop believing in God they believe in nothing. The truth is much worse: they believe in anything."**

Then He opened their minds to understand the Scriptures,
and He said to them, Thus it is written, that the Christ would suffer
and rise again from the dead the third day,
and that repentance for forgiveness of sins
would be proclaimed in His name
to all the nations, beginning from Jerusalem.
LUKE 24:45-47

Philosophy

When he who hears does not know what he who speaks means,
and when he who speaks does not know what he himself means,
that is philosophy.
Voltaire

My definition of a philosopher is of a man up in a balloon,
with his family and friends holding the ropes
which confine him to earth and trying to haul him down.
Louisa May Alcott

There is only one thing a philosopher can be relied upon to do,
and that is to contradict other philosophers.
William James

Philosophy: A route of many roads leading from nowhere to nothing.
Ambrose Bierce

One of the great mind destroyers of college education
is the belief that if it's very complex, it's very profound.
Dennis Prager

The scientists of today think deeply instead of clearly.
One must be sane to think clearly,
but one can think deeply and be quite insane.
Nikola Tesla

"I live in the spirit of prayer. I pray as I walk about, when I lie down and when I rise up. Thousands and tens of thousands of times have my prayers been answered."

GEORGE MUELLER
1805-1898 (92 years)

"God not only orders our steps, He orders our stops."

At the age of 31, Prussian born George Mueller (pronounced Mule-er) and his wife started an orphanage in Bristol, England with two children. Over a sixty-year period, Mueller became a father to 10,000 orphans. He built five homes that would eventually house 2,000 children at a time. To feed his new family, he raised today's equivalent of 7.5 million dollars. He provided support to 150 missionaries, the best known of which is Hudson Taylor. The amazing thing about this godly man was that he *never* asked for, *never* solicited, *never* even made his needs known to the general public. He is known today as a great man of faith, who trusted God for *every* need he had. He quietly prayed and God responded. Mueller was not always this righteous. As a young boy, he was a wild-eyed trouble-maker, who indulged himself in gambling, thievery, drunkenness and sexual mischief. As his mother lie dying, he was distracted by worldly pleasures. Six years later, he attended a Bible study and was introduced to God's saving grace in his life. Mueller said: **"Neither eloquence nor depth of thought makes a truly great preacher. Only a life of prayer and meditation will render him a vessel ready for the Master's use, and fit to be employed in the conversion of sinners and in the edification of the saints . . . I go on praying until the answer comes."**

Therefore, confess your sins to one another,
and pray for one another
so that you may be healed.
The effective prayer of a righteous man
can accomplish much.
JAMES 5:16

The Prayer of a Righteous Man

God always answers us in the deeps,
never in the shallows of our soul.
Amy Carmichael

——

Keep praying, but be thankful that God's answers
are wiser than your prayers.
William Culbertson

——

Prayer is a powerful thing,
for God has bound and tied Himself thereto.
None can believe how powerful prayer is,
and what it is able to effect,
but those who have learned it by experience.
Martin Luther

——

Prayer is not an argument with God
to persuade Him to move things our way,
but an exercise by which we are enabled by His Spirit
to move ourselves His way.
Leonard Ravenhill

——

Prayer is and remains always
A native and deep impulse of the soul of man.
Thomas Carlyle

"If you want a religion that makes sense,
go somewhere else. But if you want a religion
that makes life, choose Christianity."

RICH MULLINS
1955 - 1997 (41 years)

"God, in His mercy, does not answer our prayers
according to our understanding,
but according to His wisdom."

Singer / songwriter Rich Mullins, along with his group, "The Ragmuffin Band," was awarded the *"Artist of the Year"* and *"Song of the Year"* by the Gospel Music Association in 1998 and 1999. Though his collective albums over the years netted him a wealthy income, he took a meager salary and gave all of his income to mission charities around the world. With a degree in music education and a waiting list of concert appearances, he moved onto a Navajo Indian Reservation in Arizona and taught children to sing in their native language. He said: **"Christianity is about learning to love like Jesus loved, and Jesus loved the poor and Jesus loved the broken."** At his funeral, songwriter Michael W. Smith said: "Nobody on this planet wrote songs like he did, and I feel we've lost one of the only true poets in our industry." Rich rejected much of the empty tradition of the Church when he said**: "I really struggle with American Christianity. I'm not really sure that people with our cultural disabilities are capable of having souls."** His song, "Our God Is an Awesome God" has become a classic among worshippers. Lou Carlozo, music critic for the Chicago Tribune, said of Rich Mullins: "His music moves the soul like a trusted friend, gently guiding the listener to God."

Come and see the works of God,
Who is awesome in His deeds
toward the sons of men.
PSALM 66:5

Humility

Life is a long lesson in humility.
James Matthew Barrie

——

Humility makes great men twice honorable.
Benjamin Franklin

——

Pride makes us artificial and humility makes us real.
Thomas Merton

——

Humility is not thinking less of yourself, it's thinking of yourself less.
Rick Warren

——

Christianity, with its doctrine of humility, of forgiveness, of love,
is incompatible with the state, with its haughtiness, its violence,
its punishment and its wars.
Leo Tolstoy

——

Humility must always be the portion of any man who receives acclaim
earned in the blood of his followers and the sacrifices of his friends.
Dwight David Eisenhower

——

Without humility there can be no humanity.
John Buchan

"The holy work of delivering souls demands constant renewal through fellowship with God. When we pray for the Spirit's help, we will simply fall down at the Lord's feet in our weakness."

ANDREW MURRAY
1828 - 1917 (88 years)

"Nowhere can we get to know the holiness of God, and come under His influence and power, except in the inner chamber."

Andrew Murray was a South African missionary for 68 years, and the author of 240 publications, including his devotional classics: *Abide in Christ, Absolute Surrender* and *With Christ in the School of Prayer.* His father was a devout Dutch Reformed missionary who sent him to their native Scotland for college, and on for seminary training in Holland. Upon completion at the age of 20, Andrew and his brother returned to Cape Town to preach and teach. Murray prayed for revival in the villages and revival came. God blessed his ministry and he spoke throughout Europe and the United States, including a brief time of leadership for the YMCA in England. At the age of 51, he suddenly lost his voice, an unthinkable malady for a preacher of the gospel. For two years, known as "the silent years," Murray fasted and prayed and waited on God. Finally his voice returned and Murray experienced a new humility before God. He spoke with a renewed passion, as if he had never spoken before: **"No man can expect to make progress in holiness who is not often and long alone with God."**

Consecrate a fast,
Proclaim a solemn assembly;
Gather the elders and all the inhabitants
of the land to the house
of the LORD your God,
and cry out to the LORD.
Joel the Prophet, JOEL 1:14

Prayer

Prayer is a shield to the soul, a sacrifice to God
And a scourge to Satan.
John Bunyan

———

Prayer does not enable us to do a greater work.
Prayer is the greater work.
Thomas Chalmers

———

To pray is nothing more involved
than to lie in the sunshine of God's grace.
Ole Hallesby

———

Prayer is the breath of the new born soul,
and there can be no Christian life without it.
Rowland Hill

———

What a man is on his knees before God,
that he is, and nothing more.
Robert Murray McCheyne

———

The Christian on his knees sees more
than the philosopher on tiptoe.
Dwight L. Moody

"People shall never enter the kingdom of God
through our encouragement, persuasion, argument,
inducement, excitement, or attraction;
Entrance can be gained only by new birth,
by nothing less than the resurrection of the spirit."

WATCHMAN NEE
1903 - 1972 (69 years)

"To keep our hand on the plow
while wiping away our tears - THAT is Christianity!"

Watchman Nee was a Chinese Christian who wrote 55 books and started hundreds of churches in Communist China. He never attended Bible college or received formal training. Nee believed that denominations were divisive, and for that reason, he began only one church within the geography of a single city. He founded a series of churches, called "local churches," now numbering 2300 worldwide - including Philippines, Singapore, Malaysia, Thailand, and Indonesia. In 1952, Communist China imprisoned Nee for merely preaching the gospel and teaching the Bible. He remained in prison for 20 years, until the time of his death. Regarding prayer, he said this: **"Let us recognize this one thing: burden is the secret of prayer. If a person does not feel within him a burden to pray for a particular matter he can hardly succeed in prayer."** When he died, his belongings were collected, among them was found a scrap of paper which read as follows: **"Christ is the Son of God, who died for the redemption of sinners and was resurrected after three days. This is the greatest truth in the universe. I die because of my belief in Christ."**

I have no greater joy than this,
to hear of my children
walking in the truth.
3 JOHN 1:4

Sacrifice

A man (Jesus) who was completely innocent,
offered Himself as a sacrifice for the good of others,
including His enemies, and became the ransom of the world.
It was a perfect act.
Mohandas Gandhi

The greatest use of life
is to spend it for something that will outlast it.
William James

This is my commandment, that ye love one another,
even as I have loved you. Greater love hath no man than this,
that a man lay down his life for his friends.
John 15:12

A man must be sacrificed now and again
to provide for the next generation of men.
Amy Lowell

Dreams do come true, if we only wish hard enough,
You can have anything in life
if you will sacrifice everything else for it.
James Matthew Barrie

As soon as sacrifice becomes a duty and necessity,
I see no limit to the horizon which opens before him.
Ernest Renan

"This most beautiful system, the universe, could only proceed from the dominion of an intelligent and powerful Being."

ISAAC NEWTON
1643-1727 (84 Years)

"If I have seen further than others, it is by standing upon the shoulders of giants."

Thomas Jefferson considered Newton, Bacon and Locke to be three of the most influential men in history. When compared to Einstein in a survey, scientists voted Newton the more influential. He was a physicist, mathematician and astronomer, whose discovery of the three basic laws of motion would dominate scientific interpretation for the next 300 years. Ironically, Newton wrote more about the Bible than he did about science. **"The system of revealed truth which this Book contains is like that of the universe, concealed from common observation, yet the centuries have established its Divine origin."** Newton understood the order of the universe enough to marvel at the God of creation. **"Gravity explains the motions of the planets, but it cannot explain who set the planets in motion. God governs all things and knows all that is, or can be done."** He was a professor at Cambridge in England, in a day when all scientists revered the relationship of God and Science. **"In the absence of any other proof, the thumb alone would convince me of God's existence."** This brilliant man trusted God to give him wisdom. **"Yet one thing secures us whatever betide, the Scriptures assure us the Lord will provide."**

And beware not to lift up your eyes to heaven
and see the sun and the moon and the stars,
all the host of heaven,
and be drawn away and worship them
and serve them, those which the LORD your God
has allotted to all the peoples
under the whole heaven.
Moses, DEUTERONOMY 4:19

Opportunity

Master of human destinies am I.

Fame, love and fortune

On my footsteps wait.

Cities and field I walk,

I penetrate deserts and seas remote,

and passing by hovel and mart,

And palace soon or late,

I knock unbidden,

Once at every gate.

If sleeping, wake.

If feasting, rise

before I turn away.

It is the hour of fate

And those who hesitate,

Condemned to failure, penury and woe,

Seek me in vain and uselessly implore,

I answer not, and I return no more.

John James Ingalls

"Although my memory's fading,
I remember two things very clearly:
I am a great sinner and Christ is a great Savior."

JOHN NEWTON
1725-1807 (82 years)

"Amazing Grace, how sweet the sound
That saved a wretch like me.
I once was lost, but now I'm found,
Twas blind but now I see."

At the age of 17, young Newton sailed from London to become the captain of a small ship that transported slaves. He had hopes of becoming a slave master on a Jamaican plantation, but he himself was captured and made a slave to a West African merchant. Upon his release at the age of 23, he was returning to England, when the ship began to sink. During this time of desperation, John Newton prayed to God for his safety and his salvation. He committed his life to Christ, and began a new life, although for several more years he worked on slave ships. At the age of 39, he became an Anglican priest. He was especially skilled at writing hymns, the best-known of which is "Amazing Grace." Newton influenced a young Member of Parliament named William Wilberforce to fight for the abolition of slavery. Together, they fought for 26 years, until the Slave Trade Act of 1807 was enacted, the very year that Newton died. He was a humble man who said: **"I am not what I ought to be. I am not what I want to be. I am not what I hope to be. But still, I am not what I used to be. And by the grace of God, I am what I am."**

But if we walk in the Light
as He Himself is in the Light,
we have fellowship with one another,
and the blood of Jesus His Son
cleanses us from all sin.
1 JOHN 1:7

Grace

Grace is what God gives us that we don't deserve
and justice is what God doesn't give us that we do deserve.
Unknown

———

Faith is a living, daring confidence in God's grace,
so sure and certain that a man
could stake his life on it a thousand times.
Martin Luther

———

If the grace of God miraculously operates,
it probably operates through the subliminal door.
William James

———

There, but for the grace of God, go I.
Unknown

———

I am only one, but I am one.
I can't do everything, but I can do something.
The something I ought to do, I can do.
And by the grace of God, I will do.
Edward Everett Hale

———

The will of God will never take you
where the grace of God will not protect you.
Unknown

"Nothing in life is more wonderful than faith.
It is the one great moving force
which we can neither weigh in the balance
nor test in the crucible."

SIR WILLIAM OSLER
1849-1919 (70 years)

"To die daily, after the manner of St. Paul,
ensures the resurrection of a new man,
who makes each day the epitome of life."

Osler was a Canadian physician known as the "Father of Modern Medicine." He was one of the founders of Johns Hopkins Hospital in Baltimore, Maryland, and his book *Principles and Practices of Medicine* was considered for decades to be the primary textbook for medical training. He is perhaps best known for introducing the ideas of medical residency and the practice of bedside training for small groups of interns. He said, **"He who studies medicine without books sails an uncharted sea, but he who studies medicine without patients does not go to sea at all."** He was considered a great doctor, but an even greater teacher who said: **"The successful teacher is no longer on a height, pumping knowledge at high pressure into passive receptacles. No bubble floats longer than that blown by the successful teacher."** Osler left Johns Hopkins to become the Regius Professor of Medicine at Oxford University, considered at that time to be the most prestigious medical appointment in the world. Osler had considered the ministry before going into medicine and understood that God was the source of man's knowledge. **"In seeking absolute truth we aim at the unattainable and must be content with broken portions."**

Be diligent to present yourself approved to God
as a workman who does not need to be ashamed,
accurately handling the word of truth.
2 TIMOTHY 2:15

The Hippocratic Oath

(ca 500 BC, The Modern Version)

I swear to fulfill, to the best of my ability and judgment, this covenant:

I will respect the hard-won scientific gains of those physicians in whose steps I walk, and gladly share such knowledge as is mine with those who are to follow.

I will apply, for the benefit of the sick, all measures that are required, avoiding those twin traps of overtreatment and therapeutic nihilism.

I will remember that there is art to medicine as well as science, and that warmth, sympathy, and understanding may outweigh the surgeon's knife or the chemist's drug.

I will not be ashamed to say "I know not," nor will I fail to call in my colleagues when the skills of another are needed for a patient's recovery.

I will respect the privacy of my patients, for their problems are not disclosed to me that the world may know. Most especially must I tread with care in matters of life and death. If it is given me to save a life, all thanks. But it may also be within my power to take a life; this awesome responsibility must be faced with great humbleness and awareness of my own frailty. Above all, I must not play at God.

I will remember that I do not treat a fever chart, a cancerous growth, but a sick human being, whose illness may affect the person's family and economic stability. My responsibility includes these related problems, if I am to care adequately for the sick.

I will prevent disease whenever I can, for prevention is preferable to cure.

I will remember that I remain a member of society, with special obligations to all my fellow human beings, those sound of mind and body as well as the infirm.

If I do not violate this oath, may I enjoy life and art, respected while I live and remembered with affection thereafter. May I always act so as to preserve the finest traditions of my calling and may I long experience the joy of healing those who seek my help.

"The supreme function of reason is to show man
that some things are beyond reason."

BLAISE PASCAL
1623-1662 (39 years)

"Truth is so obscure in these times, and falsehood
so established, that unless we love the truth,
we cannot know it."

Pascal was a French mathematician, physicist and philosopher. At the age of 16, he developed what is now known as the Pascal Theorem of geometry, a discovery that amazed his teacher, Rene Descartes. He invented an early model of a mechanical computer, called a "Pascaline," and his research in hydraulics gave us the barometer and the syringe. His work in probability is used in economics as well as actuarial science. At the age of 24, he suffered a paralytic attack so severe that he was dependant on crutches. "His head ached, his bowels burned and his legs and feet were continually cold." His mind turned to philosophy, and his best known work *Pensees (Thoughts)* was called by Will Durant (11 volume *The Story of Civilization*) "the most eloquent book on French prose." Regarding his search for faith, Pascal said, **"In faith there is enough light for those who want to believe and enough shadows to blind those who don't."** He used his powers of reason to say: **"The gospel to me is simply irresistible. Jesus Christ is a God whom we approach without pride, and before whom we handle ourselves without despair."** He died at the age of 39, best known for this phrase: **"The heart has reasons that reason cannot know."**

And He made from one man every nation of mankind
to live on all the face of the earth, having determined
their appointed times and the boundaries of their habitation,
that they would seek God, if perhaps
they might grope for Him and find Him,
though He is not far from each one of us;
Paul the Apostle, ACTS 17:26-27

Pascal Quotes

Do you wish people to think well of you?
Don't speak well of yourself.

————

Human beings must be known to be loved;
but Divine beings must be loved to be known.

————

The immortality of the soul is a matter
which is of so great consequence to us
and which touches us so profoundly
that we must have lost all feeling to be indifferent about it.

————

There are only two kinds of men:
the righteous who think they are sinners
and the sinners who think they are righteous.

————

There are two kinds of people one can call reasonable:
those who serve God with all their heart
because they know Him,
and those who seek Him with all their heart
because they do not know Him.

————

By faith we know His existence.
in glory we shall know His nature.
Belief is a wise wager. Granted that faith cannot be proved,
but what harm will come to you
if you gamble on its truth and it proves false?
If you gain, you gain all; if you lose, you lose nothing.
Wager, then, without hesitation, that God exists.

"Posterity will someday laugh at the foolishness
of modern materialistic philosophy.
The more I study nature,
the more I am amazed at the Creator."

LOUIS PASTEUR
1822-1895 (72 years)

In the 1992 edition of Michael H. Hart's controversial book, *The 100: A Ranking of The Most Influential Persons in History,* Pasteur ranked number 11. Louis Pasteur was a French micro-biologist, one of three fathers of micro-biology, best known for giving us the process which counteracts spoilage, known as "pasteurization." He was a Professor of Chemistry at the University of Strausbourg, where his discoveries included germ theory, bacteriology and vaccines for cholera, anthrax and rabies. Pasteur first administered the rabies vaccine on a 9-year-old boy that was mauled by a bull dog. His assistants say he extracted deadly saliva from the jaws of the rabid dog - with a glass tube held between his own lips. They claimed that Dr. Pasteur fearlessly risked his own life. Had the vaccine failed, Pasteur might have faced imprisonment, since he was a Ph.D., not an M.D. With equal passion, Pasteur sought to discredit the theory called "spontaneous generation," which stated that some forms of life did not originate from a kindred seed. Pasteur used a simple experiment to disprove this false notion of the origin of life. He was a crusader who believed: **"Blessed is he who carries within himself a God, and the ideals of art and science and gospel virtues. Therein lie the springs of great thoughts and great actions."**

Before I formed you
in the womb, I knew you,
And before you were born,
I consecrated you;
I have appointed you
a prophet to the nations.
JEREMIAH 1:5

Science and God

Science has become a great power in the last century.
Man has analyzed everything divinely
handed down to us in the holy books.
After this cruel analysis the learned of this world
have left nothing of all that was sacred.
But they have only analyzed the parts and overlooked the whole,
and indeed their blindness is marvelous.
Fyodor Dostoyevsky

The Bible is true and science is true,
and therefore each, if truly read,
but proves the truth of the other.
Matthew Maury, Oceanographer

God is, by my endeavors, glorified in astronomy,
for 'the heavens declare the glory of God.'
Let my name perish if only
the name of God the Father is elevated.
Johannes Kepler, Astronomer

All human discoveries seem to be made only
for the purpose of confirming more and more
the truths contained in the sacred Scriptures.
The un-devout astronomer must be mad.
Sir William Herschel, Astronomer

Scientific concepts exist only in the minds of men.
Behind these concepts lie the reality which is being revealed to us,
but only by the grace of God.
Wernher Von Braun

"Love is the hardest lesson in Christianity;
but, for that reason, it should be most our care to learn it.
Men must be governed by God
or they will be ruled by tyrants."

WILLIAM PENN
1644-1718 (73 years)

"The country is both the philosopher's garden and his library,
in which he reads and contemplates
the power, wisdom and goodness of God."

At the age of 24, William Penn was imprisoned by King Charles II for blasphemy. He had written a scathing attack against The Church of England, The Puritans and the Catholics as hypocrites and false prophets. He believed that only the Quakers had found the true path to personal and corporate faith. Even threatened with life in prison, he contested: **"Right is right, even if everyone is against it, and wrong is wrong, even if everyone is for it. My prison shall be my grave before I will budge a jot; for I owe my conscience to no mortal man."** He was released after 8 months. Nine years later, Penn convinced the King to deport all the Quakers to America. At the age of 37, William Penn became the largest private landowner in the world when King Charles of England gave him 45,000 square miles, and named it Pennsylvania. Penn's civil charter was called the "Frame of Government," and served as the inspiration for both the Declaration of Independence and the U.S. Constitution. **"My God, who has given it (Pennsylvania) to me through many difficulties, will, I believe, bless and make it the seed of a nation."** Years later, the seed gave birth to "the land of the free."

Let no one look down on your youthfulness,
but rather in speech, conduct, love, faith and purity,
show yourself an example
of those who believe.
1 TIMOTHY 4:12

The Goodness of God

There is no greatness
where there is not simplicity, goodness, and truth.
Leo Tolstoy

———

Goodness is uneventful. It does not flash, it glows.
David Grayson

———

Receive every day as a resurrection from death,
as a new enjoyment of life; meet every rising sun
with such sentiments of God's goodness, as if you had seen it,
and all things, new - created upon your account:
and under the sense of so great a blessing.
William Law

———

The ideals which have always shone before me
and filled me with the joy of living are goodness, beauty, and truth.
Albert Einstein

———

Wisdom and goodness are twin-born, one heart
must hold both sisters, never seen apart.
William Dean Howells

"I believe a knowledge of the Bible
without a college course
is more valuable than a college course without a Bible."

WILLIAM LYON PHELPS
1865-1943 (78 years)

"God speaks to me, NOT through the thunder and the
earthquake, nor through the ocean and the stars,
but through the Son of Man, and speaks in a language
adapted to my imperfect sight and hearing."

Phelps was an American author who received a Ph.D. from Yale and became a professor of English for 41 years. In Steven D. Price's compilation *1001 Smartest Things Ever Said,* Phelps was sited for saying these noble words: **"This is the first test of a gentleman: his respect for those who can be of no possible value to him."** Phelps was a consummate teacher, who enjoyed spirited debate, and basked in the privilege of investing in the lives of the students. He said the following: **"I cannot explain to another the joy and the happiness I get out of teaching. It is more than a profession, an occupation, a vocation, a struggle; it is a passion, for I love to teach. I love to teach as a painter loves to paint, as a singer loves to sing, and as a musician loves to play."** In Phelps' book, *Human Nature in the Bible,* he dedicates the first chapter of the book to Adam and Eve, and the biblical account of Creation - a position that most college professors would mock in today's classroom. He said, **"God is the Supreme Artist. The world has always loved artists - in books, paintings, buildings, statues and music. One reason why I love God is because the beauty of the universe came from Him."** We can only hope more men of Yale will learn to bow down.

But from the beginning of creation,
God made them male and female.
For this reason a man shall leave
his father and mother
and the two shall become one flesh.
MARK 10:6-8

The Goodness of God

The country is both the philosopher's garden and his library,
in which he reads and contemplates the power,
wisdom and goodness of God.
William Penn

It is amazing how complete
is the delusion that beauty is goodness.
Leo Tolstoy

The ideals which have always shone before me,
and filled me with the joy of living are goodness, beauty, and truth.
To make a goal of comfort or happiness has never appealed to me;
a system of ethics built on this basis
would be sufficient only for a herd of cattle.
Albert Einstein

There is not enough love and goodness in the world
for us to be permitted to give any of it away to imaginary things.
Friedrich Nietzsche

Gratitude is not only the memory but the homage of the heart,
rendered to God for His goodness.
Nathaniel Parker Willis

I believe firmly that it was the Almighty's goodness,
to check my consummate vanity.
Lord Mountbatten

"All are but parts of one stupendous whole,
whose body Nature is, and God the soul."

ALEXANDER POPE
1688-1744 (56 years)

"A God without dominion, providence,
and final causes, is nothing else but fate and nature."

Alexander Pope follows Shakespeare and Tennyson as one of the most quoted authors in history, according to the *Oxford Dictionary of Quotations*,   He was considered the greatest English poet of the 1700s, and is perhaps best known for some of his one liners: **"A little learning is a dangerous thing - To err is human, to forgive, divine - Hope springs eternal in each human breast - Fools rush in where angels fear to tread."** Pope was a small man, standing 4'6" with a severe hunchback due to a crippling respiratory disease as a child. Perhaps his best known work was *Essay on Man,* in which he justified the exalted nature of God and the base nature of man , calling man **"a brain of feathers and a heart of lead."** He referred to man as **"the glory, jests and riddle of the world."** He gave the native that roams the prairies more credit than the average man when he said, **"Lo! The poor Indian, whose untutored mind sees God in the clouds, or hears him in the wind."** Of those who denied God's existence, he said: **"Atheists put on false courage in the midst of their darkness and misapprehensions, like children who, when they fear to go in the dark, will sing or whistle to keep their courage."** He reminds us: **"An honest man is the noblest work of God."**

Make it your ambition
to lead a quiet life
and attend to your own business
and work with your hands,
just as we commanded you.
1 THESSALONIANS 4:11

Quotes from Pope

Simplicity
I was not born for courts or great affairs;
I pay my debts, believe, and say my prayers.

——

Innocence
He is armed without who is innocent within.

——

Wisdom
Some people never learn anything,
because they understand everything too soon.

——

Simplicity
There is a certain majesty in simplicity.

——

Passion
The ruling passion, be it what it will,
The ruling passion conquers reason still.

——

Education
Education forms the common mind.
Just as the twig is bent, the tree's inclined.

——

Wisdom
A man should never be ashamed to own that he is wrong,
which is but saying in other words
that he is wiser today than he was yesterday.

"God is not concerned about filling empty churches,
He is concerned about filling
empty hearts that have no passion,
and empty eyes that have no vision."

LEONARD RAVENHILL
1907 - 1994 (87 years)

"My main ambition in life is to be on
the devil's most wanted list."

Perhaps Leonard Ravenhill can best be described as a "revivalist" - one who stands today as a prophetic voice, calling the world to salvation and the Church to repentance. During World War II, he was a British tent evangelist, who rallied the nation to godliness and launched a generation of missionaries. His life was a legacy of uncompromising prayer. Of prayer he said: **"No man is greater than his prayer life. Present-day preaching, with its pale interpretation of divine truths, causes us to mistake action for unction, commotion for creation, and rattles for revivals. The secret of praying is praying in secret. We are beggared and bankrupt, but not broken, nor even bent. God pity us that after years of writing, using mountains of paper and rivers of ink, we are still faced with gross corruption in every nation."** He is best known for his classic work, *Why Revival Tarries,* and also for his influence in the life of Keith Green, the Christian songwriter during the 1970s. A.W. Tozer said of him: "To such men as this the church owes a debt too heavy to pay." Ravenhill boldly proclaims: **"The Church used to be a lifeboat rescuing the perishing. Now she is a cruise ship recruiting the promising . . . How can you pull down strongholds of Satan if you don't even have the strength to turn off your TV? If we are to be much for God, we must be much with God."**

That repentance for forgiveness of sins
would be proclaimed in His name
to all the nations,
beginning from Jerusalem.
LUKE 24:47

Quotes from Ravenhill

The only time you can really say
that Christ is all I need,
is when Christ is all you have.

The pastor who is not praying is playing;
the people who are not praying are straying.
A sinning man will stop praying,
and a praying man will stop sinning.

Prayer is to the believer what capital is to the business man.

Men give advice. God gives guidance.

The self sufficient do not pray
The self satisfied will not pray
The self righteous cannot pray

If weak in prayer, we are weak everywhere.

We mistake the scaffolding for the building.

Maturity comes from obedience,
not necessarily from age.

**"Without God, democracy will not
and cannot long endure.
Freedom prospers when religion is vibrant
and the rule of law under God is acknowledged."**

RONALD REAGAN
1911-2004 (93 years)

**"If we ever forget that we are One Nation Under God,
then we will be a nation gone under."**

The 40th President of the United States was a soldier, actor and governor, who became known as "The Great Communicator." In humility, he said, **"All I did was communicate great ideas."** In 1987, he stood at the Berlin Wall and boldly said to Soviet General Secretary Gorbachev, **"Tear down this wall."** Two years later the wall came down. Two years after that, the Soviet Union collapsed. Mr. Gorbachev said at Reagan's death: "I take the death of Ronald Reagan very hard. He has already entered history as a man who was instrumental in bringing about the end of the Cold War." In many ways, it was Reagan's humor that endeared him to the American people. He once said, **"I have wondered at times what the Ten Commandments would have looked like if Moses had run them through the U.S. Congress."** Like the founding fathers, he feared the complexity and inefficiency of government when he said: **"The nine most terrifying words in the English language are: 'I'm from the government and I'm here to help.'"** But it was the Christian faith of Ronald Reagan that made him a great President. In John 1:14, Jesus was said to be FULL of "grace and truth." The world today is divided by these two words; Reagan was a rare combination of truth and grace. Perhaps his most important words were: **"Within the covers of the Bible are the answers for all the problems men face. Without God, democracy will not and cannot long endure."**

If my people who are called by My name will humble themselves and pray,
and seek My face and turn from their wicked ways, then I will hear from heaven,
will forgive their sin and will heal their land.
2 CHRONICLES 7:14
Reagan's inaugural verse, with his hand on his mother Nelle's Bible.

Quotes from Reagan

Government's view of the economy
could be summed up in a few short phrases:
If it moves, tax it. If it keeps moving, regulate it.
And if it stops moving, subsidize it.

————

We must reject the idea that every time a law's broken,
society is guilty rather than the lawbreaker.
It is time to restore the American precept
that each individual is accountable for his actions.

————

We will always remember. We will always be proud.
We will always be prepared, so we will always be free.

————

Concentrated power has always been the enemy of liberty.
Government is not the solution to our problems;
government is the problem.

————

The meaning of the Bible must be known and understood
if it is to make a difference in our lives,
and I urge all Americans to read and study the Scriptures.
The rewards of such efforts will help preserve
our heritage of freedom and signal the message
of liberty to people in all lands.

————

"Christ, who being the holiest among the mighty,
And the mightiest among the holy,
lifted with His pierced hands empires off their hinges,
and turned the stream of centuries out of its channel,
and still governs the ages."

JEAN PAUL RICHTER
1763-1825 (62 years)

"Humanity is never so beautiful as when praying
for forgiveness, or in forgiving another."

Richter was a German Romantic writer and educator who composed 60 volumes of work in his lifetime. At the age of 20, he compiled and edited *The Literary Works of Leonardo da Vinci.* His words were both profound and penetrating, as he said: **"God is the un-utterable sigh, planted in the depths of the soul . . How calmly should we commit ourselves to the hands of Him who bears up the world."** As important as his writing, was his spirit of encouragement and influence to those around him. The noted author, E.T.A Hoffmann counted Richter as a friend and mentor who deeply embedded his ideas and philosophies into the younger writer. Regarding influence, Richter wrote: **"The conscience of children is formed by the influences that surround them; their notions of good and evil are the result of the moral atmosphere they breathe . . . Only a few persons influence the formation of our character, the multitude pass us by like a distant army."** Richter wrote much about sorrow during his lifetime. Four years before his own death, Richter's talented son Max, died. Of prayer he wrote: **"Sorrows gather around great souls as storms gather around mountains . . Let prayer be the key of the day and the bolt of the night."** Of character he said: **"A man never describes his own character so clearly as when he describes another."**

For the sorrow
that is according to the will of God
produces a repentance without regret,
leading to salvation,
but the sorrow of the world produces death.
2 CORINTHIANS 7:10

Wisdom

On many of the great issues of our time,
men have lacked wisdom because they have lacked courage.
William Benton

—

Never doubt in the dark
what God told you in the light.
V. Raymond Edman

—

Encouragement is oxygen to the soul.
George M. Adams

—

A critic is one who would have you write it,
sign it, paint it, play it or carve it as he would, if he could.
Unknown

—

There are two tragedies in life.
One is to lose your heart's desire;
The other is to gain it.
George Bernard Shaw

—

Empathy is your pain in my heart.
Halford E. Luccock

—

A fanatic is one who can't change his mind
and won't change the subject.
Winston S. Churchill

"Think positively and masterfully,
with confidence and faith, and life becomes more secure . . .
richer in achievement and experience."

EDDIE RICKENBACKER
1890 - 1973 (82 years)

"I can give you a six-word formula for success:
Think things through, then follow through."

Rickenbacker was a champion race car driver before he entered World War I as a fighter pilot. During the war he flew a total of 300 combat hours and downed 26 German planes, both records which later merited him the U.S. Medal of Honor. After the war he founded the Rickenbacker Motor Co., then bought the Indianapolis Speedway, then became the owner and Chairman of Eastern Airlines. As a civilian during World War II, he was called on to encourage the troops at the age of 52 on a goodwill tour, when his plane went down in the Pacific Ocean. After three days, he and six fellow passengers ran out of food. Rickenbacker led the men in constant prayer and Bible study, encouraging them to place their trust, and their faith, in God's sovereignty. Five days later, a sea gull miraculously appeared out of nowhere and landed on his head. He caught the bird and used it for food and fish bait. Coupled with rain water, they survived for 16 more days and were finally rescued. Major Rickenbacker became a symbol of courage due to his belief that Christ controlled his destiny. He said: **"Courage is doing what you are afraid to do. There can be no courage unless you are scared."**

God is our refuge and strength,
A very present help in trouble.
Therefore we will not fear,
though the earth should change
And though the mountains slip
into the heart of the sea;
PSALM 46:1-2

Courage

Courage is almost a contradiction in terms.
It means a strong desire to live
Taking the form of readiness to die.
G. K. Chesterton

A ship is safe in harbor, but that's not what ships are for.
William Shedd

Man cannot discover new oceans
unless he has the courage to lose sight of the shore.
Andre Gide

One man with courage makes a majority.
Andrew Jackson

What would life be if we had no courage to attempt anything?
Vincent van Gogh

This will remain the land of the free
Only so long as it is the home of the brave.
Elmer Davis

The wishbone will never replace the backbone.
Will Henry

"If a man is not familiar with the Bible,
he has suffered a loss
which he had better make
all possible haste to correct."

THEODORE ROOSEVELT
1858-1919 (60 years)

"I think there is only one quality worse
than hardness of heart and that is softness of head."

Roosevelt's image on Mt. Rushmore, alongside Washington, Jefferson and Lincoln, confirms that this 26th President was one of the great leaders in American history. He was a war hero, a historian, naturalist and big game hunter who took on both parties in Washington in an effort to serve the American people. He was shot in an assassination attempt, but the bullet was slowed by a thick manuscript in his coat. He delivered a speech the same day, with blood running down his sleeve. Due to its delicate location, the bullet remained in him all his life. **"Speak softly but carry a big stick"** was his way of trying to balance the life of a gentleman and a crusader. He read thousands of books in multiple languages. He taught Sunday School at Christ Church, Oyster Bay, NY, and while in Washington he attended Grace Reformed Church. No doubt, this man's man, would bow in the presence of King Jesus. He was a champion among men, an ideological warrior whose spiritual values shaped his profound legacy. **"Far better is it to dare mighty things, to win glorious triumphs, even though checkered by failure... than to rank with those poor spirits who neither enjoy nor suffer much, because they live in a gray twilight that knows not victory nor defeat."**

These things I have spoken to you,
so that in Me you may have peace.
In the world you have tribulation,
but take courage;
I have overcome the world.
Jesus the Messiah, JOHN 16:33

Adversity

Adversity has ever been considered the state in which
a man most easily becomes acquainted with himself.
Samuel Johnson

——

We turn to God for help when our foundations are shaking,
only to learn that it is God who is shaking them.
Charles C. West

——

There is no education like adversity.
Benjamin Disraeli

——

Let me embrace thee, sour adversity,
for wise men say it is the wisest course.
William Shakespeare

——

Defeat may serve as well as victory
to shake the soul and let the glory out.
Edwin Markham

——

To have become a deeper man
is the privilege of those who have suffered.
Oscar Wilde

——

Adversity makes men, and prosperity makes monsters.
Victor Hugo

"If the life and death of Socrates
were those of a man,
the life and death of Jesus were those of a God."

JEAN JACQUES ROUSSEAU
1712-1778 (66 years)

"How petty are the books of the philosophers,
with all their pomp, compared to the Gospels."

Rousseau was born in Geneva, Switzerland, 200 years after Geneva's other favorite son, John Calvin. His religious life and views revolved from Calvinism to Catholicism to Deism and back to Calvinism. Though he is quoted as saying, **"There is no original perversity in the human heart"** (a denial of original sin), he also said, **"Everything is good when it leaves the hands of the Creator. Everything degenerates in the hands of man."** He was a philosopher whose political writings contributed much to the Enlightenment Period. His best known work, *The Social Contract,* is considered one of the most influential works of political philosophy in the western tradition. In it he proposes that the progress of knowledge has made governments too powerful and too willing to suppress individual liberty. The power of his words roused the peasants of France and The French Revolution was born. In his *Discourse on the Arts and Sciences,* he stood against the popular tide of anti-biblical reasoning to defend the spiritual origin of man and the universe. Rousseau, like Solomon, understood the vanity of life when he said: **"When a man dies, he clutches in his hands only that which he has given away in his lifetime."**

See to it that no one takes you captive
through vain philosophy and empty deception,
according to the tradition of men,
according to the elementary principles of the world,
rather than according to Christ.
Paul the Apostle, COLOSSIANS 2:8

Greatness

Great and good are seldom the same man.
Thomas Fuller, M. D.

———

There is a great man who makes every man feel small.
But the real great man is the man
who makes every man feel great.
G. K. Chesterton

———

Some are born great, some achieve greatness,
and some hire public relations officers.
Daniel J. Boorstin

———

No man was ever great without divine inspiration.
Cicero

———

The price of greatness is responsibility.
Sir Winston Churchill

———

Great men stand like solitary towers in the city of God.
Henry Wadsworth Longfellow

———

I've often said,
the only thing standing between me and greatness is me.
Woody Allen

"He who offers to God a second place
offers Him no place at all."

JOHN RUSKIN
1819 - 1900 (80 years)

"The reason preaching is so commonly ineffective is,
that it often calls on people to work for God
rather than letting God work through them."

John Ruskin was an English artist, poet and author, for whom the Ruskin College at Oxford is named. Author Leo Tolstoy described him as, "one of those rare men who thinks with his heart." Of his 250 works, he is best known for *The Seven Lamps of Architecture* and *Unto His Last,* a commentary on social justice. He believed the best of art was found in nature, as he said: **"Fine art is that in which the hand, the head, and the heart of man go together. Of all God's gifts to the sighted man, color is holiest, the most divine, the most solemn."** In his thirties he was influenced by Thomas Carlyle into a "crisis of faith" which stirred his religious conviction. He said: **"The best thing in life aren't things. If you want to work for the kingdom of God, and to enter into it, there is just one condition. You must enter it as a child or not at all."** As a historian he said: **"The root of almost every schism and heresy from which the Christian Church has suffered, has been because of the effort of men to earn, rather than receive their salvation."** He began to write stories of fantasy, and it was Ruskin's influence in Lewis Carroll to eventually write *Alice in Wonderland.* His words were profound: **"Out of suffering comes the serious mind; out of salvation comes the grateful heart. The highest reward for man's toil is not what he gets for it, but what he becomes by it."**

> That creation itself will someday
> be set free from its slavery to corruption
> into the freedom of the glory
> of the children of God.
> **ROMANS 8:21**

Creation

However far-reaching our intellectual achievements,
and however advanced our knowledge of creation,
without faith and a sense of our own spirituality
there is only isolation and despair,
and the human race is a lost cause.
Jane Hawking (wife of Steven Hawking)

———

The atheists are for the most part
impudent and misguided scholars
who reason badly, and who,
not being able to understand the creation,
the origin of evil, and other difficulties,
have no grasp of the eternity of things.
Voltaire

———

Music is the harmonious voice of creation;
an echo of the invisible world.
Giuseppe Mazzini

———

I roamed the countryside searching for answers
to things I did not understand.
Why does the lightning
becomes visible to the eye
while thunder requires time to travel?
Leonardo da Vinci

———

When our eyes see our hands doing the work of our hearts,
the circle of creation is completed inside us,
the doors of our souls fly open,
and love steps forth to heal everything in sight.
Michael Bridge

"Students today live in a generation of alienation.
Sometimes they forget that the basic alienation
which they face is a cosmic alienation.
They think nobody is home in the universe."

FRANCIS A. SCHAEFFER
1912-1984 (72 years)

Considered to be a profound philosopher and theologian, Schaeffer moved from the U.S. to Switzerland at the age of 36 to found L'abri (French for "shelter"). During the 70's and 80's he championed the cause of Christian activism against the rising assault of secular humanism. He wrote *The Christian Manifesto* as a response to the twin evils of *The Communist Manifesto* and *The Humanist Manifesto*. By definition, humanism is the worldview that "man is the measure of all things," and that spiritual and religious forces in the world today are merely mythology. The world has now shifted from "God-centered" to "man-centered". The average pagan man is like "the frog in the kettle." The temperature rises, the danger increases, and he can't even feel the heat. Regarding evolution, Schaeffer said: **"No one has yet shown how man could have been brought forth from non-man solely by time plus chance."** Schaeffer wisely understood the spirit of the age when he said: **"We should note this curious mark of our own age: the only absolute allowed is the absolute insistence that there is no absolute."** Perhaps 2 Timothy 4 (written 2000 years ago) best describes Schaeffer's prophetic voice against the pitfalls of modernism.

For the time will come when they will not endure sound doctrine;
but wanting to have their ears tickled, they will accumulate
for themselves teachers in accordance to their own desires,
and they will turn away their ears from the truth
and they will listen to myths.
2 TIMOTHY 4:3-4

Unshaken by the storms that rage,
Over all the earth in every time,
Moves one lone Man through every age
Serene, Invincible, Sublime.

Through countless centuries He goes,
His timeless journey to complete.
Divinely calm as one who knows
The way is sure beneath His feet.

Wild storms of hate beat round His head;
Earth rocks beneath the crash of war.
Yet still, with smooth, unhurried tread,
He moves, untroubled as before

Over the wrecks of fallen states,
Through fair proud nations yet to fall,
Passes the Master of their fates,
The Silent Sovereign of them all.

Unfaltering through the darkest night,
Denied by man, God's loving man,
His face gives back the morning light,
His calm eyes see God's finished plan.

One small troubled life we live,
And then find rest in beds of clay,
But our brief day is glorified,
We have seen Jesus pass this way.

George T. Liddell

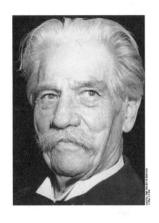

"One truth stands firm.
All that happens in world history
rests on something spiritual.
If the spiritual is strong, it <u>creates</u> world history.
If it is weak, it <u>suffers</u> world history."

<u>ALBERT SCHWEITZER</u>
1875-1965 (90 years)

Few people in history have gained mastery over three careers as did Dr. Albert Schweitzer. By age 24, he earned a Ph.D. in theology and also became widely known as a music scholar, so adept at piano and organ that he resolved to learn the works of Bach and Mendelssohn by heart. At age 30, he published his now famous book *The Quest of the Historical Jesus,* and he immediately enrolled in medical school. Seven years later he became an M.D., Now determined to give something back to society, he and his wife moved to Lambarene, West Africa (now Gabon), with the purpose of establishing a medical mission. In order to raise money for medical supplies, Schweitzer would perform organ recitals. He ministered to his African brothers for 54 years. Schweitzer considered his greatest contribution to be his philosophy of reverence for life. **"Sometimes our light goes out but is blown into flame by another human being. Each of us owes deepest thanks to those who have rekindled this light."** He wrote the book *Civilization and Ethics* in an attempt to convince mankind to turn from materialism and hedonism. In 1952 he was awarded the Nobel Peace Prize. This quote from Schweitzer best summarizes his life: **"Those among you who will be really happy are those who will have sought and found how to serve."**

It is not this way among you,
but whoever wishes to become great among you shall be your servant,
and whoever wishes to be first among you shall be your slave;
just as the Son of Man did not come
to be served, but to serve, and to give His life a ransom for many.
Jesus the Messiah, MATTHEW 20:26-28

Excerpt from

The Quest of the Historical Jesus

He comes to us as one unknown,
without a name, as of old by the lakeside,
He came to those men who knew him not.
He speaks to us the same words, "Follow me!"
and sets us to the tasks which He has to fulfill for our time.
He commands. And to those who obey Him,
whether they be wise or simple,
He will reveal himself in the toils, the conflicts, the sufferings
which they shall pass through in His fellowship,
and, as an ineffable mystery,
they shall learn in their own experience who He is.

Albert Schweitzer

"Every one of our greatest national treasures - our liberty, enterprise, vitality, wealth, military power, global authority - flow from a surprising source: our ability to give thanks. If you think Independence Day is America's defining holiday, think again. Thanksgiving deserves that title, hands-down."

TONY SNOW
1955 - 2008 (53 years)

Tony Snow rose to national fame as the host of Fox News Sunday, a weekly television political news forum. For six years, he was referred to as "the gentleman conservative warrior," proving to be a tough, but fair-minded journalist who asked hard questions that he expected Americans wanted to hear. He studied journalism at Davidson College in NC and later became a syndicated columnist for the Detroit News, Washington Post and USA Today. He hosted his own radio talk show, as well as contributing to the Paul Harvey News and National Public Radio programs. **"Many people don't give a rip about politics and know as much about public affairs as they know about the topography of Pluto."** Tony made his mark when he became the White House Press Secretary during the administration of President George W. Bush. **"To have faith is to believe that truth confers special power . . . and to know in our hearts that all these things come from God, which is why we should never get too cocky about our successes."** In the midst of battling cancer, Tony always exemplified a gracious spirit, and he always personified the heart of a journalist who is truly "fair and balanced."

Therefore I will give thanks to You,
O LORD, among the nations,
And I will sing praises to Your name.
King David, 2 SAMUEL 22:50

<u>Thanksgiving</u>

A thankful heart is not only the greatest virtue,
but the parent of all the other virtues.
Cicero

———

We can only be said to be alive in those moments
when our hearts are conscious of our treasures.
Thornton Wilder

———

As we express our gratitude, we must never forget
that the highest appreciation is not to utter words, but to live by them.
John Fitzgerald Kennedy

———

God has two dwellings; one in heaven,
and the other in a meek and thankful heart.
Izaak Walton

———

O Lord that lends me life,
Lend me a heart replete with thankfulness.
William Shakespeare

———

You say grace before meals. All right.
But I say grace before the concert and the opera,
and grace before the play and pantomime,
and grace before I open a book, and grace before sketching,
painting, swimming, fencing, boxing, walking, playing, dancing
and grace before I dip the pen in the ink.
G.K. Chesterton

"Is it true that man is above everything?
Is there no Superior Spirit above him?
Is it permissible to promote such
to the detriment of our spiritual integrity?
No one on earth has any other way left, but upward."

ALEXANDER SOLZHENITZYN
1918-2008 (89 years)

Sol-sha-neet-sin was a Russian novelist and historian who served as a commander in the Red Army during World War II. He was a twice decorated soldier, who later renounced Marxism, then criticized Stalin, and was charged with anti-Russian propaganda. For this offense, he was placed in a Gulag (a forced labor camp) and released 8 years later. He then wrote his best known work, *The Gulag Archipelago*, which has been called "one of the most consequential books of the twentieth century." He won a Nobel Peace Prize for exposing the Russian government's handling of political prisoners. He was promptly stripped of his citizenship and exiled from Russia for the next 20 years. In 1978 at a Harvard commencement address, he said the following: **"the human soul longs for things higher, warmer, and purer than those offered by today's mass living habits - by TV stupor and intolerable music."** In 1994, after suffering constant oppression by the KGB, he was finally welcomed back to Russia as a literary hero, and in 2007, just before his death, Vladimir Putin awarded him The State Prize of the Russian Federation for his work. He warned the west of continuing compromise: **"All of us are standing on the brink of a great historical cataclysm, a flood that swallows up civilization and changes whole epochs."**

The fool has said in his heart,
"There is no God."
They are corrupt,
they have committed abominable deeds;
There is no one who does good.
PSALM 14:1

Men Have Forgotten God

While I was still a child,
I recall hearing a number of old people
offer the following explanation
for the great disasters that had befallen Russia:
'Men have forgotten God; that's why all this has happened.'
Since then I have spent well-nigh 50 years working
on the history of our revolution;
And if I were asked today to formulate,
as concisely as possible, the main cause
of the ruinous revolution that swallowed up
some 60 million of our people, I could not put it
more accurately than to repeat:
'Men have forgotten God; that's why all this has happened.' "

ALEXANDER SOLZHENITZYN

"And Lord haste the day,
when my faith shall be as sight,
The clouds be rolled back as a scroll;
The trump shall resound,
and the Lord shall descend,
Even so, it is well with my soul."

HORATIO SPAFFORD
1828 - 1888 (59 years)

Spafford was a Chicago lawyer who is best known for writing the lyrics to the popular hymn, "It is Well with my Soul." The great Chicago fire of 1871 destroyed much of Spafford's financial investment in the city. Two years later he and his family made plans to travel to England, but some urgent business delayed his schedule, so he sent his wife Anna and four daughters on ahead. Crossing the Atlantic, their steamship called the Ville du Havre, was struck by an iron sailing vessel and all four daughters (with a total of 226) were lost at sea. His wife survived and sent a telegram back to him that simply read, "saved alone." He immediately set sail for England to join her, and as he crossed the spot where his daughters went down, he penned the now famous words that have provided comfort and inspiration to generations. **"When peace, like a river, attendeth my way, When sorrows like sea billows roll; Whatever my lot, Thou hast taught me to say, It is well, it is well with my soul."** Eight years later, Horatio and Anna moved to Jerusalem to form a communal society, called The American Colony, whose legacy ministered to Arabs and Jews for sixty years.

He restores my soul;
He guides me in the paths
of righteousness For His name's sake.
King David, PSALM 23:3

The Soul of Man

A billion stars go spinning through the night,
blazing high above your head.
But in you is the presence that will be,
when all the stars are dead.
Rainer Maria Rilke

———

You don't have a soul. You are a Soul. You have a body.
C.S. Lewis

———

My entire soul is a cry, and all my work is a commentary on that cry.
Nikos Kazantzakis

———

The virtue of the soul does not consist in flying high, but walking orderly;
grandeur does not exercise itself in grandeur, but in mediocrity.
Michel de Montaigne

———

Cherish your visions and your dreams as they are the children of your soul,
the blueprints of your ultimate achievements.
Napoleon Hill

———

Nowhere can man find a quieter
or more untroubled retreat than in his own soul.
Marcus Aurelius

"A good character is the best tombstone. Those who loved you and were helped by you will remember you when the flowers have withered. Carve your name on hearts, not on marble."

CHARLES HADDON SPURGEON
1834 - 1892 (57 years)

"Our misery is that we thirst SO LITTLE for the sublime things, and SO MUCH for the mocking trifles of time and space."

By the age of 19, young Charles Spurgeon was the pastor of the New Park Street Chapel (later named Metropolitan Tabernacle) in London, often preaching 10 times per week to crowds as many as 10,000. For 38 years he preached the gospel of Christ and he authored 49 volumes. Among his writings is his magnum opus, *The Treasury of David,* a masterful seven volume study of the book of Psalms, twenty years in the making. He is revered today as "the prince of preachers." During the week prior to preaching at The Crystal Palace in London (a day that amassed 23,000 people) Spurgeon was testing the acoustics when he boldly proclaimed: **"Behold the Lamb of God, who takes away the sin of the world."** A workman who overheard the simple declaration was gripped with conviction and found salvation. Spurgeon founded a college and an international children's ministry that continue today. He spoke with great authority. **"We have come to a turning point in the road. If we turn to the right, our children and our children's children will go that way; but if we turn to the left, generations yet unborn will curse our names for having been unfaithful to God and to His Word."**

Look unto me, and be ye saved,
all the ends of the earth,
for I am God, and there is none else."
ISAIAH 45:22

The Value of the Soul

There is one spectacle grander than the sea, that is the sky;
there is one spectacle grander than the sky,
that is the interior of the soul.
Victor Hugo

―――

The immortality of the soul is a matter which is of so great
consequence to us and which touches us so profoundly
that we must have lost all feeling to be indifferent about it.
Blaise Pascal

―――

Some of the greatest battles will be fought
within the silent chambers of your own soul.
Ezra Taft Benson

―――

It is perseverance, in spite of all obstacles and impossibilities,
that distinguishes the strong soul from the weak.
Thomas Carlyle

―――

One may have a blazing hearth in one's soul
and yet no one ever came to sit by it.
Passersby see only a wisp of smoke from the chimney
and continue on their way.
Vincent van Gogh

―――

Faith is the daring of the soul to go farther than it can see.
William Newton Clarke

"To me, there's a very simple solution
to the fast paced world that we live in.
If you have a relationship with Jesus Christ,
He will give you peace of mind.
My future reaches far beyond football,
and this really excites me.
Christianity is the most important part of my life."

ROGER STAUBACH
1942 -

Legendary coach Tom Landry described Roger Staubach as "possibly the best combination of a passer, an athlete and a leader to ever play in the NFL." In 2010 Staubach was named the number one Dallas Cowboy of all time according to a poll conducted by the *Dallas Morning News*. In his second season as the quarterback for the United States Naval Academy, he won the coveted Heisman Trophy, setting records along the way that stand 40 years later. In 2007, Staubach was ranked #9 on ESPN's Top 25 Players In College Football History. He was drafted by the Cowboys in 1964, but he first honored his military commitment, later starting for the Cowboys in 1969 as a 27 year old rookie. Though he could have served the Navy stateside, he chose a one year tour of Vietnam as a Navy Supply Corps officer. As a Cowboy, Staubach was called "Roger the Dodger" because of his scrambling ability. He led the club to five Super Bowl appearances and two victories, and is one of only four players in NFL history to achieve a Super Bowl MVP as well as the Heisman. Staubach introduced the now famous "Hail Mary pass" in 1975 when he launched a last second 50 yard touchdown pass to win the game. After retirement, he founded The Staubach Company, a multi-billion dollar real estate firm. In 1985 He was voted into the Pro Football Hall of Fame. A devout Christian, Staubach always promoted a noble philosophy. **"Winning isn't getting ahead of others. It's getting ahead of yourself."**

I can do all things through Christ who strengthens me.

Paul the Apostle, PHILIPPIANS 4:13

Dream, Work, Achieve

It is not the mountain we conquer but ourselves.
Sir Edmund Hillary (first to climb Mt Everest)

——

You can have everything in life you want,
if you will just help enough other people get what they want
Zig Ziglar

——

The greater danger for most of us lies not
in setting our aim too high and falling short;
but in setting our aim too low, and achieving our mark.
Michelangelo

——

To achieve great things, two things are needed;
a plan, and not quite enough time.
Leonard Bernstein

——

I long to accomplish a great and noble task; but it is my chief duty
to accomplish small tasks as if they were great and noble
Helen Keller

——

The greatest achievement of the human spirit
is to live up to one's opportunities and make the most of one's resources.
Vauvenargues, Marquis de

——

He who would accomplish little must sacrifice little;
he who would accomplish much must sacrifice much
James Allen

"There is nothing but God's grace.
We walk upon it, we breathe it.
We live and die by it.
It makes the nails and axles of the universe."

ROBERT LOUIS STEVENSON
1850-1894 (44 years)

"Quiet minds cannot be perplexed or frightened,
but go on in fortune or misfortune at their own private pace,
like a clock during a thunderstorm."

Stevenson was a Scottish writer and poet, best known for his works: *Treasure Island, Kidnapped, Dr. Jekyl and Mr Hyde,* and *A Child's Garden of Verses.* His father and brothers were all lighthouse engineers, but Robert chose the life of a wandering author, finally settling on 400 acres in the Samoan Islands. His writings influenced the later works of Hemingway, Kipling and Barrie. G.K. Chesterton said of him: "He always seemed to pick the right word up on the point of his pen." He is ranked the 25th most translated author in the world, ahead of fellow nineteenth-century writers Charles Dickens, Oscar Wilde and Edgar Allan Poe. Stevenson once wrote, **"Sooner or later, we all sit down to a banquet of consequences."** As a young man he rejected the faith of his parents, only to come full circle in later life to realize that it was the riches of God's grace that had gifted him as a writer. Grace is a commodity. Ask for it, and believe 2 Corinthians 9:8. "God is able to make all grace abound to you." Like oxygen, it is all around us; and like oxygen, without it, we cannot survive. Stevenson was buried on a mountain in Samoa, overlooking the sea: He liked to say: **"The best things are nearest to you. Breath in your nostrils, light in your eyes, flowers at your feet, duties at your hand, the path of God just before you."**

For by grace you have been saved
through faith; and that not of yourselves,
it is the gift of God; not of works, so no one may boast.
For we are His workmanship,
created in Christ Jesus for good works,
which God prepared beforehand so that we would walk in them.
EPHESIANS 2:8-10

Grace

Man is born broken. He lives by mending.
The grace of God is glue.
Eugene O'Neill

———

Above all the grace and the gifts that Christ gives
to His beloved is that of overcoming self.
St. Francis of Assisi

———

If the Lord should bring a wicked man to heaven,
heaven would be hell to him;
for he who loves not grace upon earth will never love it in heaven.
Christopher Love

———

Grace is but glory begun, and glory is but grace perfected.
Jonathan Edwards

———

Repentance is a grace of God's Spirit
whereby a sinner is inwardly humbled and visibly reformed.
Thomas J. Watson

———

Grace has been defined as the outward expression
of the inward harmony of the soul.
William Hazlitt

———

God opposes the proud, but gives grace to the humble.
James 4:6

"I'm proud of the fact that my faith in God
is so much stronger, and I'm so much more at peace
with myself than I've ever been in my life."

PAYNE STEWART
1957-1999 (42 years)

Payne Stewart became a legend as a professional golfer. He won the PGA Champi-onship in '89 and the U.S. Open in '91 and '99. He was ranked in the Top Ten of pro golfers for 5 straight years. His style was flamboyant in both dress and demeanor. He donned "the old style golf knickers and tam o'shanter cap", and he entertained the crowd with his contagious enthusiasm. Part of his philosophy of life was: **"I don't think it's healthy to take yourself too seriously."** Then came the tragic day when Payne Stewart became a legend in his death. Traveling with friends in a Learjet 35 from Orlando to Dallas, the aircraft lost cabin pressure, and the two pilots and four pas-sengers apparently lost consciousness. They died in a fiery crash in Aberdeen, South Dakota. Finally, Payne was a legend in his Christian faith. There was a time when Payne Stewart was rude, according to his mother - and arrogant, according to his wife - and impatient, lacking self-confidence, according to his caddie - "an all-around pain," according to Stewart himself. But in his final years, he surrendered his ego to Christ, and his friends said his life suddenly took on meaning and grace. **"I have to give thanks to the Lord. If it weren't for my faith in Him, I wouldn't have faith . . . in myself."** In 2001, he was inducted into the Golf Hall of Fame.

Brothers, I do not regard myself as having laid hold of it yet;
but one thing I do: forgetting what lies behind
and reaching forward to what lies ahead, I press on toward the goal
for the prize of the upward call of God in Christ Jesus.
PHILIPPIANS 3:13-14

Faith

It's faith in something
and enthusiasm for something that makes a life worth living.
Oliver Wendell Holmes

————

I know God will not give me anything I can't handle.
I just wish He didn't trust me so much.
Mother Teresa of Calcutta

————

Faith is a living, daring confidence in God's grace,
so sure and certain that a man
could stake his life on it a thousand times.
Martin Luther

————

Our misery is that we thirst so little for these sublime things,
and so much for the mocking trifles of time and space.
Charles H. Spurgeon

————

The longer I live, the more faith I have in Providence,
and the less faith in my interpretation of Providence.
Jeremiah Day

————

You can do very little with faith,
but you can do nothing without it.
Samuel Butler

"I'm against sin. I'll kick it as long as I've got a foot,
and I'll fight it as long as I've got a fist.
I'll butt it as long as I've got a head
and I'll bite it as long as I've got a tooth.
And when I'm old and fistless and footless and toothless,
I'll gum it till I go home to Glory."

BILLY SUNDAY
1862-1935 (72 years)

Sunday played National League baseball for Chicago, Pittsburgh and Philadelphia for nine years from 1883-1891. He was one of the fastest runners in the game, and he played outfield in a time that preceded wearing gloves. In his last season he was offered $3,000, but he turned it down to make $83 per month working for the YMCA. At the age of 29, he surrendered his life and his lifestyle to Christ. Two years later, he became an associate of J. Wilbur Chapman, a nationally known evangelist. After three years of training from Chapman, he set out on his own to establish the largest revival ministry until the time of Billy Graham. Sunday preached with authority and conviction, but he was also theatrical in his style, sometimes running from one side of the stage to the other, sliding into an imaginary home plate as he preached to the crowd to "come home to Jesus." It was Sunday who popularized the saying, **"Going to church doesn't make you a Christian any more than going to a garage makes you an automobile."** He preached to 100 million people during his career of 39 years, and was a friend of Presidents Roosevelt and Wilson. With a passion for lost souls he said, **"A man can slip into hell with his hand on the door-knob of heaven."**

If we say that we have no sin, we are deceiving ourselves
and the truth is not in us. If we confess our sins,
He is faithful and righteous to forgive us our sins
and to cleanse us from all unrighteousness.
John the Apostle, 1 JOHN 1:8-9

Love the Sinner, Hate the Sin

All human sin seems so much worse
in its consequences than in its intentions.
Reinhold Niebuhr

———

I would rather die than do something which I know to be a sin,
or to be against God's will.
Joan of Arc

———

One leak will sink a ship: and one sin will destroy a sinner.
John Bunyan

———

God may forgive your sins, but your nervous system won't.
Alfred Korzybski

———

Sin is the dare of God's justice, the rape of His mercy,
the jeer of His patience, the slight of His power,
and the contempt of His love.
John Bunyan

———

Cease not a day from this work;
be killing sin or it will be killing you.
John Owen

———

O miserable man, what a deformed monster has sin made you!
God made you a little lower than the angels;
sin has made you a little better than the devils.
Joseph Alleine

**"I have found that there are three stages
in every great work of God:
first, it is impossible, then it is difficult, then it is done."**

HUDSON TAYLOR
1832 - 1905 (67 years)

**"All giants have been weak men who did great things for God
because they reckoned on His power
and His presence to be with them."**

James Hudson Taylor was a missionary to China for 51 years, and he is lauded among historians as the greatest missionary since the apostle Paul. After studying medicine in London, Taylor set off for China at the age of 22. He quickly learned the Chinese language and adapted to its culture, including the native dress, the partially shaved head and pigtails. Criticized by fellow missionaries, he correctly understood the need to adapt in order to build relationships. He returned to England to recruit new workers, and at the age of 34, he founded the China Inland Mission (now Overseas Mission Fellowship), a movement that today has 1100 staff members working in 25 countries around the world. He inspired the support of godly men such as Charles Spurgeon, Dwight L. Moody and George Muller. In later years, missionaries such as Eric Liddell and Jim Elliot would attest to his influence in their lives. Taylor said: **"We are supernatural people, born again by a supernatural birth, kept by a supernatural power, sustained on supernatural food, taught by a supernatural Teacher from a supernatural Book."**

You are from God, little children,
and have overcome them;
because greater is He who is in you
than he who is in the world.
1 JOHN 4:4

Missions

We must be global Christians with a global vision
because our God is a global God.
John Stott

———

I have seen, at different times, the smoke of a thousand villages -
villages whose people are without Christ,
without God, and without hope in the world.
Robert Moffat

———

We talk of the Second Coming,
half the world has never heard of the first.
Oswald J. Smith

———

Missions is not the ultimate goal of the Church.
Worship is. Missions exists because worship doesn't.
John Piper

———

The mark of a great church is not its seating capacity,
but its sending capacity.
Mike Stachura

———

Some wish to live within the sound of a chapel bell,
I want to run a rescue shop within a yard of Hell.
C.T. Studd

"And so the Word had breath,
and wrought with human hands the creed of creeds
In loveliness of perfect deeds."

ALFRED, LORD TENNYSON

1809 - 1892 (83 years)

"The happiness of a man in this life
does not consist in the absence of his passions
but in the mastery of his passions."

In the Oxford Dictionary of Quotations, Tennyson is second only to William Shake-speare in frequency of quotes. He is best known for his words: **"Tis better to have loved and lost, than never to have loved at all,"** and, **"Theirs is not to make reply. Theirs is not to reason why. Theirs is but to do and die."** Queen Victoria admired the work of Tennyson so much that she appointed him Poet Laureate of England following the tenure of William Wordsworth. Tennyson held this position longer than any other, until his death 42 years later. Queen Victoria also appointed him as a Baron (the title, Lord), the only writer to hold that honor. Alfred was one of 11 children and the son of a Rector who was accomplished in architecture, music and poetry. Tennyson admitted his faith was flawed. **"There lives more faith in honest doubt, believe me, than in half the creeds."** In spite of this, history seems to acknowledge his problem was with the Church - not with the God of the Church. **"Our wills are ours, we know not how; Our wills are ours, to make them Thine."** He gave us one of history's best statements about prayer: **"More things are wrought by prayer than this world dreams of."**

Behold, as for the proud one,
His soul is not right within him;
But the righteous will live by his faith.
Habakkuk the Prophet, HABAKKUK 2:4

Passion

A great leader's courage to fulfill his vision
comes from passion, not position.
John C. Maxwell

———

Nothing great in the world has been accomplished without passion.
Georg Wilhelm Friedrich Hegel

———

If passion drives you, let reason hold the reins.
Benjamin Franklin

———

Who is wise? He that learns from everyone.
Who is powerful? He that governs his passions.
Who is rich? He that is content.
Who is that? Nobody.
Benjamin Franklin

———

Man is only truly great when he acts from the passions.
Benjamin Disraeli

———

He who reigns within himself and rules passions,
desires, and fears is more than a king.
John Milton

———

"The gift of mental power comes from God, Divine Being, and if we concentrate our minds on that truth, we become in tune with this great power. My mother had taught me to seek all truth in the Bible."

NIKOLA TESLA
1856-1943 (86 years)

"Thus we are inspired both by Christianity and science to do our utmost toward increasing the performance of mankind."

Tesla may be the least known great man in history. Of Serbian heritage and Austrian citizenship, he was the inventor of the following incredible list of world changing scientific discoveries: alternating current, wireless radio, the electric motor, laser and x-ray technology, robotics, remote control and hydro-electric power. At the age of 28 he moved to America, employed by Thomas Edison to redesign his (Edison's) direct current DC motors. He and Edison parted company (and remained lifelong adversaries) because of Tesla's insistence on developing AC power instead of DC power. Edison admitted, just prior to his death, that he should have focused his energy on AC power. It was Tesla who first harnessed Niagara Falls, and in 1893 he illuminated the Chicago World's Fair for the very first time. He was a brilliant man who was tormented by Obsessive Compulsive Disorder (OCD). His hotel room number had to be divisible by 3. Three napkins always adorned the dinner table, and he would walk 3 times around a building before entering. Combined with his profound brilliance was his simple sense of wit: **"The last 29 days of the month are the hardest."**

Seeing that His divine POWER
has granted to us everything
pertaining to life and godliness,
through the true knowledge of Him
who called us by His own glory and excellence.
Peter the Apostle, 2 PETER 1:3

Scientists Proclaim Their Faith

I had the intention of becoming a theologian…
but now I see how God is, by my endeavors,
also glorified in astronomy, for "the heavens declare the glory of God."
Let my name perish if only the name
of God the Father is thereby elevated.
God is the kind Creator who brought forth nature out of nothing.
Johannes Kepler, Astronomer

———

I have fled from Christ, denied Him, crucified Him.
Let me never be separated from Him.
We keep hold of Him only by the ways taught in the Gospel.
Blaise Pascal

———

Christ's passion, His death, His resurrection and ascension,
and all of those wonderful works which He did
during His stay upon earth, confirm for mankind the belief
of His being God as well as man.
Robert Boyle

———

About the time of the end, a body of men
will be raised up who will turn their attention to the Prophecies,
and insist upon their literal interpretation,
in the midst of much clamor and opposition.
There are more sure marks of authenticity
in the Bible than in any profane history.
Isaac Newton

———

I am a believer in the fundamental doctrines of Christianity.
Sir Joseph Lister

**"The only significance of life
consists in helping to establish the Kingdom of God;
and this can be done only by means
of the acknowledgment and profession
of the truth by each one of us."**

COUNT LEO TOLSTOY
1828-1910 (82 years)

Tolstoy's novel, *War and Peace*, (containing 580 characters and 1400 pages) is generally considered to be the greatest novel ever written. Anton Chekov said of Tolstoy, "If not for him, literature would be a flock without a shepherd." Chesterton said he had "immense genius, colossal faith . . and vast knowledge of life." Tolstoy was born into Russian nobility. Later in life, he rejected his inheritance, his earnings and his copyrights - in favor of living a life of simplicity and poverty. He became known as a "Christian Anarchist," one who rejects both the Government and the Church as undeserving of authority. He said**, "Christianity, with its doctrine of humility, of forgiveness, of love - is incompatible with the State - with its haughtiness, its violence, its punishment and its wars."** He learned pacifism from the Quakers, and his book, *The Kingdom of God is Within You,* became a textbook of non-violent resistance for both Gandhi and Martin Luther King, Jr. Though he appeared to reject much of orthodox Christian doctrine, he focused on Jesus' teaching of The Sermon on the Mount. In moments of humility he said: **"The only thing that we know is that we know nothing, and that is the highest flight of human wisdom."**

He opened His mouth and began to teach them, saying,
Blessed are the poor in spirit, for theirs is the kingdom of heaven.
Blessed are those who mourn, for they shall be comforted.
Blessed are the gentle, for they shall inherit the earth.
Blessed are those who hunger and thirst
for righteousness, for they shall be satisfied.
Jesus the Messiah, MATTHEW 5:3

Truth

Whoever is careless with the truth in small matters
cannot be trusted with important matters.
Albert Einstein

———

The truth is incontrovertible,
malice may attack it, ignorance may deride it,
but in the end; there it is.
Winston Churchill

———

The first reaction to truth is hatred.
Tertullian

———

If one tells the truth,
one is sure sooner or later to be found out.
Oscar Wilde

———

The truth, of course,
is that a billion falsehoods told a billion times
by a billion people are still false.
Travis Walton

———

Truth is the property of no individual
but is the treasure of all men.
Ralph Waldo Emerson

"Not until I went into the churches of America
and heard her pulpits aflame with righteousness
did I understand the secret of her genius and power."

ALEXIS DE TOQUEVILLE
1805 - 1859 (53 years)

"Christianity is the companion of liberty
in all its conflicts, the cradle of its infancy
and the divine source of its claims."

Toqueville was a French historian and politician whose best known work was his two-volume analysis called *Democracy in America*. At the age of 25, after his training in law school, he spent 21 years as a government official of the district of Manche. During this time he traveled to England and America, observing their systems of government, and he later became France's Minister of Foreign Affairs for a brief time. During the French Revolution of 1848, he helped to write the constitution for the Second Republic, but he later resisted the new leader, Louis Napoleon, when he violated term limits in favor of an empire. His insight into capitalism and socialism remains to this day a classic work in political science. Of political history he said, **"History is a gallery of pictures in which there are few originals and many copies."** He was a political prophet who understood the potential weakness of our great democracy when he said: **"The American Republic will endure until the day Congress discovers that it can bribe the public with the public's money."** Of America he said: **"America is great because America is good. If America ceases to be good, America will cease to be great."**

Surely goodness and lovingkindness
will follow me all the days of my life,
and I will dwell in the house
of the LORD forever.
King David, PSALM 23:6

History

We learn from history
that we never learn anything from history.
Hegel

A page of history is worth a volume of logic.
O. W. Holmes

That which is past and gone is irrevocable.
Wise men have enough to do with the present and things to come.
Francis Bacon

History is not history unless it is the truth.
Abraham Lincoln

How real is history? Is it just an enormous soup
so full of disparate ingredients that it is uncharacterizable.
Thomas Cahill

When the past no longer illuminates the future,
the spirit walks in darkness.
Alexis de Tocqueville

History is filled with the sound of silken slippers
going downstairs and wooden shoes coming up.
Voltaire

"No doubt historians will conclude that we
of the twentieth century had intelligence enough
to create a great civilization,
but not the moral wisdom to preserve it."

A. W. TOZER
1897 - 1963 (66 years)

"It is delightful to worship God, but it is also
a humbling thing; and the man who has not been
humbled in the presence of God
will never be a worshiper of God at all."

Among the 40 books written by Dr. Aiden Wilson Tozer are two classics in Christian literature: *The Pursuit of God* and *The Knowledge of the Holy*. Without formal theological training, this former Pennsylvania tire salesman became a pastor at the age of 22. For the next forty-four years, this humble man of God spoke as a prophetic voice through the Christian Missionary Alliance churches that he pastored in Chicago and Toronto. He firmly believed, **"Nothing less than a whole Bible can make a whole Christian. I think a new world will arise out of the religious mists when we approach our Bible with the idea that it is not only a book which was once spoken, but a book which is now speaking."** Perhaps his favorite subject was that of worship, which he called . . . **"the missing jewel of the evangelical church; there is a point in true worship where the mind may cease to understand and goes to a kind of delightful astonishment - probably to what Carlyle described as transcendent wonder, a degree of wonder without limit and beyond expression!"** Tozer's gravestone simple reads: "A Man of God." His words encouraged us to greatness: **"Keep your feet on the ground, but let your heart soar as high as it will. Refuse to be average or to surrender to the chill of your spiritual environment."**

Who will not fear, O Lord, and glorify Your name?
For You alone are holy;
For all the nations will come
And worship before You
And Your righteous acts
Have been revealed"
REVELATION 15:4

The Speaking Voice

Exerpts from A.W. Tozer

One of the great realities with which we have to deal is
The Voice of God in this world.
The briefest and only satisfying cosmogony (world origin) is this:
"He spoke and it was done."
The why of natural law is the living Voice of God
Immanent in His creation.

This Word of God is the breath of God
filling the world with living potentiality.
The Voice of God is the most powerful force in nature,
Indeed the only force in nature.
For all energy is here only because
The power-filled word is being spoken.

In the living, breathing cosmos there is a mysterious Something,
Too wonderful, too awful for any mind to understand.
The believing man does not claim to understand
He falls to his knees and whispers, "God."
The man of earth kneels also, but not to worship.
He kneels to examine, to search, to find the cause and the how of things.

Religion has accepted the monstrous heresy
that noise, size, activity and bluster make a man dear to God.
But we may take heart.
To a people caught in the tempest of the last great conflict, God says,
"Be still and know that I am God"
And still He says it,
As if He means to tell us that our strength and safety
Lie not in noise but in silence.

The facts are that God is not silent, has never been silent.
It is the nature of God to speak.
I think a new world will arise out of the religious mists
when we approach our Bible with the idea that it is not only a book
which was once spoken,
but a book which is now speaking.

"Soul winners are not soul winners
because of what they know,
but because of Whom they know;
and how well they know Him,
and how much they long for others to know Him."

DAWSON TROTMAN
1906 - 1956 (50 years)

The July 2, 1956 issue of *Time* Magazine featured a story called The Navigator. Dawson Trotman had just died trying to rescue someone from a boating mishap. He lived the way he died - trying to rescue someone. Trotman was the founder of an organization called "The Navigators," so named because he began sharing his Christian faith with sailors, who learned from him how to share their own faith with other sailors. During World War II, it was estimated that Navigators could be found on a thousand ships at sea. Today the Navigator organization, founded in 1934, has 3600 staff members working in 101 countries around the world. Daws, as he was called, was a valedictorian and athlete in high school, but he soon drifted into a life of gambling and drunkenness. His life changed when he experienced a dramatic Christian conversion. He began memorizing Scripture and training young men to be godly leaders. Daws popularized the term "discipleship" to describe his obedience to Christ. He said: **"God works through men. I see nowhere in the Word where God picks an organization."** Evangelist Billy Graham said of him: "Dawson loved the Word of God. I think more than anybody else, he taught me to love it."

The things which you have heard from me
in the presence of many witnesses,
entrust these to faithful men
who will be able to teach others also.
Paul the Apostle, 2 TIMOTHY 2:2

Influence

I love you not because of who you are,
but because of who I am when I am with you.
Roy Croft

———

You don't have to be a "person of influence" to be influential.
In fact, the most influential people in my life
are probably not even aware of the things they've taught me.
Scott Adams

———

Be not angry that you cannot make others
as you wish them to be,
since you cannot make yourself as you wish to be.
Thomas Kempis

———

For the great majority of mankind are satisfied with appearance,
and are often more influenced by the things that seem
than by those that are.
Niccolo Machiavelli

———

Because everything we say and do
is the length and shadow of our own souls,
our influence is determined by the quality of our being.
Dale E. Turner

———

"It is by the goodness of God that in our country
we have those three unspeakably precious things:
freedom of speech, freedom of conscience,
and the prudence never to practice either of them."

MARK TWAIN
1835 - 1910 (74 years)

"It ain't those parts of the Bible that I can't understand
that bother me, it is the parts that I do understand."

Samuel Langhorne Clemens has been called "the father of American literature" and his keen wit and humor made him one of the most quoted men in American history. Growing up on the Mississippi he was a riverboat captain for two years. His pen name, Mark Twain, came from the practice of calling out the boat's water depth when it reached two fathoms, or twelve feet. Twain was born two weeks after Halley's comet made its 75-year visit close to planet earth's surface, and he died the same year that Halley returned to earth, 74 years later. He referred to himself and Halley as **"two freaks of nature."** He worked as a newspaper journalist, and later became an author, speaker and world traveler. He loved science, and holds a patent on three inventions, though he lost millions on an invention that was shadowed by the linotype printer. Twain was very critical of organized religion, as evidenced by his statement: **"If Christ were here now there is one thing He would not be - a Christian."** Nevertheless, he confessed his own humility when he said: **"The human race is a race of cowards; and I am not only marching in that procession but carrying a banner."**

If anyone thinks himself to be religious,
and yet does not bridle his tongue,
but deceives his own heart,
this man's religion is worthless.
James, Brother of Jesus, JAMES 1:26

The Goodness of God

Goodness is the only investment that never fails.
Henry David Thoreau

———

The ideals which have always shone before me and filled me
with the joy of living are goodness, beauty, and truth.
Albert Einstein

———

Seek goodness everywhere, and when it is found,
bring it out of its hiding place and let it be free and unashamed.
William Saroyan

———

Surely goodness and mercy shall follow me all the days of my life:
and I will dwell in the house of the LORD forever.
Psalm 23:6

———

Of all virtues and dignities of the mind, goodness is the greatest,
being the character of the Deity; and without it,
man is a busy, mischievous, wretched thing.
Francis Bacon

———

"Joyful, joyful, we adore Thee, God of glory,
Lord of love; Hearts unfold like flowers before Thee,
opening to the sun above. Melt the clouds of sin
and sadness; drive the dark of doubt away;
Giver of immortal gladness, fill us with the light of day!"

HENRY VAN DYKE
1852 - 1933 (81 years)

"The Bible teaches that God owns the world.
He distributes to every man according to His own good pleasure."

He was a professor of English Literature at Princeton University for 24 years, and in 1913, President Wilson appointed him to be the Minister to the Netherlands. After teaching at the University of Paris, on his return to America, he penned the now famous poem, *AMERICA FOR ME:* "So it's home again, and home again, America for me! My heart is turning home again and there I long to be, In the land of youth and freedom, beyond the ocean bars, Where the air is full of sunlight and the flag is full of stars." Van Dyke loved Christmas, and he wrote the well known story, *THE OTHER WISE MAN,* as well as the beloved Christmas song, *JOYFUL, JOYFUL,* which is set to the music of Beethoven's *ODE TO JOY.* Regarding Christmas he said: "The blessed life which began in Bethlehem two thousand years ago is the image and brightness of Eternal love." His simple philosophy: "To think without confusion clearly, To love my fellow men sincerely, To act from honest motives purely, To trust in God and heaven securely."

He has shown you, O man, what *is* good;
and what the LORD requires of you,
but to do justly, and to love mercy, and to walk humbly with thy God?
Micah the Prophet, MICAH 6:8

America For Me

'Tis fine to see the Old World, and travel up and down
Among the famous palaces and cities of renown,
To admire the crumbly castles and the statues of the kings,
But now I think I've had enough of antiquated things.
So it's home again, and home again, America for me!
My heart is turning home again, and there I long to be,
In the land of youth and freedom beyond the ocean bars,
Where the air is full of sunlight and the flag is full of stars!

Oh, London is a man's town, there's power in the air;
And Paris is a woman's town, with flowers in her hair;
And it's sweet to dream in Venice, and it's great to study Rome;
But when it comes to living, there is no place like home.
I like the German fir-woods, in green battalions drilled;
I like the gardens of Versailles with flashing fountains filled;
But, oh, to take your hand, my dear, and ramble for a day
In the friendly western woodland where Nature has her way!

I know that Europe's wonderful, yet something seems to lack:
The Past is too much with her, and the people looking back.
But the glory of the Present is to make the Future free,—
We love our land for what she is and what she is to be.
Oh, it's home again, and home again, America for me!
I want a ship that's westward bound to plough the rolling sea,
To the blessed land of room enough beyond the ocean bars,
Where the air is full of sunlight and the flag is full of stars.

HENRY VAN DYKE

"Scripture was written for us all,
and scholars have no corner on its truth.
Those who sincerely and diligently
seek God's truth can find it."

ROBERT VAN KAMPEN
1938 - 1999 (60 years)

As a young Chicago stock broker, Van Kampen became known as "the Charger." At the age of 36 he founded the investment banking firm known as Van Kampen Merrit. Within 9 years, the company sold seven billion dollars worth of bond funds to become the 3rd largest company of its kind in the country. Xerox Corporation purchased the company for approximately 200 million dollars, and Van Kampen shifted his investment strategy into eternal things. He began to purchase what is now one of the largest collections of rare scrolls and Bibles in the world, housed in the Scriptorium at the Holy Land Experience in Orlando, Florida. For the next 14 years he dedicated himself to the authorship and defense of a 500 page scholarly work, *The Sign*, which challenged the timing of the popular evangelical theology known as "pretribulation rapture." Van Kampen single handedly shook the theological world by introducing the endtime concept known as "the pre-wrath rapture." Van Kampen's book challenges the reader to revisit Jesus' Olivet Discourse in Matthew 24 for new insight into the book of Revelation. He boldly claims: **"Scripture teaches that the Church of the last days will, in general, be a compromised, confused church, and much of its affliction will come because of improper teaching about the Second Coming of Christ."**

At that time Jesus said,
"I praise You, Father,
Lord of heaven and earth,
that You have hidden these things
from the wise and intelligent
and have revealed them to infants.
MATTHEW 11:25

The Mystery of God

Men go abroad to wonder at the heights of mountains,
at the huge waves of the sea, at the long courses of the rivers,
at the vast compass of the ocean, at the circular motions of the stars,
and they pass by themselves without wondering.
Augustine

———

I claim credit for nothing. Everything is determined,
the beginning as well as the end,
by forces over which we have no control.
It is determined for the insect as well as for the star.
Human beings, vegetables, or cosmic dust, we all dance
to a mysterious tune, intoned in the distance by an invisible piper.
Albert Einstein

———

I would rather live in a world where my life
is surrounded by mystery than live in a world so small
that my mind could comprehend it.
Harry Emerson Fosdick

———

There is nothing in history
like the union of contrasts that confronts us in the Gospels.
The mystery of Jesus is the mystery of Divine personality.
James Stewart

"In this age of space flight,
when we use the modern tools of science
to advance into new regions of human activity,
the Bible, this grandiose, stirring history of the gradual
revelation and unfolding of the moral law,
remains in every way an up-to-date book."

WERNHER VON BRAUN
1912-1977 (65 years)

In the words of NASA, he is, "without doubt, the greatest rocket scientist in history." His crowning achievement was to lead the development of the Saturn V booster rocket that helped land the first men on the Moon in July 1969. Von Braun received a Ph.D. in aerospace physics from the University of Berlin, and he was coerced into the Nazi Party during World War II. His desire was to send rockets to other planets, but under Hitler's authority, he launched a V-2 rocket at England in 1944. With regrets for his participation, he said: **"The rocket worked perfectly except for landing on the wrong planet."** He was briefly imprisoned by the Gestapo for expressing his doubts about the legitimacy of the war. After the war, he became a U.S. citizen and was gradually given authority to become the first director of the Marshall Space Flight Center in Huntsville, Alabama. He combined humility and humor when he said: **"Research is what I'm doing when I don't know what I'm doing."** He feared that rockets would once again become a threat to mankind: **"The guidelines of what we ought to do are furnished in the moral law of God."** He quoted Lincoln as he said: **"It is no longer enough that we pray that God may be on our side. We must learn again to pray that we may be on God's side."**

When I consider Your heavens,
the work of Your fingers,
The moon and the stars,
which You have ordained;
What is man that You take thought of him,
And the son of man that You care for him?
King David, PSALM 8:3-4

Science and the Bible

Speculations? I have none. I am resting on certainties.
A Christian commits the keeping of his soul into the hands of God.
Michael Faraday

———

It is evident that an acquaintance with natural laws
means no less than an acquaintance with the mind of God.
Order is manifestly maintained in the universe
and governed by the sovereign will of God.
After the knowledge of, and obedience to, the will of God,
the next aim must be to know something
of His attributes of wisdom, power, and goodness,
as evidenced by His handiwork.
James Prescott Joule

———

Christ's passion, His death, His resurrection and ascension . . .
confirm for mankind His being God as well as man.
Robert Boyle

———

Almighty God, teach us to study the works of Thy hands,
that we may subdue the earth for our use, and for Your service.
James Clerk Maxwell

———

Without Him, I understand nothing; without Him, all is darkness.
I regard atheism as a mania. It is the malady of the age.
You could take my skin from me more easily than my faith in God.
Jean Henri Fabre

"Let mental culture go on advancing, let the natural sciences progress in even greater extent and depth, and the human mind widen itself as much as it desires: beyond the elevation and moral culture of Christianity, as it shines forth in the Gospels, it will not go."

JOHANN WOLFGANG VON GOETHE
1749-1832 (82 years)

"A man should hear a little music, read a little poetry, and see a fine picture every day of his life, in order that worldly cares may not obliterate the sense of the beautiful which God has implanted in the human soul."

Goethe (pronounced Guh Tuh) was considered to be the greatest of German writers, and ranks among those called a "polymath", a genius who excelled in the fields of literature, drama, art, poetry, philosophy, law, theology and science. The "von" was added to his name at the age of 33, when the Duke raised his status to a Noble. His "magnum opus" (greatest work) was called *Faust*, the story of a young man who bargained his soul with a demon (named Mephistopheles) for a life of pleasure on earth. Though Goethe's personal life was morally loose, and his personal religion did not follow the orthodox Christian faith, nevertheless, his writings acknowledged the sovereignty of God, and the struggles we all face between good and evil. He reflected this struggle when he said: **"I laugh at my heart, yet I do its will."** He spoke much about the heart of man, and he understood the passion and influence of the heart when he said: **"What is uttered from the heart alone, will win the heart of others to your own."**

"But you said in your heart, 'I will ascend to heaven;
I will raise my throne above the stars of God,
And I will sit on the mount of assembly
In the recesses of the north.
I will ascend above the heights of the clouds;
I will make myself like the Most High.' "
ISAIAH 14:13-14

The Human Heart

One of the hardest things in life
is having words in your heart that you can't utter.
James Earl Jones

———

I would rather have eyes that cannot see;
ears that cannot hear; lips that cannot speak,
than a heart that cannot love.
Robert Tizon

———

The heart is the only broken instrument that works.
The heart has reasons that reason cannot know.
Blaise Pascal

———

In prayer it is better to have a heart without words
than words without a heart.
John Bunyan

———

Educating the mind without educating the heart
is no education at all.
Aristotle

———

In love, somehow, a man's heart
is always either exceeding the speed limit,
or getting parked in the wrong place.
Helen Rowland

———

"I have but one passion: It is He, it is He alone.
The world is the field and the field is the world;
and henceforth that country shall be my home
where I can be most used
in winning souls for Christ."

NIKOLAUS LUDWIG Von ZINZENDORF
1700-1760 (59 years)

Count von Zinzendorf was a Nobleman of German and Austrian heritage, trained as a lawyer, and groomed as an imperial diplomat. Though his family were Lutherans (at that time, a state supported church), he was influenced by the Pietist movement which resisted denominational identity, and emphasized biblical authority and personal purity. A group from neighboring Morava (called the Moravian Brethren) asked permission to live on his land, and they established a bond with him which motivated Zinzendorf to give up any ambition as a German statesman. Instead, he spent his life organizing groups of Christians into Moravian communities. He began to send out missionaries into regions as far away as Greenland to South Africa. Eventually, he traveled to America. On Christmas day, 1741, he and a small band of believers founded the city of Bethlehem, Pennsylvania, and for a hundred years, only Moravians were allowed to live there. The Moravians were an industrious, innovative people, and Bethlehem had the distinction of being the first city in the U.S. to have a public water system. It also was the home of Bethlehem Steel, which produced the first wide flange steel "I" beams. Zinzendorf sacrificed his personal fame and fortune to spread the gospel. In so doing, he began the Protestant world mission movement.

He said to them, "But who do you say that I am?"
Simon Peter answered, "You are the Christ,
the Son of the living God." And Jesus said to him,
"Blessed are you, Simon Barjona,
because flesh and blood did not reveal this to you,
but My Father who is in heaven.
MATTHEW 16:15-17

Christ

Christ is the great central fact in life.
All the lines of history converge upon Him.
All the great purposes of God culminate in Him.
Charles H. Spurgeon

The ground of our hope is Christ in the world,
But the evidence of our hope is Christ in the heart.
Matthew Henry

The hinge of history is on the door of a Bethlehem stable.
Ralph W. Sockman

He became what we are
in order that He might make us what He is.
Athanasius

To see His star is good,
But to see His face is better.
Dwight L. Moody

I came to Christ as a country boy.
I did not understand all about the plan of salvation.
One does not have to understand it; one has only to stand on it.
I do not understand all about electricity,
But I do not intend to sit around in the dark till I do.
One thing I did understand, even as a lad.
I understood that I was under new management.
I belonged to Christ and He was Lord.
Vance Havner

"I cannot too greatly emphasize the importance and value of Bible study - more important than ever before in these days of uncertainties, when men and women are apt to decide questions from the standpoint of expediency rather than on the eternal principles laid down by God Himself."

JOHN WANAMAKER
1838 - 1922 (84 years)

Wanamaker was the U.S. Postmaster General in 1889, and he is generally known today as the "Father of Modern Advertising." At the age of 23, he opened the first department store in Philadelphia, and later moved to the corner of 13th and Market Street across from City Hall. His now famous 12-story Wanamaker Building displays a 2500 pound bronze eagle in the Grand Court. Wanamaker began the First Penny Savings Bank in Philadelphia in order to encourage financial responsibility. It must have worked for him. At his death in 1922, he was worth an estimated 100 million dollars, valued 90 years later at approximately 1.2 billion dollars. He was a generous man who gave his employees free medical care, education, recreational facilities, pensions and profit-sharing plans long before such plans became standards in American business. A bust of Wanamaker stands next to the Chicago River, among six other industrial giants who contributed to America's vibrant free enterprise system. Thomas Edison was a pall bearer at his funeral. Regarding his strategies in advertising, he said: **"Half the money I spend on advertising is wasted; the trouble is, I don't know which half."**

If I give all my possessions to feed the poor,
and if I surrender my body to be burned,
but do not have love,
it profits me nothing.
1CORINTHIANS 13:3

Generosity

Do all the good you can,
By all the means you can,
In all the ways you can,
In all the places you can,
At all the times you can,
To all the people you can,
As long as ever you can.
John Wesley

———

What we have done for ourselves alone dies with us;
what we have done for others and the world
remains, and is immortal.
Albert Pike

———

Many men have been capable of doing a wise thing,
more a cunning thing, but very few a generous thing.
Alexander Pope

———

I can remember way back when a liberal
was generous with his own money.
Will Rogers

———

We make a living by what we get,
but we make a life by what we give.
Winston Churchill

———

The value of a man resides in what he gives
and not in what he is capable of receiving.
Albert Einstein

"While we are contending for our own liberty,
we should be very cautious not to violate
the rights of conscience in others,
ever considering that God alone
is the judge of the hearts of men,
and to Him only . . . they are answerable."

GEORGE WASHINGTON
1732-1799 (67 years)

"It is impossible to rightly govern a nation
without God and the Bible."

At the age of 42, George Washington was appointed Commander of the Continental Army during the Revolutionary War. He was elected the first President of the U.S. fourteen years later. As a framer of the Constitution, he believed in a strong government, but not an imposing government, as he said**: "Government is not reason; it is not eloquent; it is force. Like fire, it is a dangerous servant and a fearful master."** He was highly respected as a man of integrity who said: **"I hope I shall always possess firmness and virtue enough to maintain what I consider the most enviable of all titles, the character of an honest man."** Gladstone said of him, "He is the purest figure in history." Napoleon ordered ten days of mourning throughout France at his death. He died prematurely, most likely from the combined treatment of bloodletting (5 pints), and a treatment called "calomel," now known to be a form of mercury chloride poisoning. He was a true public servant who encouraged those around him: **"Labor to keep alive in your breast that little spark of celestial fire, called conscience."**

For whatever is born of God
overcomes the world;
and this is the victory
that has overcome the world - our faith.
1 JOHN 5:4

Words of Washington

The propitious smiles of Heaven can never be expected
on a nation that disregards the eternal rules
of order and right which Heaven itself has ordained.

———

The foolish and wicked practice of profane cursing and swearing
is a vice so mean and low that every person
of sense and character detests and despises it.

———

Without a humble imitation of the characteristics
of the Divine Author of our blessed religion,
we can never hope to be a happy nation.

———

Reason and experience both forbid us to expect that national morality
can prevail in exclusion of religious principle.

———

Almighty God, we make our earnest prayer
that You will keep the United States in Your holy protection;
that You will incline the hearts of the citizens
to cultivate a spirit of subordination and obedience to government.

———

Providence has at all times been my only dependence,
for all other resources seem to have failed us.

———

**"All that is best in the civilization of today
is the fruit of Christ's appearance among men."**

DANIEL WEBSTER
1782-1852 (70 years)

**"A solemn regard for spiritual and eternal things
is an indispensable element of all true greatness."**

Webster was a lawyer, Senator and U.S. Secretary of State (twice) in the days leading up to the Civil War. In 1957, he was acknowledged by the U.S. Senate as "one of the five most outstanding members in Senate history." Daniel Webster ran for, and lost, the Presidency on 3 separate occasions. Oddly enough, he was asked to be the Vice Presidential nominee by two men (William Henry Harrison and Zachary Taylor) who both died in their first 16 months of office. Ralph Waldo Emerson said of Webster, "Nature had not, in our days or since Napoleon, cut out such a master-piece." It is noteworthy to comment that the Webster's Dictionary was compiled by Noah Webster, of no apparent relation. Daniel Webster's claim to fame was his outstanding oratorical skills. He understood the impact of verbal influence, and he used it powerfully and diplomatically to hold off the polarizing ferment that eventually became the War Between the States. Needless to say, we need more statesmen today whose philosophy reflects his sobering words: **"The most important thought that ever occupied my mind is that of my individual responsibility to God."**

By common confession, great is the mystery of godliness.
He who was revealed in the flesh,
was vindicated in the Spirit, seen by angels,
proclaimed among the nations,
believed on in the world, taken up in glory.
Paul the Apostle, 1 TIMOTHY 3:16

Responsibility

Let everyone sweep in front of his own door,
and the whole world will be clean.
Johann Wolfgang von Goethe

———

Responsibility is the price of greatness.
Winston Churchill

———

If you want children to keep their feet on the ground,
put some responsibility on their shoulders.
Abigail Van Buren

———

When government accepts responsibility for people,
then people no longer take responsibility for themselves.
George Pataki

———

In times like these men should utter nothing
for which they would not be willingly responsible
through time and in eternity.
Abraham Lincoln

———

We're in a fight for our principles
and our first responsibility is to live by them.
George W. Bush

———

Responsibility is a tremendous engine in a free government.
Thomas Jefferson

"The doctrine of the Kingdom of Heaven,
which was the main teaching of Jesus,
is certainly one of the most revolutionary doctrines
that ever stirred and changed human thought."

H.G. WELLS
1866-1946 (79 years)

"We must not allow the clock and the calendar
to blind us to the fact that each moment of life
is a miracle and mystery."

Herbert George Wells is an English author perhaps best known for his science fiction writings *The War of the Worlds, The Invisible Man* and *The Time Machine.* Also prominent among his writings is the two-volume work, *The Outline of History.* The *War of the Worlds* became especially famous in 1938 when actor Orson Welles performed a radio broadcast of the story, personifying it as a real invasion from Mars. For a brief time, there was panic across the nation. Wells was a utopian, one who championed the ideas of a social and political society that decentralized powers and balanced freedom and authority. He was on a list of influential men targeted by the Nazis to be killed when Hitler took over England. He said that **"History is a race between education and catastrophe."** In his book, *God the Invisible King*, he portrays God as a **"personal and intimate God,"** though he broadly rejects all world religions because of their inability to measure up to their own standards. His conclusion: **"The world has a greater purpose than happiness; our lives are to serve God's purpose, and that purpose aims not at man as an end, but works through him to greater issues."**

Make my joy complete
by being of the same mind,
maintaining the same love,
united in spirit,
intent on one purpose.
PHILIPPIANS 2:2

Purpose

A ship is safe in harbor, but that's not what ships are for.
William Shedd

———

I am here for a purpose and that purpose is to grow into a mountain,
not to shrink to a grain of sand. Henceforth will I apply ALL my efforts
to become the highest mountain of all,
and I will strain my potential until it cries for mercy.
Og Mandino

———

Our minds are finite, and yet even in these circumstances of finitude
we are surrounded by possibilities that are infinite,
and the purpose of life is to grasp
as much as we can out of that infinitude.
Alfred North Whitehead

———

I believe in human dignity as the source of national purpose,
human liberty as the source of national action,
the human heart as the source of national compassion,
and in the human mind as the source of our invention and our ideas.
John Fitzgerald Kennedy

———

Life without a purpose is a languid, drifting thing;
every day we ought to review our purpose, saying to ourselves,
'This day let me make a sound beginning,
for what I have done thus far is nothing!'
Thomas a Kempis

"God in Scripture commands me, according to my power,
to instruct the ignorant, reform the wicked,
and confirm the virtuous."

JOHN WESLEY
1703 - 1791 (87 years)

"Catch on fire with enthusiasm and people will come
for miles to watch you burn."

John Wesley was the fifteenth of 19 children born to Samuel Wesley, the pastor of an Anglican church in Epworth, England. At the age of 5, John was barely rescued when his home was destroyed in a fire. He became known as a "brand plucked from the burning" (Zechariah 3:2), a term which later characterized his spiritual life. Following his father in ministry, he earned a master's degree from Oxford, and he was ordained a priest in the Church of England. The influence of Moravians altered his view of personal salvation as he said: **"The Church recruited people who had been starched and ironed before they were washed."** His friend George Whitefield altered his view of preaching, and he began to assemble laymen to preach to crowds in the open air. He traveled on horseback 250,000 miles, from town to town, believing **"the whole world is my parish."** Though he remained an Anglican all his life, his lasting legacy was the formation of the Protestant denomination known today as the Methodist Church. Wesley is listed as number 50 on the BBC's list of the 100 Greatest Britons.

And he was preaching, and saying,
"After me One is coming
who is mightier than I,
and I am not fit to stoop down
and untie the thong of His sandals."
John the Baptist, MARK 1:7

Goodness

It is only from the belief of the goodness and wisdom
of a Supreme Being, that our calamities can be borne
in the manner which becomes a man.
Henry MacKenzie

It is a grand mistake to think of being great without goodness,
and I pronounce it as certain that there was never
a truly great man that was not at the same time truly virtuous.
Benjamin Franklin

Wisdom has its root in goodness,
not goodness its root in wisdom.
Ralph Waldo Emerson

Above all, it is not decency or goodness of gentleness
that impresses the Middle East, but strength.
Meir Kahane

Oh that men would praise the LORD for his goodness,
and for His wonderful works to the children of men!
Psalm 107:8, 15, 21, 31

Goodness and hard work are rewarded with respect.
Luther Campbell

"The worship of God is not a rule of safety -
it is an adventure of the Spirit,
a flight after the unattainable."

ALFRED NORTH WHITEHEAD
1861-1947 (86 years)

"God is the poet of the world,
With tender patience leading it by His vision,
Of truth, beauty and goodness."

Whitehead was a professor of Mathematics at Cambridge University for 30 years, and is perhaps best known for challenging Einstein's Theory of Relativity in a losing battle. He co-authored (with Bertrand Russell), a three-volume work on the logic of Math, entitled *Principia Mathematica*. Random House publishers considers this book to be 23rd in a list of the 100 most important non-fiction books of the twentieth century. Most of us cannot begin to imagine three volumes on the foundation of mathematics! From Cambridge, he broadened his scope of teaching for 16 years to include physics and education at the University of London. On the subject of education he said: **"In all education the main cause of failure is staleness. . . Scraps of information have nothing to do with it."** At age 63, he became a professor of philosophy at Harvard and further developed a metaphysical concept called "process theology." Like many philosophers, his quest for truth was clouded with deep ramblings, but he understood the heart's desire to commune with God when he said: **"Religion is the reaction of human nature to its search for God. Religion is what the individual does with his own solitariness."**

Pure and undefiled religion
in the sight of our God and Father is this:
to visit orphans and widows in their distress,
and to keep oneself unstained by the world.
JAMES 1:27

Worship

Worship is the submission of all of our nature to God.
It is the quickening of conscience by His holiness,
the nourishment of mind by His truth,
the purifying of imagination by His beauty,
the opening of the heart to His love,
and the submission of will to His purpose.
And all of this gathered up in adoration
is the greatest expression of which we are capable.
William Temple

Men are idolaters, and want something to look at and kiss and hug,
or throw themselves down before;
they always did, they always will;
and if you don't make it of wood,
you must make it of words.
Oliver Wendell Holmes

When this age is over, and the countless millions
of the redeemed fall on their faces before the throne of God,
missions will be no more. It is a temporary necessity.
But worship abides forever.
John Piper

I have in my heart a small, shy plant called reverence,
that I cultivate every week by worshiping with the people of God.
Oliver Wendell Holmes

To gather with God's people in united adoration of the Father
is as necessary to the Christian life as prayer.
Martin Luther

**"The central purpose of Christ's life. . .
is to destroy the life of loneliness
and to establish here on earth the life of love."**

THOMAS WOLFE
1900 - 1938 (37 years)

**"The only real possession you'll ever have
is your own character."**

Thomas Wolfe, the American author, was a contemporary of great award-winning writers such as Hemingway, Faulkner and F. Scott Fitzgerald. Faulkner praised Wolfe above himself, saying, "he was the best author of his generation." Wolfe grew up in Asheville, North Carolina, graduated from UNC, and then earned a master's degree at Harvard. His best known work, *Look Homeward Angel*, was a veiled auto-biographical work based on a phrase from author John Milton, and an angel statue standing in the neighboring town of Hendersonville, NC. Another of his popular novels, *You Can't Go Home Again*, was written as early 20th century Americana literature, describing the life and times of a Depression-born struggler in small town America. One of Wolfe's recurring themes was loneliness: **"The whole conviction of my life now rests upon the belief that loneliness, far from being a rare and curious phenomenon, peculiar to myself and to a few other solitary men, is the central and inevitable fact of human existence."** He died of miliary tuberculosis, so called because a legion of bacteria, like little tiny millet seeds, attack the organs. In his final moments he wrote, **"Death the last voyage, the longest, and the best."**

Therefore, prepare your minds for action,
keep sober in spirit,
fix your hope completely
on the grace to be brought to you
at the revelation of Jesus Christ.
Peter the Apostle, 1 PETER 1:13

Adversity

All the adversity I've had in my life, all my troubles and obstacles,
have strengthened me. You may not realize it when it happens,
but a kick in the teeth may be the best thing in the world for you.
Walt Disney

When everything seems to be going against you,
remember that the airplane takes off against the wind, not with it.
Henry Ford

There is no education like adversity.
Benjamin Disraeli

In times of great stress or adversity,
it's always best to keep busy,
to plow your anger and your energy into something positive.
Lee Iacocca

By trying, we can easily learn
to endure adversity - another man's, I mean.
Mark Twain

"Character and success, two things contradictory
as they may seem, must go together. . .
humble dependence on God
and manly reliance on self."

WILLIAM WORDSWORTH
1770 - 1850 (80 years)

"The love of God is passionate.
He pursues each of us even when we know it not."

Queen Victoria of England conferred to Wordsworth the title Poet Laureate of England from 1843 until his death in 1850. The term "laureate" dates back to ancient Greece, where honor was bestowed by placing a crown of laurel leaves on the recipient. Today we use the term baccalaureate to describe the honor of receiving a bachelor's degree. Wordsworth seemed to have two recurring themes throughout his poems: nature and the immortal soul. He lamented: **"The world is too much with us; late and soon, getting and spending, we lay waste our powers: Little we see in Nature that is ours."** He understood the power of poetry when he said: **"The poet binds together by passion and knowledge the vast empire of human society."** In his 200-line verse called "Intimations of Immortality" he said: **"Though inland far we be, our souls have sight of that immortal sea, which brought us here, and can, in a moment, take us away. And see the children sport upon the shore, and hear the mighty waters rolling evermore."**

Beloved, I pray that in all respects
you may prosper and be in good health,
just as your soul prospers.
3 JOHN 1:2

Immortality

Life is the childhood of our immortality.
Johann Wolfgang von Goethe

———

Surely God would not have created such a being as man,
with an ability to grasp the infinite, to exist only for a day!
No, no, man was made for immortality.
Abraham Lincoln

———

What a man does for others, not what they do for him,
gives him immortality.
Daniel Webster

———

Our Creator would never have made such lovely days,
and have given us the deep hearts to enjoy them,
above and beyond all thought,
unless we were meant to be immortal.
Nathaniel Hawthorne

———

The immortality of the soul is a matter which is
of so great consequence to us and which touches us so profoundly
that we must have lost all feeling to be indifferent about it.
Blaise Pascal

———

Millions long for immortality who do not know
what to do with themselves on a rainy Sunday afternoon.
Susan Ertz

**"It was character that got us out of bed,
commitment that moved us into action,
and discipline that enabled us to follow through."**

Zig Ziglar
1926-

**"Success is not measured by what you do
compared to what others do, it is measured
by what you do with the ability God gave you."**

His birth certificate said Hilary Hinton Ziglar, but everyone just called him Zig. For 35 years he has been America's favorite motivational speaker, telling stories about growing up in Yazoo City Mississippi that always inspired you to work harder, sell smarter, earn more, learn more and generally just live better. Perhaps his trade-mark challenge was: **"You can have everything in life you want, if you will just help enough other people get what they want."** He served in the Navy during World War II, afterwards going on the road selling pots and pans to make a living. Customers did-n't know how to say 'no' to this super salesman. **"I am a real optimist. I would go after Moby Dick in a row boat and take the tarter sauce with me."** He worked for numerous direct sales companies, eventually rising to become a top earner in a sales force of 7000. Standing before tens of thousands of people in the Positive Thinking Rallies of the '70s and 80s, he would explain, **"You do not pay the price of success, you ENJOY the price of success. Your attitude, not your aptitude, will determine your altitude."** But Zig would quickly tell you that all his enthusiasm and motivation comes from his faith in Christ. **"If a man can take moldy bread and make penicillin, imagine what God can do with you. I win, not because of my own efforts or goodness, but through the grace of Je-sus Christ."** He closes out his meetings by saying, **"And I'll see you at the top!"**

And God is able to make all grace abound to you,
so that always having all sufficiency in everything,
you may have an abundance for every good deed;
Paul the Apostle, 2 CORINTHIANS 9:8

Encouragement

Encouragement is the oxygen of the soul.
Zig Ziglar

———

Flatter me, and I may not believe you. Criticize me, and I may not like you.
Ignore me, and I may not forgive you. Encourage me, and I will not forget you.
William Arthur Ward

———

Only as high as I reach can I grow, only as far as I seek can I go,
only as deep as I look can I see, only as much as I dream can I be.
Karen Ravn

———

Correction does much, but encouragement does more.
Johann Wolfgang von Goethe

———

Remember, man does not live on bread alone:
sometimes he needs a little buttering up.
John C. Maxwell

———

Taking an interest in what others are thinking and doing
is often a much more powerful form of encouragement than praise.
Robert Martin

———

At times our own light goes out and is rekindled
by a spark from another person.
Albert Schweitzer

———

What You Believe

and

How You Pray

Seven Words of Transformation

What You Believe and How You Pray

On the following pages you will find two chapters that have the potential for dramatically changing the way you relate to God and to the world around you. The first chapter, entitled "**Backbone of the Believer**", is a list of the seven primary doctrinal beliefs within orthodox Christianity. When properly understood, they provide the framework for a theology that rightly defines your relationship to the God of the universe. It is my position that these are the non-negotiable, essential elements - the "backbone" of truth. To be orthodox means that you adhere to a standard that is not based on culture, or generation, or politics. The orthodox truth rises above the fog of man-made ideology to reveal a clear, eternal reality. The orthodox Christian faith is offensive to the world because it is exclusive. It presumes that we have been introduced to a truth that transcends the temporal world and its fallenness. When you embrace an exclusive truth, the world around you will call you arrogant. It should be pointed out that most religions consider themselves exclusive. Judaism through the ages faithfully holds to the belief in one God, and Jesus is not their Messiah. Islam vehemently believes that all who are not Muslim are insolent unbelievers who should be subservient to their rigid ideology. Christianity believes that Jesus is "the way, the truth and the life."

The next chapter is entitled **"Reporting for Duty."** It is an outline model from Genesis 1:28 to help you order your prayer. Evangelical Christians claim that ours is not so much a religion as it is a relationship with God through Christ. The implication of this statement is that church for most folks is merely a religion, but prayer is the true key to a relationship with God. For this reason, we need all the help we can get with the systematic (or spontaneous) nature of how we approach our Father God in private, intimate communication. This prayer model provides a subconscious background for you to work through as you commune with the Lord. My former prayer life was static and lifeless before I began to employ this simple prayer outline. I now look forward to my times of praise, intercession and dialogue, and every day I vary the outline in such a way as to exercise a creative interchange with my Creator God.

Backbone
of the Believer

Seven Basic Doctrines
of the Christian Faith

"What You Believe and How You Pray"

Backbone of the Believer

Every religious faith has dozens, if not hundreds, of beliefs that comprise the sum total of a position called "orthodox". By definition, ortho-dox means "straight thinking" , or perhaps "rigid beliefs." To be orthodox means to adhere with conviction to a prescribed definable position based on a common list of beliefs. This list of beliefs is often called creeds, confessions or doctrines. Within the Christian faith, each denomination has its own interpretation of the definable orthodox position. The Mennonite Confession dating back to 1527, has now been updated to 24 articles. The Westminster Confession of 1646 has 28 articles, and the Baptist Confession of Faith in 1689 had 32 points of doctrine. Each of these confessions, to name only a few, have been crafted by godly men over hundreds of years to disseminate a systematic view of faith and practice.

With highest of respect for the exhaustive nature of denominational creeds, it is my contention in this book that the following seven doctrinal positions are one of the clearest and simplest ways to communicate the Christian faith. It is not exhaustive, but it is comprehensive in addressing the major themes of God's redemptive history. It is my position that each of the great men in this book have professed to at least ONE of these seven doctrines. I also believe that any and all of the exhaustive points of the historic doctrines of faith will fit neatly into the framework of this "very simplified approach." The reason for a simplified approach is that most people cannot tell you much about what they believe. My hope is that this seven point outline can be memorized and used to defend the faith and strengthen the believer.

The following is my approach to memorizing the order of these seven great truths. Studying the **Sovereignty of God** teaches us about the **Deity of Christ**, which teaches us about the **Authority of Scripture**, which teaches us about the **Reality of Sin**, which teaches us about the **Necessity of Salvation**, which teaches us about the **Ministry of the Spirit**, which finally teaches us about the **Destiny of Man.**

1. The <u>Sovereignty</u> of God

I believe that Jehovah God created and sustains the vast universe, from the largest galaxy to the smallest cell.

2. The <u>Deity</u> of Christ

I believe that Jesus is God's son, whose death, burial and resurrection have redeemed mankind from sin and death.

3. The <u>Authority</u> of Scripture

I believe the Bible to be the inspired Word of God, the singular document of divine revelation, truth without error.

4. The <u>Reality</u> of Sin

I believe that sin is a curse upon all creation and is a result of man's fall from Grace and the work of Satan.

5. The <u>Necessity</u> of Salvation

I believe that salvation is an act of God's elective grace, activated by the willful, faithful confession of a humble man.

6. The <u>Ministry</u> of the Spirit

I believe that God's eternal Spirit indwells and empowers those who receive Christ as their personal Lord.

7. The <u>Destiny</u> of Man

I believe that mankind awaits the return of Christ, to spend eternity in the destination of either Heaven or Hell.

The Sovereignty of God

Man has chosen to define "sovereignty" as the absolute and independent authority over a certain domain. Encyclopedias go to great length to describe the sovereignty of nations and the sovereignty of individuals, but they say nothing about the absolute dominion that God has over the entire universe. The attributes of God are infinite, and the sovereignty of God is the umbrella term that we use to understand His greatness. We use the term "anthropomorphic" to describe man-like features and qualities that we assign to God. But in our own finite limitations, we are unable to define that which is undefinable. We speak of the holiness of God as the ability to be completely set apart and different than all of His creation. He is entirely "other." The reality is that God is wholly, and entirely, and uniquely, a being that is supremely unlike anything else in the universe.

The simplicity of Psalm 115:3 is perhaps incomprehensible. **"But our God is in the heavens; He does whatever He pleases."** In our own little sphere of reality, we THINK sometimes that we do whatever we please. Because of our money or authority or influence or intelligence, we think that we go where we want, spend what we want and say anything we choose. But unlike God, we suffer consequences for everything we do. You may say, "I can fly like a bird, if I choose, because I do what I want." But gravity will soon remind you that the consequence of that thought and that action will be the death of all your supposed sovereignty. You may callously say what you want to people, but in the end, you will suffer their lack of respect and perhaps their own retribution. In classic theology we have chosen three words to begin to describe the sovereignty of God.

1.**His Omnipotence.** God is all powerful. He created everything and He has absolute power over everything. We like to pose the riddle: "Can God create something that is too heavy for Him to move?" Obviously, we want to say God can create anything, which He can. But can He then, create something beyond His own ability? Not at all. This riddle poses for us an inexplicable paradox. God cannot place limits on Himself. The space adventures called Star Trek defined for us an ultimate purpose. It was called "The Prime Directive." This was the reason for being. This was the purpose for which the crew of The Enterprise spent their lives. They lived for the Prime Directive. God's prime directive is that He will always be sovereign, with absolute control and undefinable dominion over everything that He has sovereignly created. Not only does He command authority over the natural world, but He lives in a far more powerful domain called the spiritual world, where power is exercised through the silent invisible realm of the Spirit, which exerts great magnitude by merely breathing life into substance or speaking something into reality.

2. His Omniscience. Notice the word "science" embedded here, which infers that science is knowledge. God is all knowing. Though we cannot begin to grasp this truth, God knows the mind and heart of every man. He knows not only the past and present, but He also knows the future. Perhaps the best way to describe science is the word "mystery." All of life is a mystery, and God has concealed vast treasures in a time continuum that is gradually being revealed to those He chooses, as stewards of great truths, which are far more valuable than great wealth. The greatest of mystery is Jesus Himself, who is spoken of in 1Timothy 3:16. *"By common confession, great is the mystery of godliness: He who was revealed in the flesh, Was vindicated in the Spirit, Seen by angels, Proclaimed among the nations, Believed on in the world, Taken up in glory."*

3. His Omni-Presence. To be omni-present means that the great God of the universe can inhabit, at His choosing, to be present in every square inch of the created order. Pantheism wrongly believes that God is a tree or a rock. Scripture teaches that God is Spirit, far beyond the limitations of rocks or trees. Certainly God is able to be present at the location of a rock or a tree. He may animate the tree if He so chooses, but He is not a tree. From this very idea of pantheism has come the world's erroneous religious interpretations of idol worship to things that we deem to be manifestations of God.

God is Sovereign. It is important that we worship Him as sovereign - first of all, over the planets and the mountains and trees, but more importantly, He is sovereign in our lives. It is God who has foreordained salvation to those we call "the elect." This same sovereign God has chosen certain pagans in human history, vessels of wrath, fit for destruction, (Romans 9:22) which are used for His purpose, to prove the curse of mankind in the last days. It should become a primary thesis of our lives, to bow before Creator God as the Great Sovereign, who simultaneously rules the planets and the microbes. The amazing paradox about Almighty God is that He does not rule over us as a dictator. He chooses instead to reveal Himself as a loving Father, whose commands we obey because we want to obey. In this great truth we live, that God is sovereign.

The Deity of Christ

John 1:14

And the Word became flesh, and dwelt among us, and we beheld His glory, glory as of the only begotten from the Father, FULL of grace and truth.

Full of grace and truth. What exactly does that mean? Talk about pregnant terms! Full, grace, truth. Do we really understand the word "full" in this context? I believe it means *"the absolute, unequivocal concentration of a substance in one place at one time."* Let's use shaving cream as an example. If you emptied a can of shaving cream on the floor, you would find that it oozes enough cream to fill up a suitcase. So how do manufacturers get all that foam into that little can? It is the power of concentration. Let's compare a tennis ball and a billiard ball side by side. The tennis ball is lighter than the pool ball. There is less concentration of matter and density and weight in the tennis ball. Now imagine that next to the tennis ball and the pool ball, you place a ball of equivalent size made out of lead. Clearly the lead ball is much heavier than the pool ball. Imagine now that somewhere in the universe, there is a supernatural substance much more concentrated, much more dense than even the lead ball. Imagine that instead of weighing 2 pounds, this cosmic pool ball weighs 2 tons! Impossible you say? Maybe not. Science tells us that somewhere in the universe there is the concentration of matter so dense that a marble weighs as much as the earth. That is what I would call "the absolute concentration of matter."

Now let's compare this analogy to Jesus. Colossians 2:9 says, "For in Him, the fulness of deity dwells in bodily form." Now imagine that God packed Himself inside a shaving cream can the size of Jesus. Tighter, tighter, until this human container that we call Jesus could not contain any more of the substance of God. If this substance is the "absolute concentration of God, in one place, in one time," then only now do we BEGIN to get the idea who Jesus really is - the pre-eminent personality of all time. Imagine for a moment a dozen of the tallest, strongest, wisest, noblest and most handsome of men. Imagine that they are the rulers of nations. Now picture a scene where Jesus walks into the room, and without any introduction, they all bow before Him. Why? Because they innately understand that Jesus is greater than them all. He is the perfect personality - strong, yet humble, engaging in conversation with a sparkling wit, a commanding presence among world leaders - a man that kings and princes would acknowledge as their leader. Someday that will be the profile of King Jesus. In order to understand the deity of Christ, we must look at the seven stages of His life.

His Pre-Existence - Before the foundations of the world -   HE WAS.
His Incarnation - Through time and space -   HE CAME.
His Ministry - Teaching and praying and healing -   HE LOVED.
His Crucifixion - Bearing the sins of the world -   HE SUFFERED.
His Resurrection - Defying the natural order -   HE CONQUERED.
His Ascension - As our great High Priest -   HE INTERCEDES.
His Second Coming - Closing the pages of history -   HE RETURNS.

To quote James Allen Francis:

> "all the armies that ever marched,
> all the navies that were ever built;
> all the parliaments that ever sat
> and all the kings that ever reigned, put together,
> have not affected the life of man upon this earth
> as powerfully as that one solitary life."

Galatians 4:4 says, *"But when the fullness of time came, God sent forth His Son, born of a woman, born under the law."* The fullness of God came in the fullness of time - a time of Roman government, Greek philosophy and Jewish religion. Jesus came at a time in which government, philosophy and religion all proved to be bankrupt before Almighty God. Today, like 2000 years ago, government and philosophy and religion are still bankrupt, still seeking their own worldly means to solve life's problems. Only the fullness of God can solve the fullness - the immensity, of the problems in the world today. The world desperately needs to be salvaged and restored to the glory of God's original blueprint for His creation.

The very last line of the gospel story has this to say about Jesus: *"there were many other things Jesus did, which, if they were written in detail, the world itself would not contain the books that would be written."* The world cries out for truth. The world cries out for grace. The Bible clearly teaches that Jesus was the perfect balance of grace and truth. He was the fullness of grace and truth. We wait now for the trumpet to announce His Second Coming.

The Authority of Scripture

All Scripture is inspired by God and profitable,
for doctrine, for reproof, for correction, for instruction in righteousness;
that the man of God may be adequate, equipped for every good work.
2 Timothy 3:16-17

All scripture is inspired by God. The Greek word for 'inspired' is the word "theopneustos" which means "God breathed." Into the pages of this book, written by 40 authors over a 1500-year period across 3 continents, God breathed divine revelation about Himself and His relation to the entire created order. For years I read this verse and memorized this verse but never knew what it meant. The Bible is profitable for Doctrine, Reproof, Correction, Instruction in Righteousness. What does that mean? Follow this simple illustration.

A young mother is preparing the evening meal in the kitchen while her two-year-old son, is entertaining himself with toys in the corner. She reaches into the oven to retrieve the main course, and suddenly the heat and aroma pique her son's curiosity. He drops his toys and totters over to investigate this big box which has commanded his attention. From the oven emanates a new world of sensation. The aroma of a chicken casserole with fragrant spices tells his nose that his little world just got more interesting. Undetected by his mother, he steps closer to the inviting warmth of the big box. While the oven door is still open, the little guy reaches toward the warmth to investigate the radiant heat coming from the bright glowing coils that measure about 400 degrees. His little hand inches closer and closer to the coils, now only seconds away from a visit to the emergency room. His mother is moving from one station to the next, singing to herself as she assembles the entrée. From the corner of her eye, she glances toward her precious little boy as his hand moves ominously close to the dangerous coils. She screams in absolute agony and lunges toward her baby boy, in the hopes of sparing him what could become a life changing experience.

She grabs the little hand just before it touches the coils, and in a moment of both joy and fear, she utters a powerful expression of authority. **"Don't touch the hot stove. It will burn you!"** From this story, we learn the divine meaning of 2 Timothy 3:16.

Doctrine is <u>Teaching that Declares Truth.</u>

> The mother conveyed a simple doctrinal statement. *"Don't touch the hot stove. It will burn you."* A doctrine is a teaching whose purpose is not to give you information, but to teach you a profound truth that is necessary for guidance throughout life. This was an unchanging timeless truth that deserves attention and obedience.

Reproof is <u>Conviction that Molds Behavior.</u>

> Even at age 2, the young boy is old enough to begin to embrace truth for himself. His mother's conviction must become his own. When he understands this to be an unchanging principle, and embraces that truth *with his own conviction*, he then begins to mold a noble behavior that operates from principle, not reaction.

Correction is <u>Change that Rights Wrong.</u>

> If the little boy ignores his mother's declaration of truth in Step One, and he refuses to embrace that truth with conviction in Step Two, then he will suffer the terrible consequences in Step Three. He will be burned, his body and psyche will be wounded, and then he will, by consequence, embrace with conviction his mother's warning.

Instruction in Righteousness is <u>Training that Builds Character.</u>

> Perhaps the only behavior acceptable to God is conviction. When the little boy grows into manhood, it will be his obedience to truth, and His conviction to embrace that truth, that will carry him past the precarious roads of desire and temptation and danger. In the heart of man, only obedience to the authority of biblical revelation can give us training that turns conviction into godly character.

The Bible continues through the ages to be a supernatural resource of unfathomable wealth. Christian theologians parse verses and words daily, never quite conquering the multi-faceted wisdom on each page. Hebrew scholars still today study each letter of the Torah, discovering new insight that is encoded and encrypted into every line. And yet, the metaphor we associate with our beloved Bible is that of "gathering dust." The wisdom of the ages has been revealed to us, yet we continue to chase after every new trend, rather than trusting the Word of truth.

The Reality of Sin

"Robbers on the highways, pirates on the seas,
Armies fighting, cities burning.
In the amphitheaters
men murdered to please applauding crowds,
selfishness and despair and cruelty under all roofs.
It is a bad world, my friend
an incredibly bad world."
Cyprian, 4th Century Christian Martyr

One of the compelling arguments for the authenticity of the Christian message is the Bible's ability to prophesy events and forecast social mores in today's culture. The Bible said 2000 years ago, *"for all have sinned and fall short of the glory of God."* In every corner of planet earth, there is wickedness and destruction. Modern man has had 2000 years to prove the Bible wrong. We could have created a Utopia with all our knowledge, all our technology and all of our socio-political wisdom. But alas, we live in a fallen world. The book of Genesis still rings true. The story of Satan tempting Adam and Eve forces us to reconcile in our minds and our convictions whether we believe this event to be real or merely a fairy tale. There is no middle ground. This is a watershed event for every individual. Each man and woman, child or student, white or blue collar, dropout or class prodigy, must settle in their mind an absolute sympathy or antipathy toward the Genesis account. Modern man, like it or not, is tethered to a curse that God placed upon His beloved man and planet thousands of years ago. God cursed Satan and made him eat dust throughout the ages. God cursed Eve and caused her greatest joy, childbirth, to be her greatest pain. God cursed Adam and caused the majesty of his work to be reduced to toil. God cursed the ground from which Adam would eat. Ignore this primeval curse and you will find yourself and your descendants a perpetual victim of consequence.

In order to understand (and conquer) sin, we must accept a two-fold reality: the Course of Satan, and the Curse of Creation. God, in His sovereignty, allowed free will to his Angel of Light, named Lucifer. In Isaiah 14:13-14, Lucifer (God's praise and worship leader) said: "I will ascend to heaven; I will raise my throne; I will sit on the mount of assembly; I will ascend above the heights of the clouds; and I will make myself like the Most High." As a result, God has allowed Satan to be the "god of this world, who has blinded the minds of the unbelieving." (2 Corinthians 4:4)

I believe Satan has a three fold agenda in the world today.

1) **Abuse.** Satan wants everyone to abuse everyone else. Parents against children; children against parents; husbands and wives against each other; governments against citizens and nations marching against each other. Satan delights in seeing conflict and anger and turmoil within families and cities and nations.

2) **Addiction.** Satan wants everyone to be addicted to something. It can be food, drugs, alcohol, TV or pornography. He doesn't care. He basks in the glory of watching us become distracted from our dreams, our goals and our God. He delights in addiction because it is his tool to destroy man's potential.

3) **Annihilation.**   Satan wants everyone to self destruct - to wake up one morning and say, "it's just not worth enduring another day." By whatever means, he wants us to take our lives prematurely and offer them to him as a sacrifice on the altar of death.

The second reality we must face in conquering sin is The Curse of Creation. We must accept that God has cursed man and His creation, through every generation, as an inherent, congenital disease that has only one cure. Romans 8:22 states: *"For we know that the whole creation groans and suffers the pains of childbirth together until now."* Every time a child is born with a disease, or a hurricane strikes the earth and paralyzes a community, remember that man is totally unable to harness nature, and he is totally unable to conquer disease, because it is part of the dna that is built into the fallen nature of today's world.

When I was a boy, I did not like the word "sin." I considered the church's insistence on its emphasis to be rather primitive and naïve. I now recognize its devastating power to control certain seasons of my own life, and I now run in fear when I see temptations that can undermine my own willful desire to live a godly life. We must accept that planet earth will mix its pristine beauty with the ravages of nature because of sin. We must accept that our willful desires to lie and cheat and steal and abuse are the blood-born genetic results of an age-old problem that won't go away, and cannot be solved by money, politics or education. Sin is here to stay. It is a spiritual law of the universe, and like its counterparts in the natural world, it is irreversible.

When Cain conceived evil toward his brother Abel, God said: *"Sin is crouching at the door, and its desire is to conquer you, but you must master it." (Genesis 4:7)* Generations later, we face the same painful reality. Sin is at the door.

The Necessity of Salvation

"It is a repulsive and primitive thought that I should need salvation. From what? I am educated. I'm a good person. I'm not a thief or a drunk. I've never been to jail. I've got a decent job, and I work hard at being independent. After all, isn't that the name of the game? My parents taught me I was supposed to be independent. Well, here I am. Salvation is for people who are dependent on someone else. Kinda like government welfare. That is not me. Salvation is for people who need religion - you know - some mild mannered guy telling other mild mannered people how to be more mild mannered. Well, that's just not me!"

Sounds like a lot of people I know. Independent and proud of it. It is true that independence makes it hard for a person to perceive that he needs anyone or anything. The problem with our perceived independence is that we are SEVERELY dependent upon others for our independence - unless of course you live on a farm and grow your own food, and ride a horse and catch fish out of your own pond. Even then you're dependent on equipment to farm and rain for your crops and vets for your horses. And suppose you are a college grad with an MBA. Then you're dependent upon the economy to keep your job and the grocery store for your food, and electricity for your gadgets. You're dependent upon gasoline from some foreign country to fuel your car that is run by a computer that you don't even have a clue how to maintain if it breaks. Yeah, you're independent all right.

But lets use another word for salvation. How about "entering the kingdom of God?" You want to enter the kingdom of God, right? You're just not quite sure whose standards to believe. Lets use soccer as an illustration of entrance into the kingdom of God. Now I grew up in an era of America in which baseball, basketball and football were the official sports of the American boy. Every waking moment as a kid I was outside playing one of those games. But the world is changing now and soccer has become a fever pitch passion for spectators around the world. The World Cup Championship which occurs every four years, boasts a viewership of 700 million people, by far the largest audience for any sport. Soccer even has the audacity to call itself football. Come on now. Don't go messing with the REAL game of football. (though I prefer a passing game myself.) So let's say that I get a call from the *United States Soccer Federation* and I have just won two tickets to the *World Cup* Championship. For a true soccer fan, this is heaven itself. Remember that I have no appre-

338

ciation for the game of soccer. I don't know the players and I don't know the rules. If I went to a local kids rec league game I would be bored stiff because I know nothing about this sport that everyone else is raving about. I'm sorry. I just don't care for the game of soccer.

So back to the invitation. I have been given free tickets to sit on the 50 yard line (oops, the center line) of the 2014 game in Brazil. Before the game I am ushered onto the field to meet the great players of all time - Pele, Maradona, Beckenbauer and Ronaldo. The average soccer fan would trade his wife and kids for the chance to meet these guys. The game begins and the crowd goes wild. While I'm watching the game I'm thinking to myself "I should have given these tickets to my friend Bill Ward." He loves soccer. He coaches soccer. He coaches guys who coach soccer! Bill would love to be here because Bill has spent his life loving soccer. Bill knows the rules, he knows the history. He knows the players.

Fast forward now to the kingdom of God. Jesus says, in John 14:6. **"I am the way the truth and the life. No man comes unto the Father except through me."** Act 4:12 says: "Neither is there salvation in any other: for there is none other name under heaven given among men, whereby we must be saved." If God IS the God of Israel and Jesus IS the Messiah and the Bible IS the revealed truth of God, then it follows that anyone who wants to go to heaven, to enter the kingdom of God, would expect that Jesus is going to be the centerpiece of all heavenly activity. If that is true, we spend our time on earth learning the "rules of the game" (the Bible) and the players of the game (Jesus and the old and new testament heroes). Can I truly appreciate heaven if I don't have a clue who Jesus is? Would Saddam Hussein really want to go to heaven if he understand that going to heaven means worshipping Jesus? The Bible teaches that Jesus IS the entrance into the kingdom of God. Why would anybody who rejected Him on earth want to be with Him in heaven?

You see, Jesus is the preeminent personality of all time. He is the fullness of deity. Someday, every knee shall bow and every tongue shall confess that He alone is the Lord of all Creation. When I was a kid, I learned the ABC's of salvation. ACCEPT the fact that you are a sinner. BELIEVE in your heart that Christ was raised from the dead. CONFESS that Jesus is now the Lord, the reigning influence in your life - and you will be saved. Salvation is a supernatural event in your life that gives you abundant and eternal life. To quote Edwin Markham: **"Behold this truth in a simple creed. Enough for all the roads you go. In love is all the law we need. In Christ is all the God we know."**

The Ministry of the Spirit

In Genesis 1:2, the Bible says that the Spirit of God moved across the face of the waters. The Hebrew word for Spirit is the word 'ru-ach', meaning breath or wind. At that stage of creation, there was no land, only water - and the breath of God. It is an interesting side note to observe that there are only two requirements for sustaining daily human life - water and oxygen. The human body is composed of 60% to 75% water. It is oxygen that provides fuel for blood cells, and oxygen is the engine that strengthens the body and enhances other organ functions. We were made from dust. But we trace our life-sustaining elements directly back to the primeval elements of God. The Trinity of God - Father, Son and Spirit - can be found in Matthew 3:16, where the Spirit descends on Jesus and the voice of God the Father speaks from Heaven. It is interesting to note that there are two words in the English vocabulary - 'enthusiasm' (meaning 'God in us') and 'inspiration' (meaning 'breathed in') are both superlative words of energy and joy, both connected to a God who infuses us with His supernatural love and power.

The Spirit of God is a mysterious entity to us - in part, because we can relate to God the Father as our paternal (and eternal) guardian, and we can relate to Jesus because He is the Word made Flesh, as the gospel account personifies Him. But the Spirit of God is less defined. Jesus refers to Him as the Paraclete, a Greek word meaning "one who comes alongside." We translate that as "the comforter" or "the helper." Perhaps the job description of the Holy Spirit of God can best be defined in the words "presence" and "power." As a comforter, **HIS PRESENCE** consoles us that everything will be OK. As a helper, **HIS POWER** is activated to protect us and to provide for us.

My son and I took a fly fishing trip to the San Juan River in New Mexico, touted to be among the most hallowed trout fishing waters in all of North America. We had fished many times before so we had confidence that we knew how to catch fish. But we had never been to the San Juan River, we didn't bring a boat, and we didn't know how to find the best fishing spots. So we hired a local GUIDE. After all, he knows the way. He has been there many times before. He has all the proper equipment, and he knows how to avoid the danger spots and take us right to our destination. He knows how to protect us, and he knows how to provide a safe journey that will end with predictable fulfillment. After all, we only have a short time. We can't afford to squander it, dependent upon our own limited knowledge. For us, the GUIDE is not optional. We need the GUIDE if we're going to make this trip. The San Juan River is 400 miles long, a tributary of the mighty Colorado River. But there is one spot that is sacred to fly fisherman - a four-mile stretch just below the Navajo Dam in northwest New Mexico, near the small town of Aztec. At one time, there was an estimated 80,000 fish averaging 17" in length. We had a great day of fishing with our GUIDE named Mark. He guided us through the murky waters to all the right places. Our day ended with 22 beautiful rainbow and brown trout, ranging from 14" to 20."

Jesus refers to the Holy Spirit as our GUIDE. The spiritual trip that we take through life is not fishing for trout, but fishing for TRUTH. After all, He knows the way. He has been there many times before. He has all the proper equipment, and He knows how to avoid the danger spots and take us right to our destination. He knows how to protect us, and He knows how to provide a safe journey that will end with predictable fulfillment. After all, we only have a short time. We can't afford to squander it, dependent upon our own limited knowledge. For us, the GUIDE is not optional. We need the GUIDE if we're going to make this trip.

The Spirit of God is our GUIDE through the murky waters of the meandering, unpredictable river of life. When Jesus ascended into Heaven, he appointed the Holy Spirit to be our GUIDE. Unlike man-made obstacles and unpredictable people, the **PRESENCE** of our guide, the Holy Spirit, assures us that we are on the right path - and the **POWER** of our guide, the Holy Spirit, protects us and provides for us, giving us a safe and fulfilling journey.

Just as God the Father had fellowship with man in the Garden, and just as Jesus had fellowship with His disciples during His days on the earth, so it is that The Holy Spirit of God provides fellowship for you and I in the age that we live in today. He is the silent, ever present partner that protects us and provides for us, always guiding us to a life of fulfillment. Recently, I have begun to pray every day the seven words of Samuel: "Speak, Lord, for your servant is listening." Many times, I am surprised during the day, when the Spirit of God speaks to me, in a "still small voice" - giving direction and wisdom when I need it most.

When I was a young father, my son and I missed the adventure of learning the art of trout fishing from an experienced guide. But even today, with measured achievement under my belt, I still look forward to my next trip, allowing the GUIDE to lead us on new adventures.

The Destiny of Man

Down through the ages, there are three words that loom mysteriously before the sages and scientists - those who boast of a transcendent knowledge to explain things to the rest of us. Those words are *Origin, Meaning and Destiny*. The Evolutionist will try to convince us he knows the Origin of life because he can predict what took place in the universe 100 millions years ago. The Philosopher will try to convince us he knows the Meaning of life because he has studied the psyche of modern man and found that everything is relative and nothing is absolute. The Theologian will try to convince us that he alone holds the keys to understanding the Destiny of man, that spiritual realm of the "hereafter," a world that man paradoxically anticipates and dreads. Man's destiny has been described in the biblical account of Heaven and Hell. Heaven, for most of the world, is some kind of an ethereal state of spiritual consciousness somewhere in a mystical realm of space. Hell is described as a lake of fire, of wailing and gnashing of teeth - reserved for those whose souls were bought by Satan to carry out his diabolical plan on earth.

According to the biblical account, there will be a new heaven and new earth, made necessary by the destruction of the original planet. The new earth will be the restored Eden, a global garden place of unthinkable splendor, where physical men and physical women will live physical lives in an eternal state of physical activity and ultimate fulfillment. We use the expression "heaven on earth" - that was God's idea all along. Hell, which is considered to be mythology to the average modern man, will yet prove to be a place of eternal torment for Satan and those who have chosen to reject the Kingdom of Christ. Just seven verses before the end of the Bible we find a clue to validate the future kingdoms of Heaven and Hell.

Revelation 22:15 "Outside {the gates of the city} are the dogs and the sorcerers and the immoral persons and the murderers and the idolaters, and everyone who loves and practices lying." What a mysterious verse that is.

There are six characteristics given to describe this unholy tribe that dwells outside the gates. Six is the mark of man. These six traits personify that man or woman throughout the ages who has sought to elevate man above God. Their hearts at last have betrayed what their actions have always implied; they have worshipped the creature more than the Creator and now they get their just reward. But here's the question. What are the idolaters and liars doing outside the gates of the heavenly city of Jerusalem? Shouldn't they be in some counter opposite corner of the universe serving out their eternal sentence of doom?

Here's one explanation for this verse that makes sense. The ancient city of Jerusalem sits on a mountain. The new city of Jerusalem will sit on a mountain. The ancient city of Jerusalem has walls and gates. The new city of Jerusalem has walls and gates (estimated to be 200 miles apart). The ancient city of Jerusalem had a valley known as Ge'enna (a landfill of waste and fire and human sacrifice) symbolizing for us the domain of Hell. I believe, counter to our traditional vague imaginary model of Hell, that Satan's place of eternal torment will be a lake of fire just outside the gates of the city, where he will watch in silent torment as the citizens of God's kingdom travel from the new Eden into the city gates (most likely the abode of the Jews) to worship Christ the King and to celebrate the majesty of God's ultimate city, the city of Peace, ruled of course, by the Prince of Peace. Revelation 21:24 says, *"The nations will walk by its light, and the kings of the earth will bring their glory into it."* This implies that there will still be nations, and that there will even be kings that rule over these nations. Perhaps the kings are those noble personalities that lived godly lives of innocence and humility, deserving of the crown of righteousness.

What greater torment could there be for the residents of Hell, but to rise from their bottomless pit of darkness, wailing and gnashing of teeth, only to surface on the edge of the lake of fire, with a view of the translucent golden city of Jerusalem, which they themselves will never enjoy. What torment, what agony - an eternal lakeside memorial to the spiritual warfare waged by Satan and his demons against the God of Glory. But enough about hell.

What is the most exciting verse of scripture in all the Bible? Perhaps it is 1 Corinthians 2:9 which says, *"Eyes have not seen, nor ears heard, nor entered into the heart of man, the things which God has prepared for them that love him."* What is heaven like? I can only imagine. Heaven is not about streets of gold, or living in resurrected bodies. The focus of Heaven is King Jesus, as sung so beautifully by the group *Mercy Me:*

> *Surrounded by Your glory, what will my heart feel*
> *Will I dance for you Jesus or in awe of you be still*
> *Will I stand in your presence or to my knees will I fall*
> *Will I sing hallelujah, will I be able to speak at all*
> *I can only imagine.*

Conclusion - Backbone of the Believer

Before his untimely death at 41, songwriter Rich Mullins wrote the words to his well known song "Creed". Based on the confession of faith written in the 4th century a.d. called "The Apostle's Creed", it is embraced today by many liturgical churches throughout Western culture. Mullins merely paraphrased the words in verses one and two, as follows, but it is the chorus that demands our attention.

I believe in God the Father almighty, Maker of Heaven and Maker of Earth
And in Jesus Christ, His only begotten Son, our Lord
He was conceived by the Holy Spirit, Born of the virgin Mary
Suffered under Pontius Pilate, He was crucified and dead and buried
I believe that He who suffered, Was crucified, buried, and dead
He descended into hell and, On the third day, rose again
He ascended into Heaven where He sits at God's mighty right hand
I believe that He's returning to Judge the quick and the dead of the sons of men.
Chorus
"And I believe what I believe is what makes me what I am
I did not make it, no, it is making me.
It is the very truth of God, and not the invention of any man."

I enjoy asking the question, "Does your theology shape your philosophy or does your philosophy shape your theology?" I suppose the right answer to the question is merely 'yes'. You cannot separate your theology (your view of, and relationship to God) from your philosophy (or worldview, as we call it today). What you believe makes you what you are, whether you call it religion or not. One of the great lies of secular humanism today is that anti-religious people are somehow above religion. They are not. They have merely redefined who and how they worship. It is my hope for you that "The Backbone of the Believer" can help you galvanize what you believe into a confession of faith, that becomes a habit, that becomes a lifestyle, that becomes a conviction. Thomas Carlyle said: **"Conviction is worthless unless it is converted into conduct."** What you believe makes you what you are. Be sure you know what you believe. There is someone in the world right now that would like to steal your belief and crush your convictions.

Reporting

For Duty

A Model Prayer

From Genesis 1:28

"What You Believe and How You Pray"

The greatest concern of Satan
Is to keep us from praying.
He laughs at our toil
He mocks at our wisdom
But he trembles when we pray.

- Samuel Chadwick -

Reporting For Duty
A Model Prayer From Genesis 1:28

"And God
blessed them and said,
'Be
fruitful,
and multiply,
and replenish the earth,
and subdue it,
and have dominion . . .
over every living thing.' "

Verse	Interpretation
And God	1. We Pray to Honor God
blessed them and said,	2. We Pray for Blessing
Be	3. We Pray for Obedience
fruitful,	4. We Pray to Enjoy Creation
and multiply,	5. We Pray for Productivity
and replenish the earth,	6. We Pray for Fulfillment
and subdue it,	7. We Pray to Conquer Obstacles
and have dominion over every living thing.	8. We Pray for Dominion

---

9. We Pray in Jesus' Name

10. The Dark Night of the Soul

Reporting for Duty

"And <u>God</u> <u>blessed</u> them and said, "<u>Be</u> <u>fruitful</u>, and <u>multiply</u>, and <u>replenish</u> the earth, and <u>subdue</u> it, and have <u>dominion</u> - over ever living thing."

1) God - We Pray to Honor God

Dear <u>God</u>, You are my Father, You are sovereign and I acknowledge You as Creator, Sustainer and Redeemer of my life.

2) Blessing - We Pray for Blessing

Dear God, this day I thank You for Your <u>blessings</u> that are all around me <u>Bless</u> those I lift up to You and make me a <u>blessing</u> to someone today.

3) Be - We Pray for Obedience

Dear God, this day I want to <u>be obedient</u> to the instruction of Your Word and the leading of Your Spirit.

4) Fruitful - We Pray to Enjoy Creation

Dear God, this day I want to be fruitful - to <u>enjoy You</u> and all of Your Creation.

5) Multiply - We Pray for Productivity

Dear God, this day I want to be <u>productive</u> in all my endeavors, and I want to multiply all my efforts.

6) Replenish - We Pray for Fulfillment

Dear God, this day I want to be <u>fulfilled</u> - at the end of the day I want to be satisfied that I was productive.

7) Subdue - We Pray to Conquer Obstacles

Dear God, this day I want to conquer those <u>sins and fears and problems</u> that keep me from experiencing victory in life.

8) Dominion - We Pray for Dominion

Dear God, this day I want to be <u>a good steward</u>, <u>a good manager</u>, of all that you have given me to have <u>dominion</u> over.

9) Conclusion - We Pray in Jesus' Name

Lord Jesus, I am your ambassador this day. In Jesus name, Amen.

10) The Dark Night of the Soul

I cry out in anguish. Hear my prayer O God.

Reporting For Duty

An Interpretative Outline of Genesis 1:28

According to the Jewish rabbi scholar Samlai, there are 613 commandments of God listed in the Torah, the laws of God, as recorded in the first five books of Scripture. Those 613 laws were reduced to a list of superlatives that God gave to Moses in Exodus 20 that we call the ten Commandments. Micah further refined and reduced those commandments in Micah 6:8 with his admonition *"to do justice, love kindness and walk humbly with your God."* In Mark 12:30-31 Jesus gave us the supreme singular commandment which says that you are to love the Lord *"with all your heart, and with all your soul, and with all your mind, and with all your strength, and you shall love your neighbor as yourself."*

I would suggest to you that the FIRST commandment of God is coded into Genesis 1:28 as an interpretive injunction and a beautiful model for guiding your thinking as you communicate with Almighty God. This verse says, *"God blessed them and said, 'Be fruitful and multiply and replenish the earth, and subdue it, and have dominion over every living thing.'"* On the surface this verse is stating a fact - that God gave a blessing and mandate to Adam and Eve which declared His intention that the human race spread across the planet. Is that all there is to this verse? Is this verse simply describing the reproductive process that all of life would follow? Certainly, this is a clear statement which chronicles the beginning of creation. But let's compare the literal interpretation with a spiritual parallel. I believe that there is a beautiful model for prayer embedded in this single verse. There are many models for prayer available to the Church today. Some form the acrostic PRAY, or PRAYER; some alliterate, some use The Prayer of Jabez, etc. This model is intended to capture a single verse, Genesis 1:28, and use a creative interpretation to guide through a meaningful prayer time.

Since I began to employ this model in my own life, I have enjoyed a richer time of communing with God. On those mornings when my mind was wandering or my thoughts were scattered, this model kept me on task. Every morning I get on my knees and pray the interpretive prayer of Genesis 1:28. I continually find new insight and new inspiration from this simple commandment as I learn better how to commune with Almighty God. It was Samuel Chadwick who said, *"Prayer does not equip us for the greater work; Prayer is the greater work."* The true mark of relationship to God the Father is found in the timeless act of praying. It is my hope that God can use this simple model in your life to draw you closer to His Word, and to His Spirit, and to His will for your life.

Dear God,
You are my Father in heaven,
You are <u>sovereign</u> in all the universe,
and I acknowledge You as Creator,
Sustainer and Redeemer of my life.

1. We Pray to Honor God

Genesis 1:28
And God blessed them and said,
"Be fruitful, and multiply, and replenish the earth,
and subdue it, and have dominion - over ever living thing.

When you endeavor to pray to Jehovah God, who is all knowing and all powerful, perhaps it is a good idea to prepare yourself for this encounter. On the one hand, we acknowledge that time with God is to be a simple, personal, intimate dialogue between a child and a Heavenly Father. But on the other hand, we should come to our Father God in a sense of awestruck wonder that He would <u>even</u> listen to our prayer. You do believe that, don't you? You do believe that the God of Heaven can somehow suspend His sovereign multi-tasking abilities to turn His attention to you when you call out to Him. Can I explain that? No. But I know that my Father in Heaven gives heed to my simple attempts to reach out to Him. Psalm 116:1 says, *"I love the Lord because He hears my voice and my requests. Because He has inclined His ear to me, I will follow Him all the days of my life."*

When you endeavor to pray, take a moment, just a moment, to begin your prayer in adoration of who God is. Acknowledge His sovereignty, His majesty, His power, His glory. Perhaps you choose only one different attribute every day. Don't recite the dictionary in giving Him honor. At some point that becomes vain repetition. Begin your prayer in a simple act of honor. What if you were only allowed <u>ONE PRAYER</u> to almighty God in all of your life. How would you approach Him then? You would prepare weeks in advance for what to say. You would bow in utter humility at the very notion that the God of all Creation would give you audience. Should our daily prayer be any different? I also HONOR God by getting on my knees (and elbows) to HUMBLE myself before the Lord. Is this required to commune with God? No, but this position of my body alerts my mind and prepares my heart to submit myself before the Lord. This also reminds me of the title I have chosen - "Reporting for Duty," which prepares me for the reality that prayer is not just communication. It is preparation for service. If I truly honor God, I will confess once again that I am a sinner, saved by God's grace, and set apart to experience abundant life.

"It matters not how oft you kneel, in attitude of prayer so true,
Unless, inside, where no man sees, your very soul is kneeling too."
Victor Hugo

Dear God, this day I thank You
for all Your <u>blessings</u>
that surround me.
<u>Bless</u> those that I lift up to You
and make me a <u>blessing</u>
to someone today.

2. We Pray for Blessing

"And God blessed them and said,
"Be fruitful, and multiply, and replenish the earth,
and subdue it, and have dominion - over ever living thing."

On one of my trips to Israel, I was privileged to visit Petra, the red rock city which reportedly has 10,000 homes carved into the rock. Among these is the treasury building, made famous by Indiana Jones as "the temple" in *The Last Crusade.* I wandered into one of the little shops carved into the mountainside and was met by a little Jordanian man selling trinkets. Amazingly, this little man spoke six languages and had never traveled more than 100 miles from Petra. Suddenly, even more amazing to me was the fact that I was a hundred feet inside a mountainside in which every square inch was saturated by oxygen, allowing me to breathe. I have always taken for granted this blessing. Oxygen is everywhere. It permeates every little nook and cranny of planet earth. For the first time, I thanked God for the blessing of oxygen.

Then, I had a greater revelation. The blessings of God are like oxygen. They are literally everywhere, and every bit as unappreciated as the air we breathe. At that moment, I began to understand the profoundness of God's blessings. We take them so much for granted, yet God continues to shower us with His grace. This part of the prayer to God is three-fold. 1) Thank You, God for Your Blessings. 2) Bless those that I lift up to You today (this is the intercessory part of the prayer) 3) Make me a channel of Blessing to someone today.

In Genesis 27, Jacob and Esau vie for the blessing of their Father Isaac. The blessing was not just words, otherwise they could have been retracted by Isaac when Jacob deceived him. Somehow, the blessing was literal. It was irrevocable. It reminds us of Romans 11:29, where Paul says *"the gifts and the calling of God are irrevocable."* Once God has given a blessing, it cannot be retrieved.

It is not wrong to pray for God's blessing. First, thank Him for the blessings of life and opportunity. Then intercede for God's hand of blessing for healing, salvation, encouragement and comfort for those who need a touch from God. And then pray that you will be a channel of blessing through which God can manifest His glory.

Dear God,
this day I want to <u>be obedient</u>
to the instruction of Your Word
and the leading of Your Spirit.

3. We Pray for Obedience

"And God blessed them and said,
"Be fruitful, and multiply, and replenish the earth,
and subdue it, and have dominion - over ever living thing."

This is the <u>very first commandment</u> in the Bible. God blessed them and said, "Be." Stop right there. The word "be" is an imperative. It is a commandment from God. And what do we do with commandments from God? We obey them. So we begin our model prayer by "honoring God." Then we pray for blessing. And now we pray for obedience. God makes it very clear to the nation of Israel in 1 Samuel 15:22 that *"to obey is better than sacrifice."* Obedience to the commands of Scripture sets in motion blessings and protection and the provision of God. Notice in Deuteronomy 28:1-2 the reward of obedience. God not only blesses, but the blessings of obedience literally CHASE AFTER YOU.

Now it shall be, if you diligently obey the LORD your God,
being careful to do all His commandments which I command you today,
the LORD your God will set you high above all the nations of the earth.
<u>"All these blessings will come upon you and overtake you</u>
if you obey the LORD your God."

Consequently, in Leviticus 26:18, God punishes for disobedience.

If also after these things you do not obey Me,
then I will punish you seven times more for your sins."

When I pray to God, I ask to be obedient to two things. The first is the mandate of Scripture. The second is obedience to the leading of the Spirit of God. Notice in Romans 16:26 a very important principle.

But now is manifested by the Scriptures of the prophets
and according to the commandment of the eternal God,
(the gospel) which has been made known to all the nations,
leading to obedience of faith;

Obedience is the result of salvation, not the effort to achieve salvation. We do not obey in order to fulfill a mechanical quest to please God. We obey because it is the natural by-product of a life that desires to please God. We obey traffic laws because we understand that obedience provides order which contributes to our personal welfare. We obey the laws of God because we understand that God has promised two wonderful supernatural results - **abundant life** (John 10:10) and **eternal life** (1 John 5:13)

Dear God,
this day I want to be fruitful -
to <u>enjoy You</u>
and all of <u>Your Creation</u>.

4. We Pray to Enjoy Creation

"And God blessed them and said,
"Be fruitful, and multiply, and replenish the earth,
and subdue it, and have dominion - over ever living thing."

The commandment says to "be fruitful." Traditional interpretation of this phrase means to reproduce, or to experience the fruit of the womb, which is childbirth. But I suggest to you there is another spiritual counterpart to this phrase. As I studied this passage of Scripture, I realized that I had never done a word study of the word "fruit, or fruitful." Upon examining the Hebrew, the word is "parah," which yields the traditional meaning, "to bring forth, to grow, to increase." But let's go to the Latin translation of fruit, which is the word "fructus." The word simply means - "to enjoy." In other words, when God made fruit, He said to Adam and Eve, "Here, enjoy this." Take this orange, this pineapple, this pomegranate, and enjoy it!. Notice that God didn't say the same thing about vegetables. He didn't say, "Here, take this brussel sprout and enjoy it."

My creative interpretation of this portion of Genesis 1:28 is that fruitful means "to enjoy God's created order." I believe this is a worthy component of this model prayer because you and I are so busy, so distracted by the cares and anxieties of a busy life, that we are sometimes unaware of the beauty of God's creation. For the Christian, it is especially important that we be reminded of the magnificence and wonder of creation because the secular humanist philosophy of evolution would have us believe that the beauty of nature is nothing more than a cosmic accident.

Many days, I am guilty of driving to the office in the early morning oblivious to the beauty of a spectacular sun that is 93 million miles away, rising with a precise calibration that far exceeds man's finite technology. I drive by majestic trees and manicured landscaping framed against the backdrop of morning skies of purple and orange. I have recently begun the practice of focusing on one tree every day which becomes my "tree of the day." My logic is that if God had only created one tree in all the universe, this one tree would be worthy of drawing a crowd of tourists from around the world to celebrate its beauty. Romans 1:20 says, *"For since the creation of the world His invisible attributes, His eternal power and divine nature, have been clearly seen, being understood through what has been made, so that they are without excuse."* God has made us the caretakers of the garden, and we honor Him when we are captivated by His created order.

Dear God,
this day I want to be <u>productive</u>
in all my endeavors,
and I ask you to multiply all my efforts.

5. We Pray to Be Productive

"And God blessed them and said,
"Be fruitful, and multiply, and replenish the earth,
and subdue it, and have dominion - over ever living thing."

Genesis 1:28 uses the word "multiply" as a metaphor for the reproductive process that increases the population across the planet. I would suggest another interpretation for this word. When we use the word "multiply," we are describing a process that implies "success." For the farm family, it was a mark of success to have a houseful of kids that could help contribute to the growth of the family business. The industrial revolution marked the beginning of repetitive manufacturing, later expanded into the mechanical cadence known as the assembly line. Whether you're manufacturing car parts or plastic widgets, multiplication is the name of the game. In the realm of a person's life, we multiply our efforts by becoming more skilled and more efficient at whatever line of work we are in. We want our stocks to multiply, we want our interest to multiply and we hope that year by year we see the fruit of our efforts turn from singular addition to an ever increasing geometric proportion.

Another word for multiplication is the word "productivity." The more that I employ multiplication in my work, the more productive I am. When I wake every morning, part of my prayer life is to ask God to make me productive for the day. Without productivity, life is not fulfilling. You can only work so long at a task or a profession without feeling that you are productive in some way. There are days that I have a hundred things to do, but I only accomplish a small percent. Not every day feels productive. Not every day can be calibrated on a scale of success. As an employer, I have to be careful to make sure that my employees are not only productive, but are also fulfilled.

Is it selfish to ask God to make me productive for the day? Not at all. Deuteronomy 33:11 says *"O LORD, bless his substance, And accept the work of his hands."* Whatever your work, it is a calling. after all, the word "vocation" is derived from the root "voca," meaning "to call." God wants you to be productive, to enjoy the work of your hands - and to consider your work, whatever the task, to be anointed by God as a divine calling and a personal ministry offered to God as an act of worship.

Dear God,
this day I want to be <u>fulfilled</u> -
at the end of the day
I want to be satisfied
that I was productive.

6. We Pray to be Fulfilled

"And God blessed them and said,
"Be fruitful, and multiply, and replenish the earth,
and subdue it, and have dominion - over ever living thing."

Once again, we see the words which imply reproduction - fruitful, multiply, and now, replenish. God's original intent when voicing this mandate was to suggest that mankind would continue to repopulate generation after generation - to make the earth full, and then to re-plenish it - to make it full again.

The root word "plen" is a multi-faceted term. It basically means to make full. A plenum in a house is the primary ductwork which is full of air circulating through the house. A plenary session of Congress would be a building full of politicians. Maybe there's a correlation between the hot air in the house and the hot air in Washington. To be plentiful simply means to be full. So the idea of replenishing something is very near to the more common vernacular today of using the word "fulfill."

Just as the words "multiply and replenish" were coupled together, so are the words "productive and fulfilled." When I begin my day praying for productivity, I also pray that at the end of the day, I will be fulfilled. It seems to me this is an inherent quality in every human being. We want to be productive and we want to be fulfilled. I can't pretend to understand the mind of a woman, and I am too far removed from the mind of a child, but I do believe that for every man on the planet there is a wiring diagram that connects productivity and fulfillment very close to his heart. Notice the words "produce" and "altogether" in Deuteronomy 16:15 - synonyms for productivity and fulfillment.

"The LORD your God will bless you
in all your produce and in all the work of your hands,
so that you will be altogether joyful. "

Alas, we complicate life so much. All that man needs, and all that God intended is that we live lives of simply productivity . . . and at the end of the day we have a sense of fulfillment. Perhaps the problem with the world today is that we postpone daily fulfillment, building anticipation for some great event that never comes - and we miss the joy of knowing God's peace in daily increments.

Psalm 145:16 says, *"You open Your hand and satisfy the desire of every living thing."*

Dear God,
this day I want to conquer
those <u>sins and fears and obstacles</u>
that keep me from experiencing
victory in my life.

7. We Pray to Conquer Obstacles

"And God blessed them and said,
"Be fruitful, and multiply, and replenish the earth,
and subdue it, and have dominion - over ever living thing."

The word "subdue" is a shortened version of "subduct," which means "to lead or force downward." In other words, to conquer. When Scripture says "subdue it," it refers to the earth, a general term implying that man has been genetically and spiritually placed in charge of the planet as the caretaker of the garden. So I ask myself, "How does 'submit' fit into my model prayer? Am I praying to conquer the earth, am I praying to conquer the animal kingdom, or am I even praying to conquer other individuals? Unfortunately, too many of the world's population think that conquering your neighbor is the way society works - survival of the fittest - eat or be eaten.

Yes, it is God's plan for us to have a conquering mentality - but not for other people. When I first began to contemplate the idea of conquering, the word that came to mind was "fear." God wants me to conquer my fears. That is certainly reasonable. Psalm 27:1 says *"The LORD is my light and my salvation; Whom shall I fear? The LORD is the defense of my life; Whom shall I be afraid?"* Yes, God wants me to conquer my fears. But there's more to it than that. I discussed this issue with my young friend Brett and he adjusted my thinking to add the word "sin" to those things I need to conquer. I John 3:4 says, *"Everyone who practices sin also practices lawlessness; and sin is lawlessness."* Baseball player turned evangelist Billy Sunday said, "I hate sin. I'll fight it while I have a fist and I'll bite it while I have teeth, and when I'm old and fistless and toothless, I'll gum it till I go home to glory!"

In general, God wants me to conquer sin and fear and any other obstacle that stands in the way of achieving the noble goals of loving God and serving Him. He also wants me to face those challenges and goals He has placed before me in order to conquer those in the name of Christ. Are we in a battle? Yes. Is life simply a rose garden that we wander through on our way to the grave? No. God has called us to be warriors. Psalm 18:39 says, *"For You have girded me with strength for battle; You have subdued under me those who rose up against me."* Our time of prayer should also be a preparation for battle - to stand against the forces of evil who desire to bring me down, who try to compromise my conviction and ultimately neutralize my ability to stand strong for the Lord. God give me strength, give me courage and give me victory!

Dear God,
this day I want to be
a good steward and a good manager,
to have dominion over
all that you have entrusted to me.

8. We Pray for Dominion

"And God blessed them and said,
"Be fruitful, and multiply, and replenish the earth,
and subdue it, and have dominion - over ever living thing."

The dictionary defines dominion as sovereign rule or authority over some municipality. The root word is domus, or dome, which implies a house or household. The idea is that dominion begins at home. The man is king of his castle and head of his home - but the wife will always remind him that she is the neck that turns the head. Something short circuited when man got his marching orders for dominion. God said to have dominion over the animals and plants. The idea was not that one man was to have dominion over another. Nevertheless, the strong arm among governments today dictates whose army has dominion over another.

I'm not sure we completely understand the perks that came with being the head landscaper in the Garden of Eden. God's original intention was that every man would be a plantation owner with every exotic plant in existence in his back yard. It's very possible that fruits were the only food on the menu. God's first couple were intended to live in a garden paradise similar (no comparison really) to the words in the musical "Camelot."

> A law was made a distant moon ago here, July and August cannot be too hot.
> And there's a legal limit to the snow here, in Camelot.
> The winter is forbidden till December, and exits March the second on the dot.
> By order, summer lingers through September, in Camelot.

When I pray for dominion, I ask God to give me dominion over everything I touch that day. Midas doesn't hold a candle to the dominion that God had originally prepared for you and I. I understand that I am merely a steward, a manger, operating an enterprise that God has entrusted to me to care for. Whether it be a garden on the Euphrates River or a small architectural firm, such as I own, I operate it with full understanding that it is God's business. Dominion for man is not sovereign authority. God is sovereign and He delegates to us as He chooses. The success of my company is in God's hands. I am called to be faithful. I will trust God to sustain this enterprise for His glory and for whatever tenure He chooses. If I truly believe that God owns the cattle on a thousand hills (Psalm 50:10), then I should trust God to be the Chief Executive Officer of my company. Wherever you work, you still operate as a manager or a steward, serving Him. Pray to allow Christ to direct you along the path of critical decisions.

Lord Jesus,
I am your ambassador this day.
In the strong name of Jesus,
I pray this prayer.
Amen.

9. We Pray in Jesus' Name.

"And God blessed them and said,
"Be fruitful, and multiply, and replenish the earth,
and subdue it, and have dominion - over ever living thing."

When I began to create "Reporting for Duty," there were only 7 points in this out- line. It began with Blessing and ended with Dominion. Then I realized that God was truly the first component of the verse, so I added number 8 in the outline. "We Pray to Honor God." Then I realized that God the Father was mentioned and the Holy Spirit was mentioned, but Christ was not yet part of my model prayer. It was obvious to me that "We Pray in Jesus' Name" was the crowning conclusion for this simple model of communion with God.

In the name of Jesus. On twelve occasions in scripture the name of Jesus was invoked - for baptism, for healing, for preaching and for casting out demons. One of the most majestic tributes to Jesus is made in Philippians 2:9-11, which says,

"at the name of Jesus EVERY KNEE WILL BOW,
of those in heaven and those on earth and those under the earth,
and that every tongue will confess that Jesus Christ is Lord,
to the glory of God the Father."

There is a terrible irony involved in closing a prayer "in Jesus name we pray, amen." The irony is that many times we use that phrase as a punctuation mark to close a sentence. We are sometimes unaware that we have just invoked the name of He who is called in 1 Timothy 3:16, the mystery of godliness: "He who was revealed in the flesh, was vindicated in the Spirit, seen by angels, proclaimed among the nations, believed on in the world, taken up in glory."

When you close your prayer, find a creative way to acknowledge Jesus. In the name of Jesus, who is our Savior and our Lord. In the name of Jesus, the Alpha and the Omega. In the name of Jesus, who gives us abundant and eternal life. In the name of Jesus, the King of kings and Lord of lords.

Edwin Markham gave us this simple way of remembering Jesus the Messiah.

"Behold this truth in a simple creed, Enough for all the roads you go
In Love is all the law you need, In Christ is all the God we know."

Dear God,
I cry out in anguish.
Hear my prayer, O God,
and restore the joy of my salvation.

10. The Dark Night of the Soul

To develop a model, a formula, a guide for how to pray, is a precarious endeavor. Prayer cannot be manufactured and packaged like a product, and neither should it be predictable. It is a highly personal, intimate adventure of the believer with his God - at a special juncture in his own private history. It should be so unique as to be unduplicated from day to day.

There are some days, which turn into periods of time, when my simple prayer to God is not enough. Those times become the "dark night of the soul." This phrase was coined by St. John of the Cross, a 16th century mystic, to describe a time of anxiety, desperation, or deep burden, which can only be satisfied by crying out to God for mercy.

Victor Hugo said, *"There are times in a man's life, when, regardless of the attitude of the body, the soul is on its knees in prayer."* That is the dark night of the soul. I just received news of a friend named Matt who is in a coma from a golfing accident. Several weeks prior to that a young friend named Josh was paralyzed in a swimming accident. The prayer to be offered on their behalf must be an agonizing painful prayer that pleads with God to supernaturally heal them and make sense of their suffering. It is the dark night of the soul.

Jesus tells the story in Luke 18 about the arrogant judge who would not recognize the pleas of a helpless woman. The woman kept coming to him, pleading with him day after day. She begged and begged the judge, and finally the judge relented and honored her request. Jesus says, *"will not God bring about justice for His elect who cry to Him day and night?"*

In Matthew 17:21, Jesus refers to a pure faith, the size of a mustard seed, which can move mountains. He then goes on to say, *"this kind is only effective by prayer and fasting."* I learned long ago "if you want something, you pay for it and take it." I believe every prayer request has a price. Sometimes the price is a simple act of faith turned toward God. Sometimes God requires that the prayers of many saints are offered up like incense, in a time of withdrawal, sacrifice and agonizing humility before the Lord. Psalm 55:22 says, *"Cast your burdens upon the Lord and He will sustain you. He will never allow the righteous to be shaken."* It is in the darkest of nights, when we bare our hearts to the Lord, that He, the God of all comfort, reveals Himself to us. God is sovereign. Sometimes He answers our cries of anguish and satisfies our requests. Sometimes only later, can we understand His fellowship in the dark night of the soul.

Appendix

Table of Contents - Topical

Quotes by Subject

(Opposite page of Great Men)

Achievement	Roger Staubach
Adversity	Theodore Roosevelt, Thomas Wolfe
Bible	John Quincy Adams, Galileo
Character	Omar Bradley, Horace Greeley, Herbert Hoover
Christ	Columbus, Dag Hammerskjold, Von Zinzendorf
Christmas	Charles Dickens
Compassion	William Booth
Consecration	Dwight L. Moody
Conviction	John Bunyan, Chuck Colson
Courage	A. Kuyper, D. Livingstone, Martin Luther, E. Rickenbacker
Creation	William Jennings Bryan, Wm. Cullen Bryant, John Ruskin
Death	John Donne, Stonewall Jackson
Devotion	Dwight L. Moody
Discipline	Pierre DeChardin, J. Edgar Hoover, Tom Landry
Discovery	Michael Faraday
Encouragement	Zig Ziglar
Existence of God	William Carey
Faith	William Buckley, Payne Stewart
Forgiveness	William Blake
Freedom	Friberg, Gorbachev
Generosity	Andrew Carnegie, John Wanamaker
Goodness	William Penn, Wm Lyon Phelps, Mark Twain, Wesley
Government	James Madison
Grace	John Newton, Robert Louis Stevenson
Greatness	Thomas Carlyle, Oswald Chambers, Jean Rousseau
Heart	Johann Wolfgang von Goethe, Haydn
Heaven	George Frideric Handel
History	Will Durant, Alexis de Toqueville
Honor	Stanley Jones, Immanuel Kant

Hope	Matthew Henry
Humility	Nathaniel Hawthorne, Eric Liddell, Rich Mullins
Immortality	William Wordsworth
Infinity	Peter Marshall
Influence	Dawson Trotman
Innocence	Robert E. Lee
Integrity	Dwight Eisenhower
Israel	Benjamin Disraeli, Theodor Hertzl
Kingdom	Leo Tolstoy
Liberty	Learned Hand
Missions	Hudson Taylor
Music	Ludwig van Beethoven
Mystery	Albert Einstein, Robert Van Kampen
Nature	George Washington Carver, Ralph Waldo Emerson,
Obedience	Dietrich Bonhoeffer
Opportunity	Isaac Newton
Paradise	John Milton
Passion	Alfred Tennyson, Nicholas von Zinzendorf
Patriotism	Patrick Henry
Peace	Henry Cabot Lodge
Perfection	Vince Lombardi
Philosophy	Malcolm Muggeridge
Politics	McGeoge Bundy
Power	Napoleon Bonaparte
Prayer	E.M. Bounds, George Mueller, Andrew Murray
Purpose	David Brainerd, H. G. Wells
Religion	Williams James
Repentance	Jonathan Edwards
Resurrection	Watchman Nee
Responsibility	Daniel Webster
Revival	Leonard Ravenhill
Sacrifice	Jim Elliot, Watchman Nee,

Science	Louis Pasteur, Nikola Tesla, Werner Von Braun
Simplicity	Thomas a Kempis,
Sin	Billy Sunday
Solitude	Charles Lindbergh
Soul	Henry Longfellow, Horatio Spafford, Charles Spurgeon
Thanksgiving	Tony Snow
Truth	M. Gandhi, Keith Green, Soren Kierkegaard, Leo Tolstoy
Wisdom	Henri Frederic Amiel, John Locke, Richter
Worship	John Jay, Alfred North Whitehead

Inspirational Poems and Prose

Dear Master	Cash
My Symphony	Channing
Slow me down Lord	Coleridge
Greatest of all Love	Cowper
This is a Cheerful World	Dante
I asked God for strength	Dostoyevski
Who Drives the Horses	Fenelon
The Anvil	Fenelon
If	Foreman
Poor Richard	Franklin
Desiderata	Gladstone
One Solitary Life	Graham
Touch of the Master's Hand	Grant
We are suffering	Havner
Almost 2000 years ago today	M. Henry
Mark Twain	Hertzl
Ten Commandments	Heston
Sermon on the Mount	Holmes
Declaration	Jefferson
L'envoi	Kipling
Mere Christianity	Lewis
Gettysburg	Lincoln
I live for those	Lodge
Christmas	Longfellow
The Lord's Prayer	MacArthur
Man with a Hoe	Markham
Opportunity	I. Newton
Hippocratic Oath	Osler
Unshaken by the storms	Schaeffer
Quest of the Historical Jesus	Schweitzer
America for Me	Van Dyke

Scripture References

Genesis 1:27,28	Bryan	Psalm 42:5	Dostoyevski
Exodus 4:11	Beethoven	Psalm 51:10-12	Augustine
Exodus 20:1-17	Heston	Psalm 66:5	Mullins
Exodus 34:14	Gandhi	Proverbs 2:2-4	Faraday
Deuteronomy 4:19	I. Newton	Proverbs 2:6-8	Locke
2 Samuel 22:50	Snow	Proverbs 25:2	Bacon
Psalm 1:1,2	Foreman	Psalm 96:10	Galilei
Psalm 2:8	King	Isaiah 2:17	Lindbergh
Psalm 8:3-4	Von Braun	Isaiah 9:6	Bundy
Psalm 8:3-5	Da Vinci	Isaiah 14:13	Von Goethe
Psalm 14:1	Solzhenitzyn	Isaiah 40:31	Liddell
Psalm 14:7	Hertzl	Isaiah 45:22	Spurgeon
Psalm 23:3	Spafford	Isaiah 55:12	Bryant
Psalm 23:6	Toqueville	Isaiah 58:6	Kennedy
Psalm 33:12	Eisenhower	Isaiah 66:2	Havner
Psalm 33:12	Gladstone	Jeremiah 1:5	Pasteur
Psalm 37:4	Franklin	Jeremiah 29:11	Gorbachev
Psalm 46:1,2	Rickenbacker	Ezekiel 5:5	Disraeli
Psalm 42:1,2	Kuyper	Daniel 7:14	Carey

Joel 1:14	Murray	Luke 4:18-19	Green
Amos 5:24	Hand	Luke 8:15	Van Dyke
Habakkuk 1:5	Adams	Luke 15:7	J. E. Hoover
Habakkuk 2:4	Tennyson	Luke 24:45	Muggeridge
Habakkuk 13:15	Amiel	Luke 24:47	Ravenhill
Zechariah 2:8	Disraeli	John 14:26	Blake
Zechaiah 4:6	Moody	John 16:33	Roosevelt
Matthew 5:3	Tolstoy	Acts 17:23	Emerson
Matthew 5:44-45	Holmes	Acts 17:24-25	Durant
Matthew 6:6	Bunyan	Acts 17:26	Pascal
Matthew 10:28	Cash	Romans 1:16-17	Luther
Matthew 11:25	Van Kampen	Romans 1:20	Hawthorne
Matthew 14:31	Kipling	Romans 7:23	Lee
Matthew 16:15-17	Von Zinzendorf	Romans 8:18	Bonhoeffer
Matthew 20:26-28	Schweitzer	Romans 8:21	Ruskin
Matthew 25:35	Booth	Romans 8:28	Milton
Mark 1:7	Wesley	Romans 8:38-39	Longfellow
Mark 10:6-8	Phelps	Romans 9:22	Calvin
Mark 10:43	Wilson	Romans 10:9-10	Colson
Luke 2:11	Dickens	Romans 10:12-13	Disraeli
Luke 14:13,14	Marshall	Romans 13:1	Reagan

Romans 13:5-6	Madison	Ephesians 2:8-10	Stevenson
Romans 16:17	Heston	Ephesians 6:12	MacArthur
1 Corinthians 2:7-8	Einstein	Philippians 2:2	Wells
1 Corinthians 2:9	Alighieri	Philippians 2:17	Brainerd
1 Corinthians 2:9	Columbus	Philippians 3:8	Elliot
1 Corinthians 2:9	James	Philippians 3:10	Chambers
1 Corinthians 9:24	Lombardi	Philippians 3:13-14	Stewart
1 Corinthians 13:3	Wanamaker	Philippians 4:6	Hugo
1 Corinthians 15:10	Haydn	Philippians 4:13	Staubach
1 Corinthians 15:55-57	Donne	Colossians 1:15-16	Markham
2 Corinthians 3:16-17	P. Henry	Colossians 1:27	Carver
2 Corinthians 5:18	E. S. Jones	Colossians 1:28	Graham
2 Corinthians 7:10	Richter	Colossians 1:29	Cowper
2 Corinithians 9:8	Ziglar	Colossians 2:8	Buckley,
2 Corinthians 10:3-4	Bonaparte	Colossians 2:8	Rousseau
2 Corinthians 11:26-27	Livingstone	Colossians 4:2	Bounds
2 Corinthians 13:5	Bradley	I Thessalonians 1:5	Lincoln
Galatians 5:1	Jay	1 Thessalonians 4:11	Pope
Galatians 2:20	Lewis	1 Timothy 1:12	H. Hoover
Ephesians 1:4-5	Hammarskjold	1 Timothy 3:16	Webster
Ephesians 1:18,19	Carlyle	1 Timothy 4:12	Penn

1 Timothy 6:10	Carnegie	1 John 1:7	J. Newton
2 Timothy 2:2	Trotman	1 John 4:4	H. Taylor
2 Timothy 2:15	Osler	1 John 5:4	Friburg,
2 Timothy 4:3-4	Schaeffer	1 John 5:4	Washington
2 Timothy 4:7-8	Grant	3 John 1:2	Wordsworth
Titus 1:9	Coleridge	3 John 1:4	Nee
James 1:25	Jefferson	Jude 1:24	Chesterton
James 1:26	Twain	Revelation 1:8	De Chardin
James 1;27	Whitehead	Revelation 1:10	Jackson
James 5:16	Mueller	Revelation 6:16	Edwards
Hebrews 1:1-2	Channing,	Revelation 7:12	M. Henry
Hebrews 11:1-3	Kierkegaard	Revelation 15:4	Tozer
Hebrews 11:6	Kant,	Revelation 19:6	Handel
Hebrews 11:6	Kempis	Revelation 22:14	Fenelon
Hebrews 12:14	Lodge		
Hebrews 12:7	Landry		
Hebrews 13:15	Amiel		
1 Peter 1:13	Wolfe		
2 Peter 1:3	Tesla		
1 John 1:8-9	Sunday		
1 John 2:16	Greeley		

Great Men by Vocation

Acting
- Charleston Heston
- Ronald Reagan

Art
- Leonardo da Vinci
- William Blake
- John Ruskin

Business
- Andrew Carnegie
- Herbert Hoover
- Eddie Rickenbacker
- Robert van Kampen
- John Wanamaker
- Zig Ziglar

Education
- MacGeorge Bundy
- Will Durant
- William James
- Immanuel Kant
- Henry Wadsworth Longfellow
- William Lyon Phelps
- Henry Van Dyke
- Alfred North Whitehead

Exploration
- Christopher Columbus
- Charles Lindbergh
- David Livingstone
- Theodore Roosevelt

Government
- John Quincy Adams
- Francis Bacon
- Napoleon Bonaparte
- MacGeorge Bundy
- Chuck Colson
- Benjamin Disraeli
- Dwight D. Eisenhower
- Benjamin Franklin
- William E. Gladstone
- Mikhail Gorbachev
- Ulysses S. Grant
- Dag Hammarskjold
- Patrick Henry
- Herbert Hoover
- J. Edgar Hoover
- John Jay
- Thomas Jefferson
- Abraham Kuyper
- Abrham Lincoln
- Henry Cabot Lodge
- James Madison
- William Penn
- Ronald Reagan
- Theodore Roosevelt
- George Washington
- Daniel Webster

Journalism

    Horace Greeley

    Tony Snow

Law

    William Jennings Bryan

    Mohandas Gandhi

    Learned Hand

    Theodor Hertzl

    Oliver Wendell Holmes, Jr.

    J. Edgar Hoover

    John Jay

    Horatio Spafford

    Daniel Webster

Literature

    Dante Alighieri

    William Blake

    William Cullen Bryant

    Thomas Carlyle

    G. K. Chesterton

    Samuel Taylor Coleridge

    William Cowper

    Charles Dickens

    John Donne

    Fyodor Dostoyevski

    Will Durant

    Ralph Waldo Emerson

    Nathaniel Hawthorne

    Oliver Wendell Holmes

    Victor Hugo

    Rudyard Kipling

    C.S. Lewis

    Henry Wadsworth Longfellow

    Edwin Markham

    John Milton

    Alexander Pope

    Jean Paul Richter

    John Ruskin

    Alexander Solzhenitzyn

    Robert Louis Stevenson

    Alfred, Lord Tennyson

    Leo Tolstoy

    Alexis de Toqueville

    Mark Twain

    Henry Van Dyke

    Johann Wolfgang von Goethe

    H. G. Wells

    William Wordsworth

Military

    Napoleon Bonaparte

    Omar Bradley

    Dwight D. Eisenhower

    Ulysses S. Grant

Stonewall Jackson

Robert E. Lee

Charles Lindbergh

Douglas MacArthur

Eddie Rickenbacker

George Washington

Medicine

Oliver Wendell Holmes, Sr.

Sir William Osler

Louis Pasteur

Albert Schweitzer

Music

Ludwig van Beethoven

Johnny Cash

Keith Green

George Frideric Handel

Joseph Haydn

Rich Mullins

John Newton

Albert Schweitzer

Philosophy

Henri Frederic Amiel

Pierre Teilhard de Chardin

William James

Immanuel Kant

Soren Kierkegaard

John Locke

Malcolm Muggeridge

Jean Jacques Rousseau

Alfred North Whitehead

Politics

William F. Buckley, Jr.

Mohandas Gandhi

Henry Cabot Lodge, Jr.

Religion

Augustine

Dietrich Bonhoeffer

William Booth

E. M. Bounds

David Brainerd

John Bunyan

John Calvin

William Carey

Oswald Chambers

William Ellery Channing

Jonathan Edwards

Jim Elliott

Francois Fenelon

Billy Graham

Vance Havner

Matthew Henry

E. Stanley Jones

Thomas a Kempis

C.S. Lewis

Eric Liddell

David Livingstone

Martin Luther

Peter Marshall

Dwight L. Moody

George Mueller

Rich Mullins

Andrew Murray

Watchman Nee

John Newton

Leonard Ravenhill

Francis A. Schaeffer

Albert Schweitzer

Horatio Spafford

Charles Spurgeon

Hudson Taylor

A. W. Tozer

Dawson Trotman

Robert van Kampen

Nikolaus Ludwig von Zinzendorf

John Wesley

Thomas Wolfe

Science

Leonardo da Vinci

Albert Einstein

Michael Faraday

Benjamin Franklin

Galileo Gelileio

Thomas Jefferson

Isaac Newton

Blaise Pascal

Nikola Tesla

Werner Von Braun

Sports

George Foreman

Tom Landry

Eric Liddell

Vince Lombardi

Roger Staubach

Payne Stewart

Billy Sunday

Chronology of Great Men

354	Augustine, AFRICA (a.d.)	1703	Wesley, ENGLAND
1265	Dante, ITALY	1706	Franklin, AMERICA
1380	A Kempis, GERMANY	1712	Rousseau, SWITZERLAND
1451	Columbus, ITALY	1724	Kant, GERMAN
1452	Da Vinci, ITALY	1725	J. Newton, ENGLAND
1483	Luther, GERMANY	1718	Brainerd, AMERICA
1509	Calvin, FRANCE	1731	Cowper, ENGLAND
1561	Bacon, ENGLAND	1732	Haydn, AUSTRIA
1564	Galileo, ITALY	1732	Washington, AMERICA
1572	Donne, ENGLAND	1736	P. Henry, AMERICA
1606	Milton, ENGLAND	1745	Jefferson, AMERICA
1623	Pascal, FRANCE	1745	Jay, AMERICA
1628	Bunyan, ENGLAND	1749	Von Goethe, GERMAN
1632	Locke, ENGLAND	1751	Madison, AMERICA
1643	I. Newton, ENGLAND	1757	Blake, ENGLAND
1644	Penn, ENGLAND	1761	Carey, ENGLAND
1651	Fenelon, FRANCE	1763	Richter, FRANCE
1662	M. Henry, ENGLAND	1767	Adams, AMERICA
1685	Handel, GERMANY	1769	Napoleon, ITALY
1688	Pope, ENLAND	1770	Beethoven, GERMAN
1700	Zinzendorf, GERMAN	1770	Wordsworth, ENGLAND
1703	Edwards, AMERICA	1772	Coleridge, ENGLAND

1780	Channing, AMERICA	1822	Pasteur, FRANCE
1782	Webster, AMERICA	1821	Dostoyevski, RUSSIAN
1791	Faraday, ENGLAND	1822	Jackson, AMERICA
1794	Bryant, AMERICA	1828	Murray, AFRICA
1795	Carlyle, SCOTLAND	1828	Spafford, AMERICA
1802	Hugo, FRANCE	1828	Tolstoy, RUSSIA
1803	Emerson, AMERICA	1829	Booth, ENGLAND
1804	Disraeli, ENGLAND	1832	Taylor, ENGLAND
1804	Hawthorne, AMERICA	1834	Spurgeon, ENGLAND
1805	Mueller, ENGLAND	1835	Bounds, AMERICA
1805	de Toqueville, FRANCE	1835	Carnegie, AMERICA
1807	Lee, AMERICA	1835	Twain, AMERICA
1807	Longfellow, AMERICA	1837	Kuyper, NETHERLANDS
1809	Gladstone, ENGLAND	1837	Moody, AMERICA
1809	Holmes, Sr, AMERICA	1838	Wanamaker, AMERICA
1809	Lincoln, AMERICA	1841	O. W. Holmes, Jr., AMERICA
1810	Tennyson, ENGLAND	1842	James, AMERICA
1811	Greeley, AMERICA	1849	Osler, CANADA
1812	Dickens, ENGLAND	1850	Stevenson, SCOTLAND
1813	Kierkegaard, DENMARK	1852	Markham, AMERICA
1813	Livingstone, ENGLAND	1852	Van Dyke, AMERICA
1819	Ruskin, ENGLAND	1856	Tesla, CROATIA
1821	Amiel, SWITZERLAND	1858	Roosevelt, AMERICA
1822	Grant, AMERICA	1860	Bryan, AMERICA

1869	Hertzl, HUNGARY	1898	Lewis, ENGLAND
1861	Whitehead, ENGLAND	1900	Wolfe, AMERICA
1862	Sunday, AMERICA	1901	Havner, AMERICA
1864	Carver, AMERICA	1902	Liddell, SCOTLAND
1865	Kipling, ENGLAND	1902	Lindbergh, AMERICA
1865	Phelps, AMERICA	1902	Lodge, AMERICA
1866	Wells, ENGLAND	1902	Marshall, AMERICA
1869	Gandhi, INDIA	1903	Muggeridge, ENGLAND
1872	Hand, AMERICA	1903	Nee, CHINA
1874	Chambers, SCOTLAND	1905	Hammarskjold, SWEDEN
1874	Chesterton, ENGLAND	1906	Bonhoeffer, GERMANY
1874	Hoover, AMERICA	1906	Trotman, AMERICA
1875	Schweitzer, GERMANY	1907	Ravenhill, ENGLAND
1879	Einstein, GERMANY	1911	Reagan, AMERICA
1880	MacArthur, AMERICA	1912	Schaeffer, AMERICA
1881	de Chardin, FRANCE	1912	Von Braun, GERMANY
1884	Jones, AMERICA	1913	Friberg, AMERICA
1885	Durant, AMERICA	1913	Lombardi, AMERICA
1890	Eisenhower, AMERICA	1917	Kennedy, AMERICA
1890	Rickenbacker, AMERICA	1918	Graham, AMERICA
1893	Bradley, AMERICA	1918	Solzhenitzyn, RUSSIA
1895	J. Edgar Hoover, AMERICA	1919	Bundy, AMERICA
1897	Tozer, AMERICA	1923	Heston, AMERICA

1924	Landry, AMERICA
1925	Buckley, AMERICA
1926	Ziglar, AMERICA
1927	Elliot, AMERICA
1931	Colson, AMERICA
1931	Gorbachev, RUSSIA
1932	Cash, AMERICA
1938	Van Kampen, AMERICA
1942	Staubach, AMERICA
1949	Foreman, AMERICA
1953	Green, AMERICA
1955	Mullins, AMERICA
1955	Snow, AMERICA
1957	Stewart, AMERICA

Quotes by Author

Online Bibliography

allgreatquotes.com

best-quotes-poems.com

beyondthequote.com

biography.com

brainyQuote.com

famousquotesandauthors.com

govleaders.org

great-quotes.com

greatquotesmovie.com

great-inspirational-quotes.com

inspirational-quotes-and-quotations.com

militaryquotes.com

moviequotes.com

quotationpage.com

quotegarden.com

quotesbygreats.com

thebestlifequotes.blogspot.com

thinkexist.com

thinkmenthink.com

wikipedia.org

worldquotes.com

Bibliography

70 Great Christians Changing the World, Geoffrey Hanks, Christian Focus Publications, Scotland, England, 1992.

3000 Quotations on Christian Themes, Carroll E. Simcox, Baker Book House, Grand Rapids, Michigan, 1975.

Abounding Grace, M. Scott Peck, Andrews McMeel Publishing, Kansas City, Missouri, 2000.

Amazing Grace, Kenneth W. Osbeck, Kregel Publications, Grand Rapids, Michigan, 1990.

Encyclopedia of 7700 Illustrations, Paul Lee Tan, Assurance Publishers, Rockville, Maryland, 1975.

Great Quotes and Illustrations, George Sweeting, Word Books Publisher, Waco, Texas, 1985.

Harvest of Gold, Ernest R. Miller, C.R Gibson Company, Norwalk, Conneticut, 1973.

International Thesaurus of Quotations, Eugene Ehrlick and Marshall DeBruhl, Harper Collins, New York, N.Y. 1996.

A Joy to Remember, Hallmark Cards, Inc. Kansas City Missouri, 1975.

Leaves of Gold, The Coslett Publishing Company, Williamsport, Pennsylvania, 1938.

Light from Many Lamps, Lillian Eichler Watson, Simon and Schuster, New York, 1951.

Mac's Giant Book of Quips and Quotes, E.C. McKenzie, Baker Book House, Grand Rapids, Michigan, 1980.

One Hundred and One Famous Poems, NTC Contemporary Publishing Group, 1958, Chicago, Illinois.

Oxford Dictionary of Quotations, Oxford University Press, New York, N.Y. 1979.

Men of Science, Men of God, Creation Life Publishers, El Cajon, California, 1982. Henry Morris.

Phillips' Book of Great Thoughts and Funny Sayings, Tyndale House Publishers, Wheaton, Ill, 1993, Bob Phillips.

Quote, Unquote, Lloyd Cory, Victor Books, Wheaton, Illinois, 1977.

Quotationary, Leonard Roy Frank, Random House, New York, 1999.

The 637 Best Things Anybody Ever Said, Robert Byrne, Faucett Crest, 1983.

The Goal and the Glory, Ted Simonson, Fleming H. Revell, Westwood, NJ, 1962.

The Joy of Words, J.G. Ferguson Publishing Co, Chicago, Illinois, 1960.

The International Dictionary of Thoughts, J.G. Ferguson Publishing Company, Chicago, Illinois, 1969.

The Vance Havner Quote Book, Dennis J. Hester, Baker Book House, Grand Rapids, Michigan, 1986.

Treasury of Familiar Quotations, Oppenheimer Publications, New York, N.Y. 1955.

Treasury of Religious Quotations, Gerald Tomlinson, Prentice Hall, Englewood Cliffs, New Jersey, 1991.

Variety of Men, C. P. Snow, Charles Scribner Son, New York, NY, 1966.

Words of Life, Harper and Row Pulbishers, New York, NY, 1966.

We welcome your comments about the book.

For information about upcoming books,

seminars and products from

Great Men Bow Down,

and for Gordon's new pre-release GMBD profiles,

send us your email address to

gordon@greatmenbowdown.com

Thank You.